D1601220

Leo Strauss on Political Philosophy

The Leo Strauss Transcript Series

SERIES EDITORS: NATHAN TARCOV AND GAYLE MCKEEN

 The Leo Strauss Center
The University of Chicago
HTTP://LEOSTRAUSSCENTER.UCHICAGO.EDU/

VOLUMES IN THE SERIES:

Strauss on Nietzsche's Thus Spoke Zarathustra
Edited by Richard L. Velkley

Leo Strauss on Political Philosophy
Edited by Catherine H. Zuckert

Leo Strauss on Political Philosophy

Responding to the Challenge of
Positivism and Historicism

Edited and with an introduction by
Catherine H. Zuckert

WITH ASSISTANCE FROM *Les Harris and Philip Bretton*

THE UNIVERSITY OF CHICAGO PRESS
Chicago and London

The University of Chicago Press, Chicago 60637
The University of Chicago Press, Ltd., London
© 2018 by The University of Chicago
Published 2018
Printed in the United States of America

27 26 25 24 23 22 21 20 19 18   1 2 3 4 5

ISBN-13: 978-0-226-56682-5 (cloth)
ISBN-13: 978-0-226-56696-2 (e-book)
DOI: https://doi.org/10.7208/chicago/9780226566962.001.0001

LIBRARY OF CONGRESS CATALOGING-IN-PUBLICATION DATA

Names: Strauss, Leo, author. | Zuckert, Catherine H., 1942– editor, writer of introduction. |
  Harris, Les (Editor) | Bretton, Philip.
Title: Leo Strauss on political philosophy : responding to the challenge of positivism and
  historicism / edited and with an introduction by Catherine H. Zuckert ; with assistance from
  Les Harris and Philip Bretton.
Other titles: Leo Strauss transcript series.
Description: Chicago ; London : The University of Chicago Press, 2018. | Series: The Leo Strauss
  transcript series | Includes bibliographical references and index.
Identifiers: LCCN 2017055605 | ISBN 9780226566825 (cloth : alk. paper) | ISBN 9780226566962
  (e-book)
Subjects: LCSH: Political science—Philosophy. | Political science—History.
Classification: LCC JA71 .S7937 2018 | DDC 320.01—dc23
LC record available at https://lccn.loc.gov/2017055605

♾ This paper meets the requirements of ANSI/NISO Z39.48-1992 (Permanence of Paper).

Contents

Note on the Leo Strauss Transcript Project

Leo Strauss is well known as a thinker and writer, but he also had tremendous impact as a teacher. In the transcripts of his courses one can see Strauss commenting on texts, including many he wrote little or nothing about, and responding generously to student questions and objections. The transcripts, amounting to more than twice the volume of Strauss's published work, will add immensely to the material available to scholars and students of Strauss's work.

In the early 1950s mimeographed typescripts of student notes of Strauss's courses were distributed among his students. In winter 1954, the first recording, of his course on Natural Right, was transcribed and distributed to students. Professor Herbert J. Storing obtained a grant from the Relm Foundation to support the taping and transcription, which resumed on a regular basis in the winter of 1956 with Strauss's course "Historicism and Modern Relativism." Of the 39 courses Strauss taught at the University of Chicago from 1958 until his departure in 1968, 34 were recorded and transcribed. After Strauss retired from the University of Chicago, recording of his courses continued at Claremont Men's College in the spring of 1968 and the fall and spring of 1969 (although the tapes for his last two courses there have not been located), and at St. John's College for the four years until his death in October 1973.

The surviving original audio recordings vary widely in quality and completeness, and after they had been transcribed, the audiotapes were sometimes reused, leaving the audio record very incomplete. Over time the audiotape deteriorated. Beginning in the late 1990s, Stephen Gregory, then the administrator of the University of Chicago's John M. Olin Center for Inquiry into the Theory and Practice of Democracy funded by the John M. Olin Foundation, initiated the digital remastering of the surviving tapes by Craig Harding of September Media to ensure their preservation, improve their audibility, and make possible their eventual publication. This remastering received financial support from the Olin Center and a grant from the Division of Preservation and Access of the National Endowment for the Humanities. The surviving audio files are available at the Strauss Center website: https://leostrausscenter.uchicago .edu/courses.

Strauss permitted the taping and transcribing to go forward, but he did not check the transcripts or otherwise participate in the project. Accordingly, Strauss's close associate and colleague Joseph Cropsey originally put the copyright in his own name, though he assigned copyright to the Estate of Leo Strauss in 2008. Beginning in 1958 a headnote was placed at the beginning of each transcript, which read: "This transcription is a written record of essentially oral material, much of which developed spontaneously in the classroom and none of which was prepared with publication in mind. The transcription is made available to a limited number of interested persons, with the understanding that no use will be made of it that is inconsistent with the private and partly informal origin of the material. Recipients are emphatically requested not to seek to increase the circulation of the transcription. This transcription has not been checked, seen, or passed on by the lecturer." In 2008, Strauss's heir, his daughter, Jenny Strauss, asked Nathan Tarcov to succeed Joseph Cropsey as Strauss's literary executor. They agreed that because of the widespread circulation of the old, often inaccurate and incomplete transcripts and the continuing interest in Strauss's thought and teaching, it would be a service to interested scholars and students to proceed with publication of the remastered audio files and transcripts. They were encouraged by the fact that Strauss himself signed a contract with Bantam Books to publish four of the transcripts, although in the end none were published.

The University of Chicago's Leo Strauss Center, established in 2008, launched a project, presided over by its director, Nathan Tarcov, and managed by Stephen Gregory, to correct the old transcripts on the basis of the remastered audio files as they became available, transcribe those audio files not previously transcribed, and annotate and edit for readability all the transcripts including those for which no audio files survived. This project was supported by grants from the Winiarski Family Foundation, Mr. Richard S. Shiffrin and Mrs. Barbara Z. Schiffrin, the Earhart Foundation, and the Hertog Foundation, and by contributions from numerous other donors. The Strauss Center was ably assisted in its fundraising efforts by Nina Botting-Herbst and Patrick McCusker, staff in the Office of the Dean of the Division of the Social Sciences at the University of Chicago.

Senior scholars familiar with both Strauss's work and the texts he taught were commissioned as editors, with preliminary work done in most cases by student editorial assistants. The goal in editing the transcripts has been to preserve Strauss's original words as much as possible while making the transcripts easier to read. Strauss's impact (and indeed his charm) as a teacher is revealed in the sometimes informal character of his remarks. Where no audio files survived, attempts have been made to correct likely mistranscriptions. Brackets within the text record insertions. Ellipses in transcripts without audio files have been preserved; whether they indicate deletion of something Strauss said or the trailing off of his voice or serve as a dash cannot be determined. Ellipses that have been added to transcripts with audio files indicate that the words are inaudible. Citations are provided to all passages so readers can read the transcripts with the texts in hand, and notes have been provided to identify persons, texts, and events to which Strauss refers.

Readers should make allowance for the oral character of the transcripts. There are careless phrases, slips of the tongue, repetitions, and possible mistranscriptions. However enlightening the transcripts are, they cannot be regarded as the equivalent of works that Strauss himself wrote for publication.

Nathan Tarcov, Editor-in-Chief
Gayle McKeen, Managing Editor
August 2014

Editor's Introduction

Strauss's Introduction to Political Philosophy

Leo Strauss taught very few large lecture courses during his eighteen years in the political science department at the University of Chicago. Most of his courses were graduate seminars devoted to the works of specific philosophers.[1] In the winter term of 1965, however, Strauss offered an "Introduction to Political Philosophy" open to undergraduate as well as graduate students. It attracted so many students that the course had to be moved from the medium-sized classrooms in which Strauss usually held his seminars before an audience of 40–50 students to the large, wood-paneled lecture room on the first floor of the Social Sciences Building, room 122.

The transcript of this course reveals some of the reasons Strauss was such a remarkable teacher. Not merely did he try whenever possible to find American examples to illustrate points for American students, but he also encouraged students to ask questions and displayed a genial sense of humor; the transcript notes repeated instances of laughter. The function of an introductory course is to persuade students to engage in further study, and Strauss's lectures in this course range over the entire history of political philosophy. He was extraordinarily successful in convincing members of his audience to undertake more advanced studies. As the names of students who asked questions in this course show, many of them later became professors of political science and philosophy.

Introducing students to political philosophy, Strauss also introduced them (and the readers of this transcript of his lectures) to his own distinctive approach.[2] Marking the death of Winston Churchill at the beginning of lecture 6, Strauss gave one of his most concise statements of his understanding of the glory as well as the limitations of politics and the duty of one who studies it. Recalling Churchill's adamant opposition to Hitler, Strauss proclaimed that "the contrast between the indomitable and magnanimous statesman and the insane tyrant . . . was one of the greatest lessons which men can learn, at any time" (chapter 6, xx). Yet, Strauss continued, "No less enlightening is the lesson conveyed by Churchill's failure . . . the fact that Churchill's heroic action on behalf of human freedom against Hitler only contributed, through no fault of Churchill's, to increasing the threat to freedom which is posed by Stalin or his successors." Churchill's writings were "not a whit less important than his deeds and speeches." So, Strauss reflected,

> The death of Churchill reminds us of the limitations of our craft and therewith of our duty. We have no higher duty and no more pressing duty than to remind ourselves and our students of political greatness, human greatness, of the peaks of human excellence. For we are supposed to train ourselves and others in seeing things as they are, and this means above all in seeing their greatness and their misery.[3]

And he concluded, "In our age this duty demands of us in the first place that we liberate ourselves from the supposition that value statements cannot be factual statements" (chapter 6, xx). The critique of positivism Strauss gave in the first third of this lecture course was designed to effect just such a liberation.

I. THE CONTEMPORARY OBSTACLES TO THE STUDY OF POLITICAL PHILOSOPHY: POSITIVISM AND HISTORICISM

Strauss begins his "Introduction to Political Philosophy" by emphasizing the importance of the subject. "All political action points towards the question of the good society, and the good society is *the* theme of political philosophy" (chapter 1, xx). In seeking knowledge of the best form of political association (and thus of all lesser forms, which could be understood to be such only in the light of the best), classical political philosophers like Plato and Aristotle did not distinguish between political philosophy and political science. Today, however, political philosophy and political science are not merely thought to be different: political philosophy has become incredible because people no longer believe that it is possible to know what the good society really and truly is.

Strauss begins his lectures, therefore, by critically examining the two contemporary schools of thought that have led many people to believe that political philosophy is no longer possible: "positivism" and "historicism." Similar critiques can be found in *Natural Right and History*, "An

Epilogue" to *Essays on the Scientific Study of Politics*, and "What Is Political Philosophy?"[4] The presentation and critique of these schools of thought in this lecture course is more historical than these. The course is designed to show, first, that both positivism and historicism depend upon claims about the history of human thought that need to be tested by an independent examination of that history. In the second part of the course Strauss thus presents a curtailed account of that history to show that according to the testimony of the philosophers involved, the central issue dividing the ancients from the moderns concerns the character of nature as a whole and whether it supplies a standard of justice or right. Having argued that modern philosophy leads to Kant's denial that nature supplies such a standard but that Nietzsche reveals the difficulties resulting from such a denial, in the third part of the course Strauss reexamines the classical statement in Aristotle's *Politics* of the ancient position that the moderns opposed.

By identifying the specific origins of positivism in the works of Auguste Comte and Georg Simmel, Strauss shows that neither the original nor the contemporary form of positivistic social science was a necessary or logical consequence of either philosophy or modern natural science. In "What Is Political Philosophy?" Strauss also names Comte as the first philosopher who argues that the development of modern natural science necessarily culminates in a "positive political philosophy," but in these lectures Strauss goes on to explain what Comte taught. Strauss acknowledges that the Comtean position is by no means identical to current positivism, but he declares that "we cannot understand the positivism of today without having first understood Comte" (chapter 1, xx).

Comte's "positive philosophy" consisted of an argument about the history of the development of the human mind and the necessarily comprehensive, self-reflective character of social science. In his two chief works, Strauss explains, Comte traced the intellectual development of humanity in three stages. In the first, "theological" stage human beings thought they could answer the grandest questions and exercise unlimited control over the world by substituting for the things wills they could influence. In the second, "metaphysical" stage these willing beings were replaced by abstract forces or "entities." But in the third, positive stage man abandoned the question of the origin and destiny of things, i.e., the *why*, and began asking merely how things are related.[5]

Although the theological and metaphysical approaches retained a certain practical superiority at the time because they claimed to answer all questions, Comte thought that the victory of positive philosophy was inevitable. He observed that the human mind is powerfully disposed to unity of method. However, as a result of the metaphysical critique of religion and the development of the modern sciences—beginning with mathematics, but then extending to physics, chemistry, and biology—human beings at his time lived in a state of intellectual and therefore moral and political anarchy. The development of a comprehensive science of man was thus imperative, both theoretically and practically. This science, for which Comte coined the terms "sociology" and "positive philosophy," was not merely the last science to develop. Although it presupposed biology in the way biology presupposes chemistry and physics presupposes mathematics, Comte recognized that his positive philosophy had to be the science of science, because he saw that science is a human activity and needed to be understood as such. He also observed that human beings cannot live together except on the basis of some fundamental agreements; but the critiques leveled by "metaphysical" philosophy in the seventeenth century had destroyed belief in Catholicism, the religious dogma of the Middle Ages. Science had become the only possible source of intellectual authority; but the goal and character of the science of science had not become clear until the French Revolution and its aftermath showed that humanity had a common destiny, because history is progressive.

Like contemporary positivists, Strauss points out, Comte insisted that science is the only form of true knowledge. Unlike contemporary positivists, however, Comte also thought that science could show us the best form of government. His "positive philosophy" was not value-free, and Comte continued to describe his investigations as "political philosophy." Comte's scientific approach did lead him to deny that there is any essential difference between human beings and animals. Like earlier modern philosophers he observed that human beings are driven primarily by their passions. But he opposed the "metaphysical," abstract notion of a "state of nature" in which individuals contract with one another to construct a government by observing that human beings live in society with one another at all times and in all places and that these societies are not the products of intentional design so much as spontaneous growths. Comte nevertheless thought that the progressive development of the distinctively human rational faculty would gradually change the way in which human beings organize their common life. As the division of labor that constitutes society becomes greater, individuals lose a sense of the common good. Co-

ercive authority thus becomes necessary to check the selfish, asocial passions of individuals. In earlier times the subordination of the productive
classes to the rule of warriors had to be justified by theology; but with
the advance of science and industry, religion could be replaced by positive
philosophy, and the military by captains of industry and bankers. Positive
philosophers would not hold explicitly political offices; they would tend
to the spiritual development of their people by shaping public opinion
and using a free press to critique the government.

Strauss concludes that Comte vastly overestimated the power of reason. His vision of an ever more pacific, prosperous, and rational future
was not consonant with his understanding of human nature as basically
passionate. Although Comte acknowledged the natural right of every human being to be treated in accord with the dignity of man, Comte's emphasis on the intellectual development of a few individuals in a system
of ever greater specialization meant that human beings would become
increasingly unequal. He also thought that the fate of half the human
race was biologically determined. In contrast to the "traditional" view
that Elizabeth I and Catherine the Great were quite good at governing,
Strauss reports, Comte declared that women are not naturally fit to govern. Ability to predict the future course of events is not necessarily a test
of the truth of a philosophical claim, Strauss concedes, but a mistaken
prediction does count against a thinker who claims to know the necessary course of history. Alexis de Tocqueville proved to be a better predictor of the future course of history than Comte when he declared that
progressive democratization, rather than science, would make government more stable.

Strauss emphasizes two differences between Comte and present-day
positivism. First, for Comte positive science is merely the rationalization
and universalization of common sense. He observed that human beings
at all times and places perceive the need for a theory on the basis of which
to select relevant facts to bring order to their common lives. For contemporary positivists, however, there is a radical difference between science
and common sense.[6] The second and more practically important difference is that, unlike Comte, contemporary positivists insist that social
science must be value-free. This demand might appear to arise from the
"Is-Ought" distinction, i.e., from the proposition that no statement about
what ought to be can logically be derived from a statement about what is.
But, Strauss reminds his auditors, neither of the two philosophers who

first announced the "Is-Ought" distinction (David Hume and Immanuel Kant) thought that it was impossible to know what ought to be. What is characteristic of contemporary positivism is the further assertion that we cannot know the Ought, whereas we can have scientific knowledge of the Is. And, Strauss argues, this positivist assertion rests on the conviction that there are many ultimate values (extending beyond moral duties to beauty and other nonmoral choices or commitments) that are fundamentally incompatible and hence irreducible to one.

Strauss explains that this view emerged in the last decade of the nineteenth century in Germany, but became accepted in the United States only after World War I. The first statement of it is to be found in the two-volume, six-hundred-page *Introduction to Moral Science* (*Einleitung in die Moralwissenschaft*) Georg Simmel published in 1892. "What is called normative science," Simmel explained, "is in fact only science of the normative. Science itself does not establish or prove norms, but merely explains norms and their correlations. For science always raises only causal, not teleological questions" (chapter 3, xx). But Strauss objects that the causal rather than teleological character of modern science cannot possibly be a sufficient reason for the view that social science must be value-free. Spinoza was the greatest and most outspoken enemy of all teleology, and his chief work is entitled *Ethics*. On his first reading, Strauss admits, he did not perceive the revolutionary character of Simmel's claim, because Simmel announced it so matter-of-factly.[7] Simmel could completely "break with the whole tradition of ethics in all its forms, without any apparent awareness of the immensity . . . of this change," Strauss later concluded, only because Simmel was writing in a nation that had been bombarded for a decade with Nietzsche's "immoralist" argument that no knowledge of good and evil is possible (chapter 3, xx). (And Nietzsche had clearly announced the revolutionary character of his teaching.) Reading Simmel in light of Nietzsche, Strauss saw that Simmel still accepted the positivistic view of the objectivity of science, but combined it with Nietzsche's view of the nonobjectivity of values. Max Weber announced the same view later with much greater passion; and after Weber, proscribing value judgments from scientific studies became a matter of intellectual integrity.

Strauss treats Weber's arguments in much greater detail in *Natural Right and History*. The point of the history of positivism he presents in these lectures is to show that the philosophical reasons frequently given for the now widely accepted distinction between "facts" and "values" do not justify or explain the emergence of the doctrine. People may believe that the only genuine form of knowledge is scientific knowledge, but such a conviction did not prevent Comte from thinking that science could—and should—tell us how to live. Earlier modern philosophers had emphasized the causal rather than teleological character of modern science and distinguished the "Is" from the "Ought," but neither causal analysis nor their recognition of the logical distinction between the Is and the Ought prevented these philosophers from putting forth moral arguments. The claim that human beings do not and cannot know what is good or evil originated with Nietzsche, and Nietzsche pointed out that "truth" and "knowledge," i.e., "science" itself, is among the unjustified and unjustifiable "values."

Positivistic social science cannot demonstrate that social science itself is good, Strauss concludes, because that would be a value judgment. Positivistic social science cannot even describe human social life accurately, because it is impossible to account for phenomena like corruption, crime, or degeneracy without using evaluative terms. Most fundamentally, social science presupposes the ability to tell who or what is a human being, and that ability is based, more or less articulately, on understanding what is a normal or completely developed human. Social science thus depends on prescientific "commonsense" knowledge that not only distinguishes *human* being from all other forms as a matter of fact but also entails an evaluation.

As in his published writings, so in these lectures Strauss insists that the positivist demand that a social scientist treat good and evil equally and indifferently necessarily produces moral obtuseness. But, Strauss also observes, most social scientists take a very definite moral, even political position. They do not perceive the nihilistic consequences of the fact-value distinction, because they think that if there is no reason to prefer one value to another, all values must be equal. And if all values are equal, they ought to be treated as equal. So if there is a conflict among the values people hold, the majority ought to decide. In other words, there is a close if unacknowledged connection between the widespread acceptance of the "fact-value" distinction and liberal democratic political prejudices.[8] People have not perceived the blatant inability of a "value-free" social science to provide them with politically relevant information and guidance, because the outcome of World War II and its aftermath made scientific progress and the spread of egalitarian politics appears to be "the wave of the future." And it does not make sense to ask about what is good or bad if the future is already determined.

If positivism arises as a compromise between Nietzschean historicism and objective science, as in Simmel, but science itself proves to be an unjustifiable value as much as any moral judgment or religion, we should not be surprised to learn that positivism collapses ultimately into historicism. In a rare response to his critics, Strauss shows how and why.

In *Political Theory: The Foundations of Twentieth-Century Political Thought* (1959), Arnold Brecht accused Strauss of misrepresenting Weber's position in *Natural Right and History*.[9] According to Brecht, Weber did not argue that all values are equal; he maintained simply that their validity was "equally undemonstrable" (chapter 5, xx). That was true, moreover, only of "ultimate" values. Weber "recognized of course that each value can be judged scientifically as to its accordance with known standards, *as long as these standards are not themselves at issue.*"[10] Strauss objects, however, that "from the point of view of social science, the standards are necessarily at issue, since all value judgments are rationally questioned." Social scientists have to use words like "crime" in quotation marks, because the words themselves convey disapproval. Brecht also challenged Strauss's claim that positivist social scientists cannot recognize the superiority of civilization to cannibalism. In reply Strauss points to the work of anthropologists like Ruth Benedict, and then states more generally: if social scientists could demonstrate the superiority of civilization to cannibalism, they would have shown that value judgments can be validated scientifically and so disproved the fundamental positivist contention.

Strauss then suggests that Ernest Nagel's response to his arguments in *Natural Right and History* goes further. In *The Structure of Science: Problems in the Logic of Scientific Explanation* (1961) Nagel concedes that "a large number of characterizations sometimes assumed to be purely factual descriptions of social phenomena do indeed formulate a type of value judgment."[11] He admits, moreover, that it is often difficult to separate means entirely from ends, and that values can be attached to both. Nagel thinks that he can rescue the positivist position by distinguishing value judgments that express approval or disapproval from those that express an estimate of the degree to which some commonly recognized type of action, object, or institution is embodied in a given instance. The key point, Strauss thinks, is that Nagel admits that such "characterizing" value judgments are inevitable (chapter 5, xx).

By characterizing the principle of causality, upon which all modern science rests, as "only a contingent historical fact . . . for it is logically possible that in their efforts at mastering their environments men might have aimed at something quite different," Nagel, Strauss argues, shows how positivism leads eventually to historicism without realizing that he is doing so. The reason positivism collapses into historicism is that modern science cannot answer the question, why science? "Teleological" philosophers like Aristotle had argued that science or knowledge is the fulfillment and thus the perfection of human nature. Having cut free from such a teleological view of nature, early modern philosophers like Francis Bacon and Thomas Hobbes suggested that science could relieve the human condition. But that did not explain or justify mathematicians' study of prime numbers, for example, i.e., science merely for the sake of science. Nor was it clear to later thinkers exactly what would benefit or please most if not all human beings. It was at least partly the difficulty of defining what precisely constitutes "the greatest good for the greatest number" that led social scientists like Simmel and Weber to jettison utilitarianism in favor of their positivist assertion of the indemonstrability of all ultimate values.

Strauss concludes that the inadequacy of the positivist contention that all genuine knowledge is scientific knowledge is revealed by the dependency of all social "scientific" knowledge on a prescientific understanding of humanity. Historicism constitutes a more serious challenge to the possibility of political philosophy, because historicism begins by recognizing that human existence is not like all other existence. Contrary to certain popular forms of "cultural relativism," historicism does not rest merely on the observation that human beings disagree about the answers to the most fundamental questions. Like positivism, historicism grows out of a certain understanding of the history of philosophy. The disagreements among past philosophers about the answers to the most fundamental questions may have appeared scandalous in the eyes of others, but each philosopher continued to pronounce what he thought was true in opposition to the errors of others. Only after Jean-Jacques Rousseau suggested that human nature was changeable, and that the changes occurred particularly in the rational faculty as a result of a process of socialization, did philosophers begin to think that the differences in comprehensive views from time to time and place to place might not merely be significant but have a progressive order. Both the rational and the progressive character of the development could be established, however, only after the process or change had come to completion. That argument was first made by G. W. F. Hegel. With the secularization of Christianity in the declaration of the universal rights of man during the French Revolution and the subsequent institution of states in Europe explicitly based on that principle, Hegel contended that the question that had animated political philosophy—namely, what is the just society?—had been definitively answered, and that it could not have been correctly answered earlier.

Strauss observes that Hegel's claims about the achievement of knowledge and the just state were subject to proof or disproof like any previous claims. The problem posed by history came to light only when nineteenth-century historians like Leopold von Ranke accepted the notion that every epoch has its own truth but denied that history is rational or progressive, because they thought that history is an ongoing process that has no end in the sense of completion. The historical insight thus culminated in the proposition that there is no eternal truth.

Nietzsche first disclosed the problematic consequences of this historicist insight in his essay "On the Use and Abuse of History." "History teaches a truth that is deadly," according to Nietzsche. "It shows that culture is possible only if men are fully dedicated to principles of thought and action which they do not question" (chapter 6, xx). But history also shows us that the principles of previous thought and action do not possess the validity they claim and do not, therefore, deserve to be regarded as simply true. The answer might seem to lie in the fabrication of a new myth, but Nietzsche saw that would involve a kind of deliberate self-delusion impossible for men of intellectual probity. The true solution comes to sight only when one realizes that scientific history suffices to show the relative validity of all previous principles of thought and action, but it does not allow the uncommitted "objective" observer to understand the vital source of previous history, precisely because he does not share or have a commitment. The principles that claimed to be rational or of divine origin were, Nietzsche argued, human creations. What was necessary now was for human beings to do consciously what they had done unconsciously in the past. But, Strauss explains, Nietzsche's further suggestion that all these goals were products of a universal will to power looked like a relapse into metaphysics.[12] Later historicists attempted to retain Nietzsche's insight that there cannot be historical objectivity but to avoid asserting a trans-historical truth.

In explicating and critiquing the "radical historicist" position, Strauss confronted the difficulty that the thinker he considered to be the most competent exponent of that position, Martin Heidegger, had not written in English.[13] As in *Natural Right and History*, so in these lectures Strauss thus gives a brief summary of the problem as Heidegger presents it at the beginning of *Being and Time* without grounding his discussion explicitly in Heidegger's text.[14] As in the lecture course Strauss gave in 1961, "Basic Principles of Classical Political Philosophy," he then tries to explain the basic claims and the difficulties with those claims on the basis of an admittedly less satisfactory presentation of the position in English by the historian R. G. Collingwood.

Reflecting on his own practice as an archaeologist in his *Autobiography*, Collingwood first came to a new understanding of knowledge as composed not simply of propositions, but of propositions that were answers to questions. In reading the political theories of Plato and Hobbes Collingwood then discovered that they were not giving answers to the same question. They were writing about different things: Plato about the best form of the ancient *polis*, and Hobbes about the modern state.[15] Collingwood concluded that there are no eternal questions. All human thought rests ultimately on absolute presuppositions, which differ from historical epoch to historical epoch. These absolute presuppositions cannot be judged to be true or false, because they are not answers to questions but the presuppositions of the questions. The most a historian can do is to trace the changes in comprehensive views that arise as a result of changes in these absolute presuppositions.[16] The problem with this view, Strauss points out, lies in the status of the historicist presupposition itself—that each era has its own presuppositions. The historicist contradicts himself by treating the presupposition of his own age as simply true. Because he believes that his own age is superior, he cannot take the thought of past ages seriously.[17]

II. THE NECESSITY OF STUDYING THE HISTORY OF POLITICAL PHILOSOPHY

Although Strauss concludes that the historicist position articulated by Collingwood is untenable, he nevertheless agrees with the historicists that in our time philosophy must to a certain extent become fused with history. The reason Strauss gives differs, however, from those Collingwood gave in his *Idea of History*. Strauss argues:

Every attempt at rational knowledge, philosophic or scientific, consists in replacing opinions by knowledge. This cannot be conscientiously done if one does not first know the opinions from which one starts. But . . . what we regard as our opinions consists to a considerable extent of the sediments of past discussions . . . in earlier centuries, and now we live on their results. Hence the nonhistorical concern with the clarification of our opinions insensibly shifts into historical studies. (chapter 8, xx)

Positivist political science discourages the study of the history of political philosophy, but, Strauss reminds his auditors, Comte founded positivism on the basis of a history of human thought. In order to determine whether current opinions are true or false, it thus seems necessary from any point of view to study the history of political philosophy. In opposition to both the positivists and the historicists, however, Strauss insists that we must be open to the possibility that past thinkers knew something that we have forgotten.

To study the history of political philosophy, Strauss then observes, we need to divide it into parts or periods. Looking to find divisions within the material itself, he finds the clearest break with previous thought in the works of Thomas Hobbes. Presenting a much-abbreviated version of the history he gives in much greater detail elsewhere, Strauss notes that the decisive break actually took place before Hobbes, when Machiavelli announced in chapter 15 of his *Prince* that he was departing from the writings of others in teaching a prince how not to be good if he wants to maintain his state. Strauss nevertheless concentrates on Hobbes, because Hobbes formulates the modern position in terms of natural law, and, Strauss emphasizes, "the lowering of the standards has to do with a profoundly changed posture toward nature" (chapter 8, xx). Plato, Aristotle, the whole tradition of "classical political philosophy" that stems from Socrates sought "to delineate the character of the just society by taking their bearings by men's perfection, by the highest in them. And these modern thinkers . . . tried to take their bearings by the lowest, but for this very reason the most powerful, in man" (chapter 8, xx).

According to Hobbes, Strauss reminds his auditors, human life in the "state of nature" is "solitary, nasty, brutish, and short." Because human desires can never be satisfied, it is impossible to achieve "the repose of the mind satisfied. For there is no such *finis ultimus* (utmost aim) nor *summum bonum* (greatest good), as is spoken of in the books of the old moral philosophers" (*Leviathan*, chapter 11). Human beings must have some fixed point by which to take our bearings, and "Hobbes finds it in the beginning" (chapter 8, xx). Although human beings cannot achieve happiness, Hobbes maintains that we can attain a certain amount of security and peace by fleeing the state of nature and contracting with others to relinquish our natural right to everything to a sovereign who will see that the "natural law" is enforced.

Admitting that the practical consequences Locke draws are far different from those to be found in Hobbes, in these lectures Strauss nevertheless skips Locke because he thinks that in many respects Locke's fundamental scheme is not so different from that of Hobbes. Strauss concentrates instead on Rousseau's critique of Hobbes, because this critique brings modern political philosophy to its first crisis.[18] If human beings are solitary or presocial in the state of nature, Rousseau pointed out in his *Discourse on the Origins of Inequality*, human beings must also be prerational. Rousseau thus challenges the traditional definition of man as a rational animal in a way Hobbes did not. It might seem that a stupid animal could not serve as a standard of natural right. Rousseau argues that natural liberty merely allows a person to become a slave to his passions. True human liberty can be achieved only in a society where no one is subject to a law he does not take part in making. Both the rationality and the justice of the "general will" are guaranteed by its form: each wills what he desires not only for himself but for all others as well. By living according to the general will, Rousseau adds, a person acquires moral as well as civic liberty. Rousseau does not make the grounds of this moral freedom clear, however. In the profession of faith of the Savoyard vicar in his *Emile*, Rousseau presents the issue of moral liberty in terms of traditional dualistic metaphysics. "But," Strauss observes, "according to Rousseau himself, that metaphysics is exposed to insoluble objections" (chapter 8, xx). Rousseau also clings to a notion of natural goodness, rooted in the *sentiment de son existence*, that is fundamentally different from rational moral liberty. One of Rousseau's objections to Hobbes is that human beings would not strive to preserve themselves if they did not perceive that life is good.

Strauss then explains how "Kant solved Rousseau's problem, and put therewith moral and political philosophy on an entirely new basis. And the net result . . . is that from Kant on, the moral law is no longer a natural law" (chapter 8, xx).[19] According to Kant, morality cannot be based on dualistic metaphysics, because God and the soul are unknowable. That does not mean that the opposite view, that everything is corporeal, is true. "Materialism, or the view underlying modern physics, has as its premise the principle of causality. And this principle of causality ... had been subjected to a radical critique by David Hume" (chapter 9, xx). The "gist of Hume's critique" was that science or rationality in the highest sense rests on an irrational foundation of mere custom. In opposing Hume, Kant asserts that science is rational, but that it is limited to the phenomenal world. "Reason supplies only the form of knowledge; for its content, it depends on sense experience" (chapter 9, xx).

Although in his *Critique of Pure Reason* Kant shows that reason is weak in the sphere of theory, he argues that it is sufficient to guide human practice. "Practical reason prescribes, without any borrowings whatever from experience, universally valid laws of action" (chapter 9, xx). And because the moral law is not based in any way on experience, it can no longer be called, as it was before, the natural law. The moral law must be valid, not only for men, but for *all* intelligent beings. But if the moral law is to apply to God, it cannot be based on human nature. And it must apply to God, Kant would say, because if God's actions are not to be understood in terms of the moral law, then God might conceivably do unjust things. The moral law cannot be based on anything else or deduced from anything else—God or nature. It is the law of reason, pure reason, in no way dependent on experience. If one asks where it gets its content, Kant, like Rousseau, answers: from its form—the form of law, meaning generality, universality, and rationality, is sufficient to supply the moral law. And if this is the moral law, Strauss points out, it becomes impossible to criticize political proposals like universal peace or the United Nations on the grounds that they disagree with human nature or experience.

"Morality as Kant understands it liberates man from the tutelage of nature" (chapter 9, xx). And Strauss quickly traces the consequences of that liberation. If man owes his dignity to the moral law alone, Fichte concluded, man's duty consists in subjugating everything else, in him and without him, to the moral law, because nothing else has any intrinsic worth. Marx then showed that if the moral law demands virtuous activity in the Aristotelian sense of the full development of one's distinctively human faculties, but the division of labor makes that impossible, it is necessary to abolish and overcome that division with technology. Nature is only an obstacle to be overcome; nature does not supply guidance in any way. Strauss quotes statements from Nietzsche's *Beyond Good and Evil* to show that in modern political philosophy not merely is nature understood to be "immoderately wasteful, immoderately indifferent, devoid of intentions and considerateness, devoid of compassion and sense of justice, fruitful and desolate and uncertain at the same time" (§ 9), but "every morality . . . is a work of tyranny against 'nature,' and also against 'reason'" (§ 118; chapter 9, xx). "That which for Kant was the justification of nature, namely, that nature is the only rational interpretation of sense data," Strauss concludes, ". . . has become doubtful for Nietzsche" (chapter 9, xx). In other words, the understanding of nature characteristic of modern science has become, in Nagel's terms, "a historically contingent way of interpreting things" (chapter 9, xx). Rather than knowledge of nature, modern "natural" science appears to be a human construct.

Strauss then contrasts this modern understanding of nature as the rational ordering of sense data with the classical understanding of nature as a term of distinction. The term (*physis*) first appears in *Odyssey* 10.300 where Hermes informs Odysseus about the "nature" of a certain herb—in effect, its look (*eidos*) and power (*dynamis*). It is then to be found in Thucydides's observations about the "nature" of a place, which he proceeds to describe as "the place itself" (4.3–4) and thus points to the difference between nature (or what is there) and art (what is made of it). Finally and most famously, Aristotle observes that fire burns in Persia just as it burns in Greece,[20] although the laws differ. On the basis of this distinction between nature and convention (which Strauss insists was not the invention of the sophists), classical political philosophers raised the question whether there is anything just and noble by nature.[21]

In opposition to Collingwood, Strauss suggests that ancient and modern political philosophers ask the same question. He emphasizes, however, that they answer that question in importantly different ways and quotes Hegel's description of the difference:

> The manner of study in ancient times is distinct from that of modern times, in that the former consisted in the veritable training and perfecting of the natural consciousness. . . . Philosophizing about everything it came across, the natural consciousness transformed itself into a universality of abstract understanding. . . . In modern times, however, the individual finds the abstract form ready made. (Chapter 9, xx)

"What happened in classical philosophy, especially political philosophy," Strauss emphasizes, "is the primary acquisition of concepts . . . as distinguished from the use of concepts already acquired . . . there is not a single technical term in the properly political writings . . . of Plato and Aristotle. . . . What they do, especially Aristotle, is to define [these terms] more precisely, and this more precise definition became then the great heritage of the West" (chapter 9, xx). In order for us "moderns" to unearth the experiences upon which the concepts in terms of which we understand our own experience are based, we must, therefore, study classical political philosophy—in its own terms, and not in ours.

III. THE CLASSICAL WORK OF CLASSICAL POLITICAL PHILOSOPHY: ARISTOTLE'S *POLITICS*

Where, then, should we begin our study of classical political philosophy? Strauss suggests that we begin with Aristotle, rather than with Plato, the tragedians, or Thucydides, all of whom wrote earlier, because unlike Plato, the tragedians, or Thucydides, Aristotle speaks directly in his own name.

Space constraints prevented us from including Strauss's lectures on Aristotle in this volume. However, they are available online at https://leostrausscenter.uchicago.edu/courses. The following summary is intended to indicate the contents of those lectures as well as the reasons Strauss thought it was necessary to study classical political philosophy in order to see the way in which modern political philosophy has reshaped our understanding as well as our practice.

Because Aristotle begins his *Politics* with a definition of the political association or *polis*, the question immediately arises about how the word should be translated. Strauss agrees with Collingwood that *polis* should not be translated "state," because the ancients did not distinguish between "state" and "society." *Polis* can be accurately translated as "commonwealth," but, Strauss comments, selection of an appropriate term does not resolve the substantive issue. Aristotle defines the *polis* in terms of its end, the achievement of *eudaimonia* or happiness, which he equates with a life of virtue. We moderns tend to think that happiness is subjective. Schooled in the logic of the Declaration of Independence, Americans believe that people have many different notions of happiness, but they recognize the necessity of securing the conditions for the pursuit of happiness. Since the conditions are means to achieving another end, what the state does is, in one respect, lower than the private ends it serves. However, because private notions of happiness are merely subjective, whereas the conditions of pursuing it are objective, what the states does is, in another respect, higher. Modern people have invented a concept or term for the matrix of which state and society are a part: culture. But our concept of culture includes art and thought, whereas the classics thought that "polis and wisdom are not only distinguishable, but have a fundamentally different character, insofar as the polis is always this or that polis, whereas wisdom is universal." We no longer recognize the tension the classics saw between the *polis* and philosophy, because of a great movement called the Enlightenment, which suggested that wisdom could be diffused among the whole population so that the difference between the theoretically wise and theoretically unwise ceases to be important.

Aristotle argues not only that the *polis* is the highest and most comprehensive form of human association, because it has the highest and most comprehensive end, but also that both that end and the *polis* are natural. The *polis* is natural not merely because it is composed of smaller associations or parts, households, which develop naturally. It is natural because human beings can achieve their full development or completion only in such an association. So understood, the *polis* embodies the understanding of nature as a term of distinction, and, Strauss points out, nature so understood can be used in the plural. Each kind of thing has its own nature. That nature defines it and its limits. Later in the *Politics* Aristotle thus suggests that the *polis* is natural in a third respect as well: it is a society large enough to fulfill all of man's essential natural needs, but small enough to be commensurate with the limitations of man's natural powers of knowing and caring. The proposition that the *polis* is natural also means that, in contrast to the poets, Aristotle does not think that the *polis* is sacred.

Having examined Aristotle's argument that the *polis* as a whole is natural, Strauss follows Aristotle by looking at its parts. Aristotle begins with the association between master and slave that he argues is a necessary part of the household (*oikos*), and asks whether slavery is natural or conventional. Once again, Strauss notes that nature provides the standard of what is just or unjust. Using the relation between soul and body as his primary example, Aristotle first suggests that nature as a whole is hierarchical. He then maintains that a human being who can understand and obey the commands of reason but cannot formulate such commands for himself is naturally a slave, but that it is unjust to enslave prisoners of war who are not naturally slaves as the Greeks customarily did.

The art of household management includes knowledge of how to acquire and use the nonhuman as well as human forms of property necessary to live a good life. But Aristotle distinguishes this natural form of acquisition, which is limited to what one can use, from the unlimited and therefore unnatural art of making money. Aristotle points out that everything has two kinds of uses—one proper to itself and another not. A shoe, for example, can be worn or exchanged for something else. Strauss observes that Marx picked up this Aristotelian distinction between use and exchange value but that Marx gave it a very different interpretation, because he combined it with Locke's labor theory of value. According to Locke and Marx, the origin of all true wealth is human production; nature merely supplies the almost worthless materials. At this point early in the *Politics* Aristotle suggests, on the contrary, that nature provides us with what we need. Modern thinkers consider nature to be something to be conquered, but, Strauss points out, this modern view faces the difficulty that man owes his ability or potential to conquer nature not to himself but ultimately to nature itself. Aristotle's contention that the *polis* is natural also means that it is not, contrary to early modern political philosophy, the product of a contract or convention.

In contrast not merely to modern political philosophers but also and more immediately to Plato, as Strauss emphasizes, Aristotle argues that the *polis* is a distinct kind of association, not only different from but also higher than the household.

Recognizing his inability to comment on all parts of the text, Strauss selects the arguments in book 2 that reflect Aristotle's distinctive approach. In contrast to all his other treatises, Strauss observes, Aristotle begins his examination of the ideas of others about the best regime by explaining that he is not criticizing the others for their ambition, because ambition is a passion that is particularly prominent in politics.[22] He then argues that the communistic institutions Socrates proposes in the *Republic* would not be desirable, because human beings care only for things and people they understand to be their particular responsibility, i.e., because of their natural limitations as human beings. Strauss also points out that Aristotle appeals to the sense of decency of the well-brought-up people he explicitly said he was addressing in the *Nicomachean Ethics* (1.1095b5–7), by arguing that the abolition of the private family would result in incest and that the abolition of private property would make it impossible for anyone to be temperate or generous.

Although Aristotle acknowledges both the novelty and the beauty of the proposals Socrates makes in the *Republic*, he concludes that "if these proposals were sound, then people would have become aware of them" (2.1264a1–3). And Strauss comments: "Aristotle does not say that everything that is, is reasonable. But he says that what is reasonable is some-

how known" (session 11). The political consequences of Aristotle's contention become manifest in his criticism of Hippodamus. Aristotle shows
that Hippodamus's apparently simple scheme of dividing everything—
citizens, laws, land—into thirds results in immense confusion, because
he does not take account of the distinctively political but tries to interpret
it on the basis of concepts supplied by science that deal with the subhuman. The most important example is his proposal that anyone who
invents something of use to the city should be honored. Aristotle does not
deny that human beings have made great progress since ancient times, not
only in the arts and science, but also in politics. But, he warns, improvement in politics always comes at a cost because law owes its power to
custom or habit *alone*—not to its intrinsic reasonableness.[23] Any change
in the law thus weakens the law.

Strauss makes only one more point about the contents of book 2
before he goes on to book 3, which contains "the fundamental discussion
of Aristotle's *Politics*" (session 11). One of the three actual regimes that are
supposed to be good—Sparta, Crete, and Carthage—is not a Greek city.
Contrary to some historicist claims, Aristotle's analysis of the *polis* was
not limited to "Greek city-states."

At the beginning of book 3 Aristotle again raises the question, what
is the *polis*? That's strange, Strauss comments, because Aristotle has apparently already told us what the *polis* is in book 1. Aristotle raises the
question again because the *polis* is shaped or defined most decisively by
its form of government or *politeia*. *Politeia* is often translated as "constitution," but that is too legalistic. The *politeia* refers to the group of people
who factually rule and thus make or determine what the law is. The question that animates political life is not whether people should live in a political association or not, but who should rule.[24]

Recognizing that there are different forms of government, Aristotle
develops a basic table of six forms on the basis of the number of people
ruling and whether they rule for the common benefit or in their own
interest: The one monarch, few aristocrats, or many people in a polity
rule for the common good, whereas a single tyrant, few oligarchs, and the
multitude in a democracy rule in their own interest. As Aristotle makes
clear in later books, there are varieties of these basic types and there can
be mixtures.

Strauss admits that at first glance Aristotle's understanding of democracy as the rule of the many poor in their own interest appears to be very
far from modern liberal or representative democracy. But Strauss points

out that by "poor" Aristotle means those who have to work for a living. Modern and ancient democracies have something fundamental in common because neither has a property qualification for holding office. Modern democracy is more egalitarian than ancient democracy inasmuch as it does not recognize the legitimacy of slavery, but it is less democratic insofar as it does not select public officials primarily by lot. Election of individuals on the basis of merit is from an Aristotelian point of view an aristocratic institution; it characterizes the mixture of democracy and aristocracy that Aristotle later suggests is the best regime generally possible.

Political life is characterized by conflict because different groups raise claims to rule on the basis of different understandings of justice. Democrats say that equals should receive equal amounts, but oligarchs retort that unequals should be rewarded unequally. Citing his discussion of justice in his *Ethics* (5.1134b18–1135a8), Aristotle agrees that justice is proportional. He asks, however, equal and unequal in what? Democrats assert that they are equally free; oligarchs seek recognition for their superior wealth. But, Aristotle observes, a political association is not merely a defensive league or a trading alliance. It exists for the sake of living a good or noble life. Therefore, those with the most virtue have the best claim to rule. The question, then, is how this virtue is actually distributed. Each member of the demos may be less noble than one of the few gentlemen, but the demos as a whole may possess more virtue than a few. Likewise, if virtue gives someone a right to rule, the one best man may have the most. Aristotle thus presents his strongest argument on behalf of democracy followed by the case for the other extreme, rule by the one best man. Not merely may a democratic people possess more virtue in sum than its few most distinguished citizens. Using the example of an architect and the inhabitants of a house, Aristotle observes that there are some decisions that can be made better by the many people who receive services than by the few who provide them. However, although the members of a particularly virtuous demos would be able to participate in making deliberative and judicial decisions, they are not capable of serving in the highest offices.[25] Because not all peoples are virtuous and their virtue is in the best case limited, Aristotle then turns to consider the claims of the one best man. Someone might object that not a man but the law should rule because law is intellect without passion, but, Aristotle observes, laws have to be formulated and administered by human beings. Because human beings are passionate and tend to favor themselves, it is best for more than one to rule and for them to rule and be ruled in turn.

However, if there is one person so obviously superior to all others as to be virtually a god among men, it would not be just for that person to be ruled by anyone else.

Although book 4 clearly follows book 3, Strauss observes, the last sentence in book 3 points to the discussion of the best regime in books 7 and 8. The reason for this ambiguity in the order of the text is that "one cannot see the more or less imperfect regimes discussed in the central books without awareness of the best" (session 14). Because Strauss has emphasized Aristotle's contention that the nature of a thing can be understood only from its complete development, he turns to Aristotle's discussion of the best regime before he comments on Aristotle's discussion of the lesser but more frequently encountered regimes in the central books of the *Politics*.[26]

To determine what the best regime is, Aristotle reasons, we need to know what is the most choiceworthy form of life. In his *Nicomachean Ethics* he showed that there are three kinds of goods. Since both external and bodily goods are means to the achievement of the goods of the soul or virtue, he reasons, both individuals and polities should devote themselves to the acquisition and exercise of virtue. The end of the *polis* and the individual are thus the same. Aristotle observes, however, that there are two kinds of virtue: moral and intellectual. Because happiness consists in activity and the moral virtues are matters of practice, it might seem that they are the end. However, activity does not have to involve other people; on the contrary, Aristotle argues, contemplation is the highest and most self-sufficient form of activity. And Strauss comments that that means the end of the *polis* and the end of the individual are only analogous, not identical. According to Aristotle, a *polis* should concentrate on perfecting its internal order rather than expanding imperialistically, but a *polis* does not philosophize.

In constructing the best regime, Aristotle begins with the matter. There must be a large enough number of people to make the *polis* self-sufficient, but not too many to prevent them from knowing, trusting, and supervising each other. Aristotle then observes that there are seven indispensable kinds of work in every city provided by farmers, artisans, merchants, soldiers, the wealthy who supply a store of goods, priests, and the government. Some people may perform more than one function, e.g., farmers can be soldiers. But, Aristotle insists, those who do not contribute to the end of the *polis* should not be citizens. Farmers, artisans, and merchants should be excluded, because they do not have the leisure required to acquire and exercise virtue. In the best regime, Strauss comments, there is no *demos*. The necessary tasks will be performed by slaves. To prevent them from rebelling, as in Sparta, the slaves should be promised emancipation if they behave. But, Strauss points out, if the slaves are capable of living as free men, they are not slaves by nature. This necessary injustice can be defended so long as there is an economy of scarcity. Most people do not have the leisure needed to acquire the education requisite for ruling, and no one wants to be ruled by the unwise. Aristotle goes into great detail about the generation of children, but the most important question is education. Those who participate in ruling need to be educated "liberally," i.e., not as a slave. Although Aristotle recognizes that skills in reading, writing, and arithmetic can be used in trade, he argues that citizens need to learn them in order to contemplate (but not make) beautiful works of music. Such contemplation, Strauss suggests, is a reflection, but merely a reflection, of the excellence of the truly contemplative, philosophical life.

At the beginning of book 4 Aristotle insists that political science must do more than describe the best regime, as Plato does, or praise an existing regime like Sparta. To be useful to a legislator, political science must include knowledge of all regimes, which sort is appropriate for what kind of people, how to preserve or change each regime, and what the best generally possible regime is. People often see two and only two kinds of imperfect regimes: democracy and oligarchy. In fact, however, there are several kinds of democracies and several kinds of oligarchies. The differences arise from differences in the occupations or sources of wealth of the dominant class. In the best because least extreme and thus least unjust form of democracy, as in the best because least extreme form of oligarchy, citizens are farmers who do not have time to gather in the city to attend political meetings; as a result the laws rule. Better still is a regime that mixes democratic and oligarchic elements so that rich and poor both share in rule and neither is expropriated or oppressed.[27] To indicate how such a mixture can be constructed, Aristotle distinguishes three functions of government: deliberative, magisterial, and judicial. This distinction differs from the "separation of powers" Montesquieu later advocates, Strauss points out, because Montesquieu's overriding interest in checking and balancing the powers of the government is the security of the individual, whereas Aristotle declared in book 1 that the *polis* is prior to the individual.

Investigating the causes of the preservation or change of regimes, Aristotle emphasizes that the decisive factor is "that the number of those who wish a regime to continue be greater than the number of those who do not" (1309b20). As we might infer from Aristotle's initial definition of political rule as the rule of free and equal people in turn, in contrast to the rule of a master over slaves or a father over children, Strauss points out that the *polis* is fundamentally democratic. The principle of democracy is freedom, and Aristotle shows that that means that democracy has two fundamental characteristics: first, ruling and being ruled in turn means that no citizen is simply a subject; and, second, each is to live as he pleases. "Some things in Aristotle remind one of Rousseau, but there is a very great difference. . . . Aristotle does not suggest for one moment that in a democracy there must be a total submission of everyone in every respect to the general will" (session 15). The permissiveness of ancient democracy is as important as its egalitarianism.

The most obvious limitation of Aristotle's political science from a contemporary point of view is that he does not include the regimes that concern us most—liberal democratic, fascist, or communist—in his sixfold schema. But, Strauss contends, Aristotle enables us to understand their distinctive principle. By emphasizing the polarity between the fundamentally democratic character of the *polis* and the virtue and wisdom of the one best man, Aristotle lets us see that modern regimes presuppose the harmonization of the ends of the people and the philosopher. Modern science promises not only to enlighten the people but also to overcome the economy of scarcity. Modern democracies are based on technology, as Comte recognized when he predicted the rule of scientists (or, we would say, technocrats).[28]

And, Strauss suggests, the most fundamental limitation of Aristotle's political science comes to light from the most obvious difference between his political science and ours. Aristotle understands politics in terms of its end, happiness, and he understands happiness to be a life of virtue. Aristotle therefore devotes the first part of his two-part treatise on politics to ethics. That would be inconceivable for a contemporary positivist political scientist.

What, then, does Aristotle understand the end of politics—or virtue—to be? There are two peaks of moral virtue, as Aristotle presents it in his *Nicomachean Ethics*: justice in one's relations to others and magnanimity as the sum of all virtues in an individual. In defining justice, Strauss observes, Aristotle distinguishes between conventional and natural, but he declares that both kinds of justice are variable. Human beings can discern what is right (or just) under the circumstances, if they are prudent. But prudence also has two parts or aspects. A prudent person must be able not only to calculate the best means to any given end, but also to choose the right end. And to be able to choose the right end, a person must have been brought up well. But, Strauss asks, how do we know what constitutes a sound upbringing? The answer we get from looking at the characteristics Aristotle attributes to the magnanimous man is this: opinion.

Strauss contrasts Aristotle's treatment of the moral virtues with Plato's. In the dialogues we not only hear characters like Callicles and Thrasymachus ask, as Aristotle's decent auditors never would, why be decent or virtuous? In the *Republic* we also see Socrates provide a theoretical foundation for the virtues in an analysis of the parts of the soul. Aristotle never does that. In *De Anima* he states that theoretical wisdom is the end of man, but he never presents the moral virtues merely or explicitly as the means of achieving that end. If the moral virtues are seen merely to be means, he recognizes, they are no longer chosen for their own sake or truly virtuous. The problem becomes even worse, Strauss observes, if the virtues, like justice, are seen to be the necessary means of achieving the common good. As Machiavelli dramatically points out, if virtue consists in doing what is necessary to achieve the common good, what is usually considered to be vicious behavior will in certain circumstances be virtuous. To avoid Machiavellianism, we have to understand the *polis* as being for the sake of moral virtue. That is what Aristotle explicitly does. He recognizes that moral virtue is necessary to acquire theoretical virtue, but he does not pay attention to theoretical virtue in the *Politics*, because philosophy is not part of the city. He presents moral virtue as irreducible to any other end, not because it is absolute as in Kant, but because moral virtue is the place where the requirements of the two fundamental ends of man—theoretical life and society—meet. By arguing that evils in cities will not cease until philosophers become kings but then showing that is impossible by requiring the expulsion of everyone more than ten years of age from the city, Plato in the *Republic* reveals the limits, character, and nature of political things more clearly than Aristotle does. As illustrated by the noble lie, "the political community must be ascribed a naturalness, a sacredness, which it cannot truly claim, but which is necessary for its being a unity" (session 16).

At the end of his "Introduction" Strauss thus indicates more clearly than he does in *The City and Man* why he begins his examination of classical political philosophy with Aristotle, but moves back first to Plato and ultimately to Thucydides. These lectures are explicitly only an "introduction." In them Strauss explains perhaps more clearly and directly than in his published works why he thought political philosophy, which is not inherently a historical study, must begin in our time with a study of the history of political philosophy.

Catherine Zuckert, University of Notre Dame

Editorial Headnote

This volume includes transcripts of nine of the sixteen sessions of Strauss's course, "Introduction to Political Philosophy," offered in 1965. The course was a lecture course that included both undergraduates and graduate students. Strauss himself reads passages from the text, often making use of his own translations. The primary texts discussed in the course are Auguste Comte, *Course in Positive Philosophy* (1830–42); Georg Simmel, *Introduction to Moral Science* [*Einleitung in die Moralwissenschaft*, 1892]; Arnold Brecht, *Political Theory: The Foundations of Twentieth-Century Political Thought* (Princeton: Princeton University Press, 1959); Ernest Nagel, *The Structure of Science: Problems in the Logic of Scientific Explanation* (New York: Harcourt, Brace & World, 1961); Friedrich Nietzsche, "On the Use and Abuse of History" and *Thus Spoke Zarathustra*, First Part, sec. 15; R. G. Collingwood, *The Idea of History*, ed. T. M. Knox (Oxford: Clarendon Press, 1946), and *An Autobiography* (Oxford: Oxford University Press, 1939). Citations are included for all passages read aloud.

The transcripts of chapters 1–5 and 7–9 are based on the existing remastered audiofiles. The transcript of chapter 6 is based on the original transcript, which was made by persons unknown to us and which can be consulted in the Leo Strauss archive in Special Collections at the University of Chicago Library. Audio files and a transcript of sessions 10–16 of the course, which address Aristotle's *Politics*, are available on the Leo Strauss Center website.

Minor changes to the transcript are not noted. For example, we have corrected inaccurate noun-verb agreement, rectified peculiar word order, and inserted prepositions or connecting words in the interest of readability. Sentence fragments that might not be appropriate in academic prose have been kept; some long and rambling sentences have been divided; some repeated clauses or words have been deleted. A clause that breaks the syntax or train of thought may have been moved elsewhere in the sentence or paragraph. In rare cases sentences within a paragraph may have been reordered.

Administrative details regarding paper topics or meeting rooms or times have been deleted without being noted, but reading assignments have been retained. Notes have been provided to identify persons, texts, and events to which Strauss refers.

A version of the transcript showing all deletions and insertions will become available on the Leo Strauss Center website two years after print publication of this transcript and can be made available upon request meanwhile for the same price as the printed version. The original transcript may be consulted in the Strauss archive in Special Collections at the University of Chicago Library.

This transcript was edited by Catherine Zuckert with assistance from Les Harris and Philip Bretton.

I

The Obstacles to the Study of Political Philosophy Today

A. Positivism

1 Comte as the Founder of Positivism

The Three Stages of the History of Mankind

LEO STRAUSS: [In progress] Political action is founded upon knowledge. Therefore, all political action points to knowledge of the politically good or bad. The complete political good, we call the good society. In every political action there is implied a reference to the good society. All politically acting men are concerned with that; whether they call it the good society or call it by another name is a secondary question. There are people who would deny that there is anything to be called the common good, which is another way of speaking of the good society, but these same people speak of the "open society," by which they mean the good society. President Johnson likes to speak of the Great Society, which is in its wording somewhat different from the good society. But I think President Johnson means by "the Great Society" the good society. Why he and other contemporaries prefer to speak of the Great Society rather than of the good society is an interesting question, but one which doesn't have to concern us here now.

Now if this is so, if all concern with political things, all political action, points towards the question of the good society, and the good society is *the* theme of political philosophy, one seemingly paradoxical consequence follows: that there is no fundamental distinction between political philosophy and political science. This was the older view, according to which the study of the more or less imperfect societies is part of the same study which is concerned above all with the good society. This can be compared with the relation between physiology and pathology: they are in a way separable, but obviously the study of the healthy body and its workings points to the possibility of diseases, and you cannot diagnose the diseases unless you know what a healthy body is. This is the way in which above all Plato in the *Republic* and Aristotle in the *Politics* deal with all kinds of political societies, perfect or imperfect.

The situation in which we find ourselves today is characterized by the fact that, in the first place, political philosophy is thought to be radically different from political science. In the mildest form, political science is a whole of which political philosophy is one of many parts. But it is clearer and more straightforward to say that political philosophy is no longer credible at all, and that it is partly the continuation of an ever-weakening tradition which explains the fact that political philosophy is still academically recognized. Political philosophy is no longer credible, and political science takes its place—to make this quite clear: a *nonphilosophic* political science. This is, if not the full reality today, at least the tendency.

Now while this is true and could easily be borne out by quotations, it is also true that political science is in need of what is called political theory, and in this respect I think there is unanimity. Theory, in contradistinction to philosophy, can be scientific. Think of the theory of numbers, theory of functions, theory of evolution, and so on. These are all scientific phenomena. Political theory, according to this view, is a branch of political science among others; only look at the announcements of this department to see that this is the prevailing view. All fields of political science are related to the others. For example, agricultural politics and foreign aid are in foreign relations. But political theory is more related to the other fields than any others among themselves. Political theory is the most general of the fields of political science.

What is political theory? You would help me if you would answer me that question, because I have some notion of what has been suggested in the course of the last thirty years as to what political theory is, but there is a great variety of opinions. Will the most articulate among you tell me? Well, since I seem to be unable to overcome this shyness so becoming young people, I will at least give a few of the views which I have found. [Laughter] You find the view, for example, that political theory, this universal discipline which has its finger in all pies, is needed for guiding research. It is a theory of theory-formulations, one could say. Political theory thus understood does not claim to meet the political issues, the so-called "isms." Therefore, there is another understanding of political theory according to which political theory is that pursuit which is primarily concerned with the "isms"—democracy, communism, fascism—dealing with the ideologies, the operative ideals, of course, primarily within the United States, with ideals operative within the United States. Political theory thus understood is not possible without history. For example, you cannot understand the American operative ideals without understanding what the United States Constitution was originally meant to be. You have to study the *Federalist* papers, and if you want to understand them properly, you have to go back to the authorities guiding the founding fathers, guiding especially Hamilton and Madison: Montesquieu, and so on and so on. You are led back eventually to classical antiquity.

Now a third meaning is indicated by the recollection of the fact that fifty years ago, I believe the general answer to what political theory is about would have been to say that it has to do with the state, the state understood as a sovereign state. The sovereign state, according to this doctrine, was distinguished from society. And a development took place there, around 1900, which led to what is called pluralism, according to which the state is only one of many associations, each having a function of its own but none of these associations can be said to be superior to any other. So the state in particular cannot be said to be superior to the churches, trade unions, etc. This pluralistic doctrine questioned the crucial importance of the state, and even if we take the state proper, it is easy to observe (especially in a democracy) that its action is determined by the interplay of interest groups or groups of other sorts. Furthermore, there are movements opposed to the state, denying the importance of the state: anarchism, and to some extent communism. And yet these movements, anarchism and communism, are without any question political movements. So it seems that "political" is a wider term than "state," and therefore it was suggested that *the* theme should rather be the political than the state. So in other words, the state has lost this evidence which it had for quite some time, surely throughout the nineteenth century. Now one can of course also say that political theory is sometimes meant to consist of overall reflections, comprehensive reflections, about policy in our age, reflections more elaborated than they can be elaborated in an inaugural address, but as they find their expression to some extent within an inaugural address.

These are the views of political theory which one would discover on the basis of present-day usage. Did I omit any meaning of political theory with which you are familiar? Please tell me.

Now political philosophy, as I said before, has become incredible, implausible. In order to understand what that means, we have to formulate the objections to political philosophy. The simple argument which I stated earlier, which leads from the fact that every political action is concerned with better or worse, this simple reflection has no longer the plausibility which it has had for centuries. Now what are these objections to the possibility of political philosophy? The most powerful one can be stated as follows. All genuine knowledge is scientific knowledge, but philosophic knowledge is not scientific knowledge. Hence political philosophy is not genuine knowledge. I will elaborate this while I go. Let us first reflect upon the crucial part of this reasoning: all genuine knowledge is scientific knowledge. This view is called, and may be called, positivism, and we will first discuss that.

Now the founder of positivism, the originator of that term, is the French thinker of the early nineteenth century Auguste Comte. [LS writes on the blackboard.] And I will first present the Comtean position, which is by no means identical with the positivistic position as now prevailing, but we cannot understand the positivism of today without having first understood Comte. Now I will give you the titles of his chief works, translated into English: *Course of Positive Philosophy*, six volumes from 1830 to 1842, and *System of Positive Politics*, 1851 to 1854. Auguste Comte was originally connected with Saint-Simon, one of these early socialists who were called by Marx and Engels the "utopian socialists," and there are quite a few things which Comte has in common with Saint-Simon.[1] But Comte ceased to be a socialist very early. Nevertheless, the similarity of his problem with the problem as seen by Marx is very great, as you will gradually see. Now the basis of Comte's doctrine is the well-known success of modern science since the time of Galileo and its ever-spreading impact on modern society. In order to be enabled to form an independent judgment of what this success of modern science means, let us remember the most striking features of pre-Galilean science, traditional science, Aristotelian science. The simplest thing to do is to write here. [LS writes on the blackboard.] Now according to the Aristotelian scheme, philosophy or science—there is no distinction made—consists of two main parts. One is called theoretical and the other is called practical. Each consists of three parts: the theoretical consists of mathematics, physics (which is used here in a wide sense to include all natural science), and metaphysics. Practical philosophy or science consists of three parts: ethics, economics, and politics. ("Economics" means here the management of the household or the family, not what it has come to mean in modern times.) Now in Comte's scheme, the division of the sciences is as follows: mathematics, physics, chemistry, biology, and social physics, or sociology. These terms, "sociology" and "social physics," have been coined by Comte. There is in addition a philosophy dealing with these various sciences, understanding the meaning of mathematics, biology, sociology, etc., and this overall reflection on science and the sciences is what Comte calls positive philosophy.

Now what are the decisive differences between the Comtean and the Aristotelian schemes? (The Comtean scheme is, by the way, the scheme now generally recognized, with minor additions: mathematics is a fundamental science, and so on, and social science is the last in the order of the sciences.) Now obviously in Comte's scheme there is no metaphysics. The second point, which was no longer a question for Comte at all, but which is in the light of history of immense importance, is this: that the natural sciences, or physics in the wide sense of the term, were originally not metaphysically neutral. I mean by that that up to Galileo and Newton in the seventeenth century, a student of nature was either an Aristotelian, or a Platonist, or an Epicurean, or a Stoic. There was not *physics*, but Aristotelian, Platonic, Epicurean, Stoic physics. There were pursuits which were metaphysically neutral, where it did not make any difference whether you were a Platonist or an Epicurean: for example, shoemaking, to some extent also medicine, and also mathematics. But the epoch-making event was that the study of nature became as metaphysically neutral as shoemaking, medicine, and mathematics always more or less had been. The third point which I will mention right now is this: that what Aristotle called practical science is here replaced by a theoretical science, sociology. Sociology is as theoretical as mathematics, physics, and chemistry. Every science according to Comte has its practical applications, naturally—mathematics, physics, chemistry—and so has sociology. But the science in itself, the science of man and of human affairs, is as theoretical as the other sciences. Therefore, for Aristotle, ethics—or let me speak more specifically of politics—political science is fundamentally independent of the natural sciences. I mean that it uses the natural sciences in a subsidiary fashion goes without saying, but in itself it is independent of the natural sciences. But in the Comtean scheme, sociology, the study of human society, is as much dependent on biology as biology is dependent on chemistry, and chemistry is dependent on physics, and physics is dependent on mathematics. That is a crucial difference, and this is of course very important for the understanding of what social science means today. It is no longer understood that a social scientist has had a very thorough training in mathematics, physics, and chemistry, but on the highest level of social science in the modern sense, this dependence on the preceding sciences (preceding in the order of the sciences) still is of crucial importance. Comte implies that *the* fundamental science, the science on which all others depend, is mathematics. Mathematics is the model; hence science formulates laws, equations, preferably in mathematical form.

Now positive philosophy, the understanding of all intellectual activity which has reached the level of science, this one cannot do if one does not know its history. According to Comte, this is true of every conception: one cannot completely know a science without knowing its history, and this is impossible without studying, in a general way, the history of mankind. The broad result of Comte's study of the history of mankind is that it consists of three stages, of three successive philosophies, as he calls it, so much so that every science, say, mathematics or chemistry, goes through each of these three stages. The three stages are called by Comte the theological stage, the metaphysical stage, and the positive stage. "Positive" you can almost identify with "scientific," but I have to use his terminology. At all times, man needs a philosophy for observing facts as well as a social bond. We cannot observe facts without selecting facts, and we must therefore have principles guiding our selection. To that extent, a theory, a philosophy, precedes all observation. But we need also a philosophy, in the sense of Comte, as a social bond. Men cannot live together without an agreement regarding fundamentals, as others have put it. Now what are these three stages?

The first is the theological stage, in which man believes that he can answer the grandest questions and that he can exercise an unlimited control over the external world by substituting for the things wills which he can influence. There are three stages of that, according to Comte, which he called fetishism, polytheism, and monotheism. In this early stage, which lasted in a way up to the present day, man believes he knows the origin as well as the destiny of the universe. He claims to possess absolute knowledge, and he finds this absolute knowledge supplied by the assumption of supernatural, willing agents. Comte explains the primacy of the theological philosophy as follows: that man has a tendency to transport involuntarily the intimate sentiment of his own nature to the universal explanation of all phenomena whatsoever. The anthropocentric approach, in other words, is natural to man, and it finds its perfect expression in the theological stage.

The second stage is the metaphysical stage, in which the willing beings, persons, are replaced by abstract forces, as he calls them, by personified abstractions. The highest stage of this is that in which Nature with a capital N is understood as the universal source of all phenomena. Another formula which he uses is that in the metaphysical stage, entity is substituted for divinity. These two stages take as their principles our immediate sentiments of human phenomena, our immediate sentiments of man, and hence they seek to explain the universe and all particulars in terms of will. Those who have any knowledge of what is called metaphysics may not recognize metaphysics at all in Comte's description, but let me say only this. What he has in mind is a teleological analysis, say, in the form of Aristotle, that a being tends toward something. This of course is not a will in the beings, say, as in a worm or any other being which tends toward the peak of its growth, but the very speaking of tendency implies thinking in terms of willing. That he has in mind.

The positive stage is characterized by the fact that its starting point is obviously not will, but numbers. The fundamental science is mathematics, and therewith any attempt to explain phenomena in terms of will is excluded. In the positive stage, man abandons the question of the origin and destiny of everything. It abandons the claim, or the aim, of absolute knowledge: only relative knowledge is possible. What does that mean? In the positive stage, man no longer asks for the Why but is only concerned with the How: how things operate, not why they operate in this manner. For example, there is no longer any speculation on the origin of life or the origin of the species, according to Comte. In this particular point, Comte was obviously refuted by the later development of biology, to say nothing of Lamarck, who had already preceded him.[2] But the fundamental thesis, that science is concerned with the How and not with the Why, has survived Comte up to the present day in many circles. Another example: Man is no longer concerned in the positive stage with whether inanimate and animate beings have or do not have the same or a different nature. This is according to Comte an insoluble question. In the positive stage, man studies the phenomena alone with a view to their laws, the invariable relations of succession and simultaneity. The type of this positive knowledge is this: given these and these conditions, this and this happens. This is not in Comte's view a statement about causes but about correlation: here are conditions, there are the things related, succeeding these conditions. Newton's laws of gravitation do not determine what attraction is in itself, what its cause is, but how attraction works. He says on one occasion that the question of the first causes of all motion, of all life, whatever it may be, or of the final causes, the last causes, is meaningless for us—a phrase which has recurred many times since.

Now the positive stage, which cannot be properly understood if one doesn't see it as succeeding the theological and the metaphysical stages, is the final stage in the development of the human mind. There is no possibility of visualizing anything radically different from the scientific approach which has come into being since the seventeenth century and has spread ever more. The victory of the positive spirit is inevitable, i.e., it has not yet been entirely victorious, especially not in the social sciences, but it is inevitable, for the human mind is powerfully disposed toward unity of method, and in the long run men will not leave it at proceeding in this very successful manner, say, in physics and chemistry, and proceeding in a radically different manner in the study of human affairs. For the time being, say, 1835 or thereabouts, the theological and metaphysical philosophy have still a certain practical superiority over the positive philosophy because they still can maintain the claim to universality, to answering all questions, while positive philosophy has achieved a breakthrough only in certain fields, say, physics and chemistry especially. But the human mind cannot but reach its true definitive maturity, the positive spirit, in all fields.

What makes Comte certain of the future victory of the positive spirit is the constant progress of the positive spirit from generation to generation, and the corresponding constant decline of the theological and metaphysical spirit. The most important lacuna as far as the positive spirit is concerned is the study of the social phenomena. This has surely not yet reached the positive stage—that does not yet exist for social science, in other words. And the external fact that Comte coined the term "sociology" is an indication of this state of affairs: sociology did not yet exist before Comte. Hitherto we do not yet have, as Comte says, a social physics, but only a social theology or a social metaphysics. And the examples which he gives are, for social theology, the doctrine of the divine right of kings, which was of course still lingering on in continental Europe in the thirties of the last century, and for social metaphysics, the doctrine of the sovereignty of the people. These are examples which may give you some initial guidance as to what he means by the distinction between theology and metaphysics: the doctrine of the divine right of kings, a theological doctrine; the doctrine of the sovereignty of the people, a metaphysical doctrine.

Now while there can be no doubt regarding the intellectual superiority of the spirit of science and of science to all competitors, the positive spirit is not without its intrinsic dangers. The peculiar danger which is inherent in the victory of science is specialization. It becomes ever more necessary for men of science to be either physicists, or chemists, or whatever it may be. Where do we get that comprehensive view which, in however spurious a manner, the theological and metaphysical spirit supplied? Comte's answer is: We need a new kind of specialty, namely, a special study of science in general, of science as such and its relation to society. And that is what the positive philosophy of Comte is about. The social situation now is that the positive spirit, the scientific spirit, has destroyed the old certainties, i.e., the social bonds which hitherto kept society together. The consequence is anarchy, intellectual anarchy; the reconstruction is possible only through the application of the positive spirit to the social phenomena. For men need and society requires the assent, the more or less conscious assent, of all to a certain number of general ideas. These are no longer supplied by theology and cannot be supplied by metaphysics. The only way in which we can escape the anarchy caused by the destruction of the old certainties is that science supplies these certainties. We must see how he thinks of that.

The meaning of science is clearly indicated by the fact that the first of the sciences, the science par excellence, is mathematics. (By the way, what Comte says about mathematics is of course very much dated—there is no inkling of non-Euclidean geometry, for example—but within the limits of what could be known at the time, I find it very interesting and very clear, and so I think very helpful; especially if one wants to understand or at least to get an inkling of the fundamental difference between modern mathematics, analytical geometry and calculus, in contradistinction to earlier Greek mathematics, it is quite helpful.) Now "mathematics" meant in Greek originally the same as "science."[3] According to Comte, mathematics is the science which aims at the measuring of magnitudes, a determining of unknown magnitudes through known magnitudes, according to precise relations which exist between them. This kind of precision cannot be expected in all sciences; hence science in general may be said to determine phenomena, unknown phenomena, by other phenomena according to relations which exist between these series of phenomena. Science is essentially destined to dispense, to the extent to which the various kinds of phenomena permit it, with every direct observation by permitting one to deduce from a small number of immediately given data the largest possible number of results, so that theoretical mechanics would be the model of science. Every question can in principle be conceived of as reducible to a pure question of numbers. Descartes has shown that all ideas of quality can be reduced to ideas of quantity. Think of colors, and wavelengths, and such things. In fact, however, this is possible only for very simple phenomena; it is not possible for the subjects of biology and sociology.

In these sciences dealing with more complex phenomena, there exists a fundamental impossibility of our ever obtaining true mathematical laws.

Yet this does not entitle us, according to Comte, to give up the notion that all phenomena are necessarily subject to mathematical laws, although we shall never be able to discover them in these large fields. The positive spirit in Comte's sense—does that not depend on the availability of mathematical laws in all spheres? It depends on the expectation of such laws. In a way, the positive spirit is as old as man himself. At all times men needed, in order to survive, relations between facts . . . at all times men had arts which are based on such knowledge of relationships between facts. Generally speaking, men must have a reasonable respect for, I quote, "the crude but judicious indications of vulgar common sense, the true and eternal starting point of all wise scientific speculations."[4] In other words, common sense, prescientific understanding, is highly respectable because it is already, in a germinal way, scientific thinking. Now this importance of common sense applies especially to human affairs. Ordinary common sense is perfectly competent in regard to phenomena which by their nature are constantly submitted to its attentive consideration. A man dealing all his life with this kind of activity knows more about it than a scientist as scientist who doesn't have the same familiarity can possibly know. All isolated study of the various social elements, which is the way in which it is handled by scientists as scientists, is in itself irrational and sterile. In this sphere, the sphere of social things, all understanding must start from the whole and not from the elements. For the demand that one must proceed from the simple to the complex, a demand which is in a way underlying Comte's whole scheme, from mathematics and physics to sociology, is not the primary demand of the scientific mind. The primary demand is that we proceed from the known to the unknown. But in sociology, in the study of society, the whole is the thing which is known, and the elements are those towards which we have to proceed by analysis. In the social sphere, the most vulgar phenomena are the most important ones, and therefore the procedure in sociology, to some extent even in biology, must be different from that of the mathematical sciences strictly understood. The positive spirit, we may say, is universalized common sense and therefore not in opposition to it. Comte hesitates to assert that this is due to the fact that there is an essential difference between man, the subject of sociology, and brutes, the subject of biology, to say nothing of inanimate things. For according to Comte, there cannot be natures—a nature of man different from the nature of brutes—because this is metaphysics: intimate natures, as distinguished from phenomena and their manifest relations.

But Comte's consideration regarding the primacy of the whole in sociology goes very far to compensate for this tacit denial of essential differences. The fact that sociology, which means here the study of all social phenomena (it has a very broad meaning), is not reducible to biology, etc., does not mean that it is not to some extent based on biology, for example. For instance, biology, especially anatomy and physiology, has to fulfill a most important function in regard to the intellectual government of society. Anatomy and physiology must protect common sense in its on the whole just appraisal of the various levels of intelligence against the metaphysical view that all human intelligences are fundamentally equal. Biology as he understood it (I do not have to go into the particular teachings he had in mind) made sure that the intellectual levels of different human beings are very great. The differences are very great, and therefore the belief in the equality of men intellectually is a wrong assertion. Biology does fulfill here an important political or social function. Or also the overestimation of the merely acquired abilities as distinguished from the native abilities: this—and he said without any irony—this error, the overestimation of the acquired abilities, is fostered by the scientists themselves, the majority of whom are men of very mediocre minds and therefore must put all their emphasis on their learning rather than on their native abilities.

Yet the dependence of sociology on the preceding sciences means more than that. It means the primacy of the nonsocial and the subsocial— generally speaking, of the lower. Accordingly, there is only a difference of degree between the human mind and the mind of the brutes. The scholastic definition of man as the rational animal is, according to Comte, nonsense: no higher animal could live without being rational to some extent. Ideology, which means in Comte's terminology the same as what is now called psychology, is a part of zoology. In other words, human psychology as such doesn't exist. In connection with this, Comte teaches the primacy of the passions in contradistinction to reason and intelligence. The passions are the primary motive power in human life, and so far from being dependent on intelligence or resulting from it, they are the powers which awaken intelligence and bring about its continuous development. The passions, not reason, determine the permanent goal of the intellect, and the lowest passions are the strongest. Does this important strand in Comte's thought remind you of something? Yes?

STUDENT: Hobbes.

LS: Yes, Hobbes especially, but quite a few men in between. In other words, if we generalize from that, the materialistic tradition of the seventeenth century, going through French materialism, is living on very powerfully in Comte. But the interesting thing is that Comte is no longer formally a materialist. That is the meaning, the important implication, of positivism. From the positivistic point of view, materialism as materialism is a metaphysical doctrine, and positivism is opposed to materialism as much as to spiritualism. Yet it is surely an heir to the materialistic metaphysics.

Sociology is in a way the universal science. For all sciences must be understood in the light of a general theory of human development, of the development of the human mind. So you cannot understand mathematics in terms of numbers, because mathematics is not a number. Mathematics is a human pursuit, and this human pursuit can only be understood within the context of the development of the human mind, i.e., of the law of the three stages. Furthermore, the guidance of research and of discovery in all sciences requires a rational theory, and this rational theory is ultimately supplied by the needs of man, which needs of man can only be scientifically known by a science of man, by sociology. All sciences are the work of the human mind as social mind. From this point of view, sociology is the fundamental science.

Now the supremacy of the positive spirit means simply the obvious superiority of scientific explanations to theological or metaphysical explanations. This obvious supremacy of the positive spirit proves the necessity of a positive science of society—of what, to repeat, Comte calls sociology or social physics. Why do we not yet have a social science? Why has not the positive spirit made itself the master of the study of social phenomena, as it has made itself the master in physics? Now in the first place, the logical order of the sciences, from mathematics, biophysics, and so on to sociology, is at the same time the temporal order of their emergence. Chemistry could not become a science, a positive science, before physics had become a science. So only after biology has reached the scientific stage, which according to Comte was not the case before the end of the eighteenth century, could a social science become possible. More specifically, and more importantly, the phenomena most important for making social science possible did not yet exist before our time (our time meaning 1830 or thereabouts). Why? What is the most important phenomenon for making social science possible, that phenomenon which makes it possible to see society as a whole, properly, truly? A society is in a way always a whole, but this is insufficient. The larger whole of which all societies are a part is the development of the human race, and the development of the human race finds its completion in the positive spirit and its social implications. And this did not yet exist before the reaction to the French Revolution was completed, according to Comte. Social science is not possible before the completion of the development within the elite of the human race in our times. Prior to our times, the essential direction of the social movement was not sufficiently determined, there was no certainty as regards the progressive character of the historical process.

Classical political philosophy, that of Plato and Aristotle, coincided with the state of decline of ancient society. The notion of a more perfect state of things replacing a less perfect one, i.e., of progress, is due to Christianity, according to Comte: the distinction between the new law, the perfect new law, in contradistinction to the less perfect old law. Forerunners of the positive social science, according to Comte, are especially three men: Aristotle, whom he highly respects; Montesquieu; and Condorcet—you know, the victim of the French Revolution. Those of you who know Montesquieu, Aristotle, and Condorcet, at least to some extent, will be quite surprised by this combination because one can see that someone admires Aristotle and Montesquieu because of the very solid empirical character of their studies, which of course Comte means too, but Condorcet is very far removed from that. Later on it will be clear to you why he makes this peculiar selection. But he has also a certain respect for the political economists, especially Adam Smith, and the historical school of jurisprudence in Germany.

Prior to the French Revolution and the reaction to it, it was impossible to see that the history of the human race is a whole, has a physiognomy of its own, and this is its progressive character. And that insight makes social science possible; therefore there could be no social science before. Social science is necessary now, not only theoretically, in order to round off the whole of science, but above all practically. Public morality needs a solid basis, and practical politics needs reliable guidance, a vision of the future. This indispensable agreement regarding the fundamentals can now, after the decay of theological and metaphysical thought, be supplied only by science. As it is, there is intellectual anarchy, and the intellectual anarchy is the root of the moral anarchy, which in its turn is the root of the political anarchy. At present there are no established principles regarding which all members of society can be united. Human reason needs above all fixed points, which alone are susceptible to rally in a useful way its spontaneous efforts, and for which the skepticism momentarily produced by the more or less difficult passage from one dogmatism to another constitutes a sort of morbid perturbation which cannot be prolonged without grave dangers.

In other words, there was a dogmatism in the past: religious dogmatism. This was destroyed by the revolutionary critical philosophy, and there will be no order, no stability, before there is a new dogmatism, and this new dogmatism can only be based on science, because science is the only intellectual power anymore which commands universal respect. This means—Comte doesn't hesitate to draw the conclusion from that—there cannot be universal toleration. Universal toleration for every opinion is defensible as a transitional thing, for the pulling down of the untenable old views and institutions so that room is created for the emergence of the new and final, but not in the elementary stage. Systematic tolerance cannot exist, and has never really existed, except regarding opinions regarded as indifferent or questionable, as is proven by the very practice of revolutionary politics in spite of its absolute proclamation of the freedom of conscience . . .[5] itself guaranteed in the last analysis by a kind of religious consecration, real, if vague, without which these metaphysical dogmas would necessarily be exposed to a continuous discussion, which would compromise much the efficacy of these dogmas.

He speaks in another context of the fundamental dogma of free examination and of the dogma of equality in order to indicate that the revolutionary position which he attacks is itself based on unquestionable premises without which the revolutionary position would be as little possible as any other political position. The root of the present anarchy in morals and politics is, to repeat, intellectual anarchy. Now how can Comte diagnose the situation prevailing in his time as chaotic or anarchic? He must have some notion of order, and not merely a fantastic notion which may not have any solidity, but of an order which is surely possible. Comte indeed takes it for granted that there was once an order: intellectual order, hence moral, hence political, and this existed in the Middle Ages. According to Comte, Catholicism is the most noble work of the theological spirit. But since it is based on theology, i.e., on untruth, it must be rejected, to say nothing of the fact that it has lost its social power to a considerable extent. In addition, it is already undermined by the critical revolutionary philosophy of the Enlightenment, which according to Comte stems from Protestantism, from the Protestant principle of free examination. Theological politics is no longer compatible with society and is forced into one compromise with secularized society after another. Metaphysical politics, on the other hand, let us say Rousseau (because Comte thinks of Rousseau probably more than of anybody else), is good only for pulling down, not for reconstruction. The final superiority of positive philosophy is undeniable, as our discussion of its own development will show.

> To the positive philosophy alone it belongs, in the realized state of human reason, to develop in us, within our most daring enterprises, an unshakeable vigor and a reflective constancy drawn directly from our own nature, without any external assistance and without any chimerical impediment.[6] The propriety to unite as well as to stimulate and direct belongs from now on in an ever more exclusive manner, since the decay of religious beliefs, to the whole of positive conceptions, which alone are today capable of establishing[7] spontaneously, from one end of the world to the other, on bases as durable as extended, a true intellectual community which can serve as a solid foundation to the vastest political organization.[8]

This is the practical significance of the positive philosophy. There is then an obvious need for the new order, and this new order is understood as the final order. It is final for the simple reason that modern science is the final philosophy. The new order will come inevitably; its power is based on the power of science, which destroyed the alternatives. The new order, we may say, is the order in accordance with nature, and especially in accordance with the nature of the elite of the human race. There is some difficulty in the argument which I would like to read to you.

> The elite of the human race, as the necessary and final result of all the diverse earlier evolutions, touches now at the direct coming of the social order best adapted to its nature.[9] The theological and metaphysical philosophy have alone really undertaken hitherto to operate the political reorganization of modern societies;[10] and their having failed, it follows evidently either that the problem would not be susceptible of any solution, which it would be absurd to think, or we have to have recourse to positive philosophy.[11]

Comte does not consider it possible that there might be a problem which cannot be solved by any philosophy, philosophy in his sense of the term. In the new order, men will be guided by a small elite (that is implied in everything I said before), and these men are the men devoted by nature to contemplation. In a very strange, not to say fantastic way, Comte has dared to demand and even to predict the rule of philosophers in the nineteenth century, the imminent rule of philosophers, but these philosophers being now modern scientists. One can say Comte has been refuted a hundred times by the development which has taken place, and as a predictor he surely is subject to refutation by further developments, but this doesn't mean that his suggestions are not of the utmost importance for us to consider. There is a thing which comes up time and again and which is something very actual in our society, although not preponderant, what is called technocracy. Our society requires to some extent rule by experts, which means rule by scientific experts. No one has stated the argument in favor of this possibility and half-necessity as strongly as Comte. There are a few passages regarding this Platonism which it might be good to read.

> Every individual, however inferior, has always the natural right, provided he does not behave in a pronouncedly antisocial manner, to expect from all others the scrupulous accomplishment of the general considerations following from the dignity of man.[12] But in spite of this great moral obligation, which has never been directly denied since the abolition of slavery, it is evident that men are not equal among themselves nor even equivalent; and hence could not possess in society identical right, apart of course from the fundamental right necessarily common to all, of the free and normal development of personal activity.[13] The continuous progress of civilization, far from bringing us closer to a chimerical equality, tends on the contrary by its nature to develop extremely these fundamental inequalities.[14]

And this is at the bottom of the fact that there must be a government by the simply superior people, and these are of course those who are not mediocre: scientists. We can say (although Comte never would use such a phrase) it's the rule of the philosophers; that is the only way out. And to repeat, for Comte this is not, as it is at most in Plato, a wish, a pious wish, but something which he can predict because there is no other solution to the social problem, and the social problem *must* have a solution. It would be absurd to think that it could not have a solution, as we have seen.

Let us now turn to some details of Comte's sociology, of his positive political philosophy, as he also calls it—he still speaks of political philosophy as a matter of course. I see it is rather late, and that this would lead us much beyond the time. I propose therefore that we use the remaining few minutes for discussion. There must be some—yes?

STUDENT: Earlier you said that Comte favors the passions over reason—

LS: Favors? When did I say—

SAME STUDENT: Not favors, excuse me, not favors. The passions are—

LS: Are primary and strong.

SAME STUDENT: Also, this is reminiscent of materialism, but not formally materialism, because he denies the possibility of metaphysics. And my question is: On what ground does he claim the primacy of the passions, and if these aren't metaphysical grounds, what are they?

LS: He would say: observation. The study of men, individual men, will always show that apart from very rare exceptions, due to particular circumstances, men are more passionate—passion in the wide sense. I mean of course not only noble passions, passions of any other kind than rational.

SAME STUDENT: Then you're saying that Comte would consider it a sufficient argument that an overwhelming percentage of people did something—

LS: No, not quite. I mean, there is one point into which I didn't wish to go because it would really lead us afar. Regarding biology, he thinks very highly of one writer of the early nineteenth century called Gall, the founder of a thing called phrenology, the study of the brain.[15] He was in a way a very materialistic man, believing he would find the locus of each mental activity in a special part of the brain. I've forgotten now where he localized passion and where he localized reason, and what is the bulk of the passionate part of the brain compared with the bulk of the rational part of the brain, if one may say so. These things do play a great role in Comte.

But still I would say this. This view of the preponderant power of passion in the majority of men was rather a common view. I mean, Plato and Aristotle wouldn't say anything different about it, only the *possibility* of truly rational men was more important for Plato and Aristotle than it was for Hobbes. This is, I think, the different point. I mean, what is your—in other words, you think that this is not sufficiently established in a scientific manner, according to the notion of science which he has, yet to which Comte would reply that common sense is not so untrustworthy in these matters as it is according to the now prevailing view of science. Today such assertions would be questioned by scientists if they have not been properly established by what is called scientific methods. This was not Comte's view. Comte thought that in matters of such grave importance for men, the ordinary experience of men throughout the ages is quite trustworthy, and he would contend that this general experience of men throughout the ages confirms that: that men who are rational are an exception rather than the rule. And of course Comte wants these men, these rare men, to be the rulers. He doesn't draw the conclusion that since passion is more powerful, it should not be controlled. It must be controlled—the details of how he visualizes this control I will discuss next time—because if there were not a partial control of passion by passion, reason couldn't do very much. This was already a great theme of people like Hobbes, that the passions counteracting each other creates a possibility for reason to throw its weight on the right side, and therefore reason doesn't have to be so powerful in itself. Yes?

STUDENT: Mr. Strauss, is there any significant relation between the positivism of Comte and the ideology of de Tracy?[16]

LS: Yes, there is, but Comte rejects that. I mean, what is Tracy? There was a school at the end of the eighteenth century in France, Napoleonic times, which continued more or less what Locke had done in England, and today what they did would be called psychology. This school called itself "ideologic," for this reason: because, as you know from Locke, the subject matter of Locke is ideas, the ideas in the human mind. And the study of these ideas is therefore ideology. And Napoleon, who detested these men because they were republicans, used the word ideology in order to show how incredibly stupid they were. And from this Napoleonic usage of ideology, the Marxian usage is derived. Then it came to mean, from Marx on, a *wrong* theory, a theory which is based on a fundamentally wrong perspective, ultimately due to class . . . this is a meaning which it took on in Marx and was then taken over by half-Marxists and by non-Marxists, and now it is a perfectly respectable term, so much so that Khrushchev, for example, and, as I was told, even Stalin himself, has spoken of "the Marxist ideology." Imagine! [Laughter] But . . . otherwise sensible people shout for an ideology: they want to have an ideology, by which they mean, I suppose, that they want to have a coherent body of doctrine which guides them in their actions, and they call it an ideology. But an ideology—but I would just regard the authority of Marx as absolutely decisive: an ideology is a *wrong doctrine*. And one shouldn't really speak of it except under great provocation or pressure. Someone else? Yes.

STUDENT: Would you clarify please why the reaction to the French Revolution, rather than the French Revolution—

LS: Because the French Revolution led to this thing called the Terror, don't forget that. 1793, Robespierre. And of course they got rid of Robespierre eventually, but until some order came out of it—it took Napoleon, and Napoleon is surely a reaction to the French Revolution. But still, Comte detests Napoleon because he detests the military spirit (I will take this up later), and therefore the character of the postrevolutionary society became visible only partly under Napoleon, and partly even after the defeat of Napoleon—very briefly, the industrial society. That is the point towards which Comte is working. The two powers now determining the world are science and industry. By the way, the two names are combined in the designation of a museum very close to this university:[17] science and industry, the idea being that the alternative is religion and war. This is the perspective. You see here the kinship with Marx, which kinship can be explained by a common ancestry because Saint-Simon, the original teacher of Comte, was in a way also a teacher of Marx. But Comte turned away entirely from all socialism, and Comte believed that the nerve of the whole historical development is the human mind, the intellect, and not the relations of production at all. This is radical.

STUDENT: Mr. Strauss, may I ask: you said something about Comte's relationship to Euclidean geometry and modern mathematics, as opposed to Cartesian—

LS: No, I mean the difference between classical mathematics—also mechanics, say, in Archimedes—and this radically new point in the seventeenth century, especially Descartes's analytical geometry and Leibniz, with his calculus.

SAME STUDENT: Comte accepted the latter as the . . .

LS: Of course, the modern assertion naturally is that the ancient was only an inadequate form of mathematics. Surely what he understands by the positive spirit, by the scientific spirit, is the spirit of modern science, which was prepared to some extent by Euclid. Yes?

SAME STUDENT: Could you be, if you think it's necessary, a bit more explicit on the nature of these technocrats in the final stage?

LS: Well, I will speak of that later. But regarding mathematics, one can use this simple thing: premodern mathematics, at least in the Western world, did not know of algebra. In other words, they could reckon only with numbers, not with these strangely generalized numbers . . . Yes?

STUDENT: I wonder if you could tell me what was Comte's view about human nature in this sense: you mentioned that in the transition from the second to the third stage, from the metaphysical to the positivistic, an intellectual anarchy occurs, in the sense of the old orders being destroyed, and no longer are people asking *why*-questions, they are now asking *how*-questions.

LS: Well, this is not quite correct. The chaos, the anarchy, is not during the transition from the metaphysical to the positive, but is coeval with the metaphysical period. The metaphysical philosophy is the negative, critical, skeptical, destructive thought of the seventeenth and eighteenth centuries. In the seventeenth century, the power of religion and of the old authorities was still relatively unbroken, and the situation has progressed and has become unbearable only in the nineteenth century. But the theories there, from Hobbes to Rousseau—he doesn't mention names very frequently. Rousseau he simply calls a sophist; I mean, he belongs to these people. I haven't found the reference to Hobbes or to Locke, but I'm sure he also meant them too.

SAME STUDENT: The question that I really wanted to ask was, in the last stage, when science becomes the last philosophy, does he now see the human being as no longer being concerned with moral questions?

LS: Yes, *of course* he's concerned, but these questions will be answered by science now.

SAME STUDENT: Is science the new moral authority?

LS: Sure! Oh, yes, naturally. I mean, you see here the most powerful difference between Comtean positivism and present-day positivism. In present-day positivism, science is silent about all moral questions. In other words, science can supply material with which moral men as moral men can answer their questions, but science as such does not answer the questions. You know this familiarly. This is completely absent from Comte. For Comte, science is an intrinsically moral affair. This creates certain theoretical difficulties for Comte, by the way, which are avoided by present-day positivism, but present-day positivism has some other difficulties instead. Did I answer your question?

SAME STUDENT: Yes.

LS: Mr. Landon.

STUDENT: Earlier you explained the independence of the practical sciences from the theoretical sciences in Aristotle's scheme. Yet, as I recall, and I hope I'm recalling accurately, in your introduction to *Natural Right and History*, after talking about certain political matters, you said that the answers to the highest questions were ultimately involved in the method . . . whether it was teleological or mechanistic. And I think the footnote is from the *Physics*—[18]

LS: Yes. Well, I do not remember the quotation exactly, I remember the thought. In other words, the question is whether the distinction between theoretical and practical knowledge is theoretically adequate. It is practically good enough, but theoretically perhaps not good enough. That would be a question. Could this not be that something is practically good enough and theoretically in need of clarification? I think that is so.

Let me say these words from the Aristotelian point of view. There are principles of practice which are not in need of theoretical justification in order to be evident to us. But they can be obscured by false theories. Now then, in order to fight a false theory, you need a theory. You need therefore a theory to defend sound practice and its principles against false theories. Now is this theory—let us say, this apologetic theory—a theory like theories simply, say, astronomical theories, or is it not of a peculiar character, because of its apologetic character? These are questions into which one . . . I think I will leave it at that.

2   Comte's Positive Political Philosophy

LEO STRAUSS: [In progress] . . . used here includes just. To take a simple example today, reapportionment on the basis of "one man, one vote" is based on the opinion that "one man, one vote" alone is just. Now despite that prima facie evidence of political philosophy, political philosophy has become incredible, implausible today, and this is due in the first place to the view now prevailing that the only kind of genuine knowledge is scientific knowledge. This view is called positivism.

Positivism was founded by Auguste Comte. I spoke last time of his central teaching, the law of the three stages: theological, metaphysical, and positive or scientific. The positive stage is the highest and the final stage in the development of the human mind. One cannot understand the scientific spirit if one does not understand the fundamental and typical obstacles to it, and these obstacles are precisely the theological and the metaphysical spirit. Comte, in contradistinction to present-day positivism, still holds the view that commonsense knowledge is genuine knowledge, so that scientific knowledge is only universalized commonsense knowledge. And Comte still calls the scientific study of social phenomena—what he was the first to call sociology or social physics—he still calls that political philosophy.

Now sociology in Comte's sense depends on the sciences preceding it, in the first place, biology, then chemistry, physics, and ultimately mathematics. Yet sociology does not depend completely on the preceding sciences. It has a subject matter of its own which is not reducible to that of biology, etc. Yet on the other hand, there is no essential difference between the social and the presocial, or nonsocial: more generally stated, between the human and the nonhuman. Psychology—in the language of Comte, "ideology"—is a part of zoology simply. Society consists of men, and man is the subject of biology, yet society is a whole of which men are parts. This whole is something which escapes biology as biology. So there is a certain obscurity as to the possibility of reducing the more complex phenomena to the more simple phenomena.

We must go a step further. Sociology is not only to some extent independent of the preceding sciences; it is in a way even the science of sciences, the universal science. For all sciences are the work of the human mind as social mind, and therefore the clarification of science as such is a part, perhaps the most important part, of sociology in Comte's sense. I have spoken also of what Comte teaches regarding the practical necessity of sociology. He starts from the prevailing intellectual anarchy: there is no agreement regarding fundamentals. This is due to the dissolution of the theological spirit, and that dissolution is the work of the metaphysical or revolutionary spirit, i.e., of the philosophies of the sixteenth, seventeenth, and eighteenth centuries. The intellectual anarchy necessarily leads to moral anarchy, which in its turn leads to political anarchy. Man is in a transitional stage between an order, the order of the Middle Ages, and a new order which will be the final order, and this new order can be brought about only by the consistent application of the scientific or positive spirit, by the extension of the scientific spirit to the social phenomena. In other words, science has to take over the function which theology had in the Middle Ages. The new order will be brought about by the unqualified rule of science, which means the rule of scientists. He doesn't mean the rule of any mediocre scientists; he means the rule of the most outstanding, most comprehensive scientists, whom he still calls philosophers. So what Comte demands is the rule of philosophers, but of course of positive philosophers, not of metaphysicians, who are responsible in a way for the present intellectual chaos. This much to remind you of what I will discuss today. Before I go on, I would like to know whether there is any point of those just made which you would like clarified.

STUDENT: Last time you referred to modern physics, modern science, as being metaphysically neutral. And I don't understand what that means. How can physics be considered today metaphysically neutral? It strikes me that their metaphysics, although usually undeveloped, would be more Epicurean than—

LS: Yes, but talk to any physicist or to any theorist of physics, and he would deny that. He would simply say that while modern physics emerged originally from the so-called molecular philosophy, which is Epicureanism or Democriteanism, this has long ceased to be the essence of physics. That is of course a question, but I stated only that modern science, according to the interpretation which it has of itself, is metaphysically neutral. Whether one can leave it at that is a long question. Now let us turn—yes?

STUDENT: When you say that every scientist takes from the preceding ones, do you mean anything more than that one accepts the results of the preceding ones?

LS: At least this, but also the training acquired by the use of these methods is essential for the later sciences. In other words, what Comte thinks is that a chemist, for example, must be thoroughly trained in mathematics, and the same would be true of course also of the biologist and of the sociologist. If this were not so, then the preceding sciences would be mere authorities and not truly understood. He wants more than that, than to simply say that my colleague in the other department has proved that, Joe has done it and we don't have to bother about that. It is a bit more.

Now let us turn to Comte's notion of positive political philosophy, which is the same as sociology or social physics. Sociology consists of social statics and social dynamics. You see here the connection with physics. Social statics deals equally with all societies, i.e., with the conditions of existence common to all societies and the corresponding rules of harmony in regard to, first, the individual; second, the family; and third, society properly so called. The notion of society properly so called, when it has reached its entire scientific extension, tends to embrace the whole of the human species, i.e., it is no longer a national society, and one principally of "the white race." Now why does he make this strange—in our opinion strange—qualification or limitation to the white race? I think there is no inconsistency in that, because in Comte's time the positive spirit was still a preserve of the Western world, which extended only later to the East and to Africa, and so on. The separate treatment of the individual in social statics does not mean that the individual precedes society. Man's fundamental sociability is undeniable; there never was a state of nature in the sense of Hobbes, Locke, or Rousseau.

Now regarding the individual, we must observe the preponderance of the lowest and most egoistic instincts over our social instincts. Our social instincts are weaker than our egoistic instincts. Hence the primacy of the egoistic instincts must clearly be seen; hence the notion of the common good or, as he says, of the public interest has no intelligible sense without that of the particular interest in the first place. We cannot understand the common good if we do not understand first the private good, and here Comte admires the wisdom of the biblical command "Love thy neighbor like thyself." The personal instinct, as he puts it, self-love, must serve as guide to the social instinct, love of others. The strengthening of man's benevolence, which is primarily so weak, is due to the growth of his intelligence. Intelligence weakens his passions, and man achieves greater clarity about his social relations. He sees more and more that his private interests cannot be furthered without due consideration for the interests of others, for the common interest.

Now in Comte's age people began to speak of conservative and progressive people. You know this is now a very popular distinction, but it doesn't antedate the early nineteenth century. Now the conservative spirit according to Comte is inspired above all by the purely personal instinct, by selfishness—vested interests, as it came to be called later; and the spirit of improvement, the progressive spirit, is inspired by the spontaneous combination of intellectual activity with the social instinct. In other words, the intellectuals are progressive (a thesis which is now extremely popular, as you know, and here we have one early indication of it) because the intelligence strengthens the social interests, the interest in the common good, the progressiveness. Comte has abandoned the notion of the state of nature, as we have seen. He has not entirely abandoned the notion of natural right. There is indeed no necessary connection between the state of nature and the natural right. He says: Every individual has always the natural right, unless he has behaved antisocially in a very pronounced way, to expect from all others the scrupulous and continuous fulfillment of the general regards due to the dignity of man.[1] This much about the individual. Now we turn to the question of the family.

According to Comte, the family is the school of sociability. And the main reason for this is that every society presupposes some inequalities, and the family is characterized by two fundamental inequalities: that of husband and wife, and that of parents and children. And so here we learn, so to say, the rudiments of living together by living on the basis of these fundamental inequalities. I will read to you a few passages to show you how conservative Comte was compared with his present-day successors:

> Doubtless the institution of marriage suffers necessarily, as all other institutions, spontaneous modifications through the gradual course of human evolution. Modern marriage, as Catholicism has finally constituted it, differs radically from Roman marriage, just as Roman marriage differed from Greek marriage and both of them from Egyptian or Oriental marriage, even after the establishment of monogamy.[2]
>
> However great one may suppose these spontaneous changes [from the

Oriental marriage to present-day monogamous marriage as understood by Catholicism—LS] they all rest constantly uniform with[3] the invariable fundamental spirit of the institution, which alone is here our primary subject. Now this spirit of marriage consists always in this inevitable natural subordination of the wife towards the husband, which is always reproduced in all the changes.[4]

And this is proven, according to Comte . . . not only historically, but more directly by biology.

Positive biology [i.e., scientific biology—LS] tends to represent the female sex, especially in our species [because in other animals it may be different—LS] as necessarily constituted, compared to the male, in a sort of continuous infancy, which removes her, especially in the most important respects, from the ideal type of the race.[5] [So in other words, science proves that women cannot reach the level of men.—LS] One cannot seriously doubt today, merely on the basis of biology, the evident relative inferiority of the woman, who is much less capable than man, to the indispensable continuity as well as to the high intensity of mental work either by virtue of the smaller intrinsic power of her intelligence or because of her more lifeless moral and physical susceptibility which is so opposed to every obstruction and every concentrated scientific work.[6]

And all history shows that. And especially women are wholly unfit for government. He goes much beyond the tradition because the tradition generally said that for government, women can be quite good. Proof: Queen Elizabeth I, Empress Catherine, and some others. But only the question regarding science. But I read this to you more in order to show you how very conservative Comte, in spite of his profession, is.

Now the third and most important subject: society strictly understood. Society consists of families, not of individuals. This is a clear return to the older view against the view of the seventeenth and eighteenth century, where society is based on a contract between the individuals and not families. What is characteristic of society at large is the invariable reconciliation of the separation of work, the division of labor, with cooperation. Division and yet cooperation. Individuals of very great intellectual and moral differences work together without an organization or a plan: "spontaneously," as he calls it. The principle of society is the division of labor, which leads naturally to or implies cooperation. And this is the

crucial difference between society and the family: the family is characterized by social affections—love, parents and children, husband and wife,
and vice versa. But love is of no importance in society, where solidarity is
supplied by the necessary consequence of the division of labor, that they
have to work together.

The division of labor, and hence cooperation, also explains or justi-
fies the multiplicity of nations. Each nation makes its contribution to the
one work of mankind. The division of labor constitutes principally social
solidarity. Social organization tends ever more to divide labor: the more
society progresses, the greater will be the division of labor. And this takes
place in accordance with the characteristics of each individual. Everyone
gets that parcel of social labor for which he is best fitted. Some of you
may remember the beginning of the discussion in Plato's *Republic* book
2, when he describes the division of labor, and where everyone gets that
job for which he is by nature fitted.[7] But Comte is not as strict as Plato:
he says the division of labor is in accordance with the characteristics of
each individual, regardless of whether these characteristics are natural,
i.e., congenital, or due to the education received in social position. In
other words, here the problem of justice arises but is not faced by Comte.
I mean, whether there is, say, someone who is congenitally very gifted,
naturally very gifted but does not receive the proper education because
of his social position—whether that is fair that he remains at the bottom
of the social ladder. The division of labor even produces differences both
intellectual and moral among the individuals. In other words, these are
not merely the natural inequalities there; these natural inequalities are
increased through the division of labor. If someone works all the time
intellectually, his intellect is, as a natural result, superior to the intellect of
one whose intellect is never used or hardly used.

Since through the division of labor each has a very restricted sphere,
say, making some part of some machine, he doesn't see clearly the relation of his private interest (his wages), or maybe even his class interest, to
the public interest. So a certain atomization of society takes place. There
arises therefore the need for permanent social discipline, that is to say,
for government. Government is necessary because society is necessarily
divisive. Social progress is due to society, but government renders society
possible. Comte comes here very close to the view, say, of Thomas Paine:
the true and good thing is society, and government has only a necessary
but marginal function. Yet, as you will see immediately, Comte differs
very radically from Paine and his like. For the action of the government is

not merely, as he puts it, material, by which he means coercive (the police), but also and above all intellectual and moral. For government stands for the spirit of the whole, whereas society is characterized by the division of labor. More precisely, the division of labor leads to the consequence that the more specialized kinds of labor place themselves spontaneously, naturally, under the continuous direction of those of greater generality. That is to say, there is a natural hierarchy: the simple worker who does this kind of very limited work has a foreman, and so on and so on, and this hierarchy emerges without any planning, by the nature of things. This fact increases, of course, the intellectual and moral inequality. That doesn't mean that the men at the bottom of the ladder are immoral, but simply that quite a few moral potentialities are not actualized there which are actualized on the higher level. More intellectual and moral qualities are needed at the top than at the bottom. Every human society tends then toward a spontaneous government. This tendency is in harmony with another natural phenomenon, namely, that some individuals are by nature inclined to command, and others to obey or to follow. Nature is so kind, we can say, as to provide for this distinction. Yet we have to consider that there is a need for two kinds of government.

In the first place, we need a government which vouches for the preponderance of a certain system of common opinions. There is a need for the permanent existence of a speculative class—in other words, for the continuous division between theory and practice—a privileged class which enjoys physical leisure, indispensable for the culture of the intellect. And the function of this speculative class is to organize opinion and education in the largest sense of the word, i.e., not merely what is going on in schools. Its function is limited to moral influence, i.e., these intellectual rulers, who as we know are the scientists, are excluded from political power. The medieval separation between church and state, or rather between the power spiritual and power temporal, is a not quite perfect model for Comte. Spiritual government, the government of the scientists (or we could say, intellectuals, if we understand by "intellectual" a man of science) ...[8] has also the function to approve and disapprove of the public and private life of temporal government. In other words, a power of censorship, which however has of itself no direct political effect. The temporal government was originally of a military kind, and now it must be industrial, peaceful. The temporal government will naturally consist of the captains of industry and banking. "Captain," we remember, is originally a military title, which shows a connection. At the top there would be a dictatorship of three bankers, not elected but named by their predecessors, but checked by the freedom of the press and public opinion in general, the idea being that public opinion is formed by the wisest members of the society, these men of science.

Now the need of a power spiritual is connected with the fact that no society is possible without religion, according to Comte. But Comte, being a positivist, can of course not have a religion with God, it must be a religion without God. Now, that which at that time might have seemed to be very paradoxical has in the meantime become a very popular notion. I read an article, for example, by one of the present-day positivists, that a scientist who is absolutely unbelieving is religious because of his dedication to science. This is not quite Comte's view. The object of worship of Comte's religion is the human race: a religion of humanity, a religion which consists in the worship of humanity and especially of the great benefactors of the human race. Now this is in agreement with Comte's moral teaching: morality according to Comte consists in altruism, living for others, *vivre pour autrui*. This does not mean to exclude self-love, as we have seen, because Comte accepts the biblical command "Love thy neighbor like thyself." And it is also not merely love of the present generation but of the future ones as well. This morality is very stern: it demands severe self-control. Man has no right to do what he pleases. A life of self-indulgence and mere amusement is impossible. Every citizen, high or low, must regard himself as a public functionary. Intellectual power, no less than the power of wealth, needs moral control. The mind, the intellect, must be subordinated to the heart. So in other words, these scientists, as rulers, are supposed to be permeated by the highest morality. They are not mere technocrats.

I have switched more than once from Comte's social statics to his social dynamics, because the social dynamics is the authoritative and the fundamental part of Comte's teaching. The chief content of Comte's new political philosophy as a whole is the law of the three stages, and this belongs to social dynamics, the changes that society has undergone in the course of time. More generally stated, the chief teaching of Comte's political philosophy is to the effect that the whole development of the human race constitutes a progress, that is to say, an ever-increasing power of the characteristic faculties of humanity, as distinguished from animality, of our most noble inclinations and our most generous sentiments. The conditions of progress are in the first place the continuous renovation of the ages of the social movement, that is to say, the death of the individuals—

if this would not take place, rigidity would set in—and secondly, the progressive increase in numbers. Progress requires large population centers throughout history. Comte faces for a moment the possibility of overpopulation in the future but doesn't see it as an imminent danger. The core of progress, however, is intellectual progress. The history of society is dominated by the history of the human mind, and the history of the human mind—intellectual history, history of philosophy—is the key to all history. Now history of philosophy does not of course mean philosophy as an academic field in any sense. Philosophy is the overall view which man necessarily has, whether it is theological, metaphysical, or positive. The change from military societies, feudal societies, to industrial societies is a consequence of the changes in philosophy, i.e., in *Weltanschauung*, in ways of thinking.

The military regime had always as its indispensable political base the individual slavery of the producers, so that the warriors had the free and full development of their characteristic activity. This institution of slavery was of crucial importance because the slaves, the producers, were the forerunners of the men of the industrial society because of the nonwarlike and productive character of the work. Now another point. No military regime could have established itself and, especially, lasted except by being based on a sufficient theological consecration without which the intimate subordination which it demands would never have been possible. Without this intimate correlation to the theological spirit, it is evident that the military spirit could never have fulfilled the highest social destination which it had for the development of the human race. In other words, the military spirit required the theological spirit, was based on it, and therefore the fundamental thing is the theological spirit, not the military spirit, and the whole history of the human race is intellectual history.

Now for the better understanding of Comte's new political philosophy, we shall consider at somewhat greater length his critique of what he calls metaphysical politics, in contradistinction to his critique of theological politics. This, for the following reason: metaphysical politics at least claims to be based on man's natural faculties alone, whereas theological politics claims to be based on divine revelation. But above all, metaphysical politics was not sociology, whereas positive political philosophy is sociology. What was the fundamental error of that political philosophy which was not sociology? In other words, what was the fundamental error of all political philosophy proper?

This question is answered by Comte's criticism of metaphysical politics. Generally speaking, Comte identifies metaphysical political philosophy with that of the modern age, sixteenth to eighteenth centuries. But on at least one occasion, he identifies metaphysical politics with medieval thought. Metaphysical political philosophy is legalistic political philosophy. He probably thinks of the importance of the idea of natural law in both the Middle Ages and modern times. But this is not the decisive point in Comte. Metaphysical politics appeals directly to all intelligences on whatever level, i.e., no training, scientific training, is required as you must have in order to be a chemist or a biologist. The various social questions were subject of simple inspiration, and this simple inspiration you can have without any labor and even without any native gifts. In other words, metaphysical politics treated political or social subjects as if they could be treated by men not thoroughly trained in natural science as a whole. And there is of course an element of truth in that, because the predecessors of Comte assumed that the principles of politics, i.e., the modern principles, have a source of their own, and therefore there is no need to establish them by means of biology and so on. Even Hobbes asserted— and precisely Hobbes, Hobbes indeed being a metaphysical political philosopher in Comte's sense—that his political philosophy is intelligible without natural science.

Now what is common to both theological and metaphysical politics— and here we come to a deeper level—is the belief that social phenomena are, as it were, indefinitely and arbitrarily modifiable by the legislator or by providence. In other words, metaphysical politics exaggerated in an absurd manner the influence of the individual genius. It was blind to the fact that political phenomena are subject to veritable natural laws; hence political actions are subject to fundamental limitation. From this Comte concludes the vanity of the search of the search characteristic of metaphysical politics, namely, the search for the best government absolutely, i.e., without regard to any definite state of civilization, for the invariable natural laws to which Comte appeals circumscribe for each epoch the fundamental limits and the essential character of political action. Metaphysical politics treats the political and social organization in isolation, that is to say, as independent of the corresponding civilization. In the language now prevailing today, it disregards the cultural matrix of the political and social organization. The harmony between the whole and the parts of the social system is in principle spontaneous, not due to conscious action: government is an outgrowth of society proceeding from a spontaneous consensus. In other words, government is not *made*, as the metaphysical politics according to Comte assumes. The primary action is that of society; that of government is secondary. The artificial and voluntary order, made by men, is a simple prolongation of the natural and involuntary order. We can state this view as follows. Society is natural. It comes into being naturally and it subsists naturally, without any human doing. Naturally: that means in accordance with natural laws. To use another distinction not used by Comte but parallel to what he thinks: society has grown and grows, it is not made.

Now those of you who know a bit of what Comte calls metaphysical politics must be wondering: Where do we find this metaphysical politics? Does he not set up a phantom? Or was there such a politics once, which assumed the omnipotence or quasi-omnipotence of government, of human voluntary action, and saw in it the ground of society and of government? Where do we find it? Well, you remember that Aristotle said that the *polis*, the city, society, is by nature, i.e., it grows out of families, clans, etc., so there was nothing new in that. But where do we find this view of the quasi-omnipotence of government?

STUDENT: In Hobbes, Locke, and Rousseau. The social contract idea.

LS: Yes. What does the social contract, at least as understood by these men, imply?

SAME STUDENT: It implies that there was a time when society existed without government.

LS: Oh, no, no. Perhaps Locke believes that, but surely not Hobbes and Rousseau. No, we have isolated individuals, and these isolated individuals figure out that they are in a very bad situation; and on the basis of this figuring out, they consciously form societies through this conscious act of the social contract. And these people, when setting up their government, are of course perfectly free to set up this or that or that kind of government. They deliberate: Should we have a monarchy, an aristocracy, or a democracy? And whatever they voluntarily and consciously decide upon, that government will come into being. So in other words, Comte's description of metaphysical politics is a kind of caricature, but not altogether misleading, of the most famous teachings of the seventeenth and eighteenth centuries. Aristotle's *Politics* would not be metaphysical in this sense, although Comte does not make this sufficiently clear. But still, what Comte teaches is of course not the same as what Aristotle teaches. What is the difference between Aristotle's teaching on this point and Comte's teaching?

STUDENT: One difference would be that Aristotle does not distinguish the state and society.

LS: Very good. Crucial. There are families, naturally, and there are all kinds of loose associations among citizens and so on, but there is no notion of society. That is of decisive importance. This concept of the society developed only in the modern age, in connection with the market especially, in connection with the emergence of modern political economy. That is very true. Now this is connected with something else. The political society, according to Aristotle, the *polis*, is concerned with the common good, and politics means a conscious concern with the common good. And the common good is above all the quality of the citizen body—naturally also the walls of the city, public defense, etc., etc., but the highest consideration is the quality of the citizen body. This is intrinsically a much higher object than that of what Comte calls society, the production of goods. Is this not, however, admitted by Comte too? Does not Comte admit that it is absolutely necessary to be concerned with the quality of the citizen body, with education in the widest sense of the term? To some extent, Comte surely does, and this is for Comte the function of the spiritual as distinguished from the temporal government. To some extent, what he calls spiritual government is an attempt to solve the question which Aristotle had in mind. But there is a great difference nevertheless between Comte and Aristotle on this point, because according to Comte what is decisive for society is the character of common opinion. Is that common opinion that is always there theological or scientific? And only if it is scientific is it truly good. Now how does this fit in with Aristotle's whole way of thinking? Let me leave it now at saying that Aristotle does not consider the possibility of common opinion of society molded by science. Why this is so and what this implies, that is a very broad question. I limit myself now to stating the mere fact.

Now metaphysical politics in Comte's sense has this character: a thinker finds out that this and this is the right political order; whether it is absolute monarchy of Hobbes, or constitutional monarchy of Locke, or the direct democracy of Rousseau doesn't make any difference. And then he says that what is required for its establishment is only that the legislator or founder have a sufficient force to bring about that establishment. Against this, Comte argues that the power of the natural laws is much greater than that of any human will. It is hard to find an example of this view of political philosophy according to which the founder of a society can establish *any order he pleases* on society provided he has the sufficient physical force. The closest approximation to it which I know occurs in Machiavelli's *Discourses*, book 1, chapter 18, where Machiavelli discusses the question: Can a man who wants to establish a tyranny in an incorrupt society, in a society unfit for tyrannical government, succeed in doing that? And Machiavelli says that is very hard, he needs a couple of generations to corrupt the citizen body and he won't live long enough, but if for one reason or another he has sufficient force, he can bring it about in his lifetime. I believe that Machiavelli means this with a certain irony; this has no direct basis in the character of metaphysical politics itself.

Another characterization of metaphysical politics (which is implied in what I said before, but I think I should mention it nevertheless) is the belief in the unlimited power of education. Just as there is an unlimited power of government, so too there is an unlimited power of education: you can make of men by education whatever you see fit. Impossible, according to Comte, because of the natural laws. I will read to you a passage here which describes the spirit of positive politics as Comte sees it.

> The eminently relative spirit of positive philosophy will gradually dissipate, to the evident profit of the general order, this absolute disposition, as narrow as irrational, common to theological politics and metaphysical politics, which drives them unceasingly to wish to realize uniformly, in all possible stages of civilizations, their respective types of unchangeable governments; and which, for example in our age, has led people to conceive no other means of civilizing Tahiti except with the help of the banal importation of Protestantism and parliamentary government.[9]

So positive politics does not believe that there is a single desirable form of government which can be established at any time, in any place, but which kind of government is good for a given society depends on the character of the society in question. The spirit of positive politics is described in Comte by the term "wise resignation," a resignation imposed on man by the knowledge of the natural laws which cannot be transgressed and which limit human action. True liberty can only consist in a rational submission to the preponderance, the overwhelming power, of the fundamental laws of nature, as distinguished from the arbitrary commands of rulers, where it would be foolish to resign because these arbitrary commands could be changed; the fundamental laws of nature cannot be changed.

Another point: metaphysical politics is characterized by the preponderance of purely material considerations. He means by that the view that all political evils are due to faulty institutions, and not to the social ideals and morals, i.e., to the doctrines prevailing in society. Now the belief in propaganda which you find frequently today is of course also a belief in institutions in Comte's sense, insofar as propaganda can be manipulated and is based on the view that human opinions can be manipulated, whereas Comte implies this change of opinions is a matter which cannot be manipulated, but is a very, very long process and due especially in our age to the expansion of the positive spirit, which requires time of its own. In other words, the metaphysical politics believes that the temporal rulers can do what can be done in a way only by the spiritual rulers, namely, the change of opinions taking place in a generation. Metaphysical politics expects salvation from political action, and especially revolutionary action—or, overstated, as Comte does it occasionally—from military action: by force you establish the right order. Metaphysical politics, we may say, is (although Comte doesn't use that term) unhistorical. It ascribes a chimerical fixity to essentially variable conditions, and at the same time it despises the social or historical continuity. It trusts more in conscious action, reform or revolution than in the spontaneous changes. The very ends which men pursue are themselves, according to Comte, products of the historical process, i.e., these very ends do not lie within the power of the individual thinker.

> In the real development of social evolution, the spontaneous modifications eventually produced by the gradual course of events are, generally speaking, by far superior to what the most eminent reformers could have dared to conceive in advance. A philosophy which necessarily takes history as its principal scientific base, which represents in every respect the men of all times, as well as of all places, as indispensable cooperators in the same fundamental evolution, intellectual or moral,[10] moral or political, and which in any case attempts always to attach the actual process to the whole of real antecedents, must certainly be judged to be much more proper today than any other philosophy to regularize the idea and the sentiment of social continuity, without incurring the danger of that servile and irrational admiration of the past.[11]

In other words, change is inevitable, but this change is a matter of a spontaneous occurrence rather than to be brought about by human planning. Metaphysical politics conceives of society itself as due to human making. Some individuals founded society because they became convinced of the usefulness of society to the individuals—Hobbes, Locke, Rousseau—which implies that man is not by nature sociable, which Comte denies. Metaphysical politics is characterized by the primacy of the individual and his rights, and especially this leads to the belief in the absolute right of free examination, or the dogma of the unlimited freedom of the conscience. It leads finally to distrust of the government, to the belief that government is by its nature the necessary enemy of society, a thought intimated by Rousseau in the *Social Contract* and more clearly stated by Thomas Paine. The common defect of theological and metaphysical politics: they have no awareness of historical continuity and its salutary character. Proof: the theologians condemn the modern development, and the metaphysicians condemn the Middle Ages. Comte's positive politics sees the necessity, and hence the right or the function, of both the medieval order and the modern development. Social conditions in every epoch are as perfect as possible; therefore the criticism of certain features of, say, the Middle Ages, or of modern times, or of any other society is absurd. Social conditions are in every respect as perfect as possible, which also means that they can be models for another society. Let me read to you another passage.[12]

… is the correlative to it. Social conditions are in every epoch as perfect as possible, but of course not simply perfect, and therefore the possibility and the need for progress: a higher perfection is possible in the twentieth century than was possible in the Middle Ages or in ancient China, or whatever have you. Now if this is so, this leads to the consequence—and this is crucial—of the coincidence of the Is and the Ought. At every time the perfect is actual, only the perfect for stage A is not the perfect for stage B, C, D, etc. If this is so, there is no need of course for any Ought. I will read to you a passage: "Positive philosophy alone has been constantly progressing since a long series of centuries, while its antagonists have been constantly decaying." Now listen: "Whether this is good or bad, is of little importance. The fact itself is undeniable, and this is sufficient."[13]

In other words, every wave of the future is good. We do not have to raise the question whether it is a good or a bad wave. This is one reason why already in Comte, and also in the later development of positivism, the question of the Ought tended to become less and less important, especially after the impact of the evolutionist doctrine on social science. When evolution determines what will come, we don't have to raise the question of what *should* come, because this would be of no influence whatever. And the great reaction to that trend, that tendency, in social science in the second half of the nineteenth century was the so-called fact-value distinction which is so characteristic of social science today. In other words: against this so-called evolutionism, the real assertion that the evolution does not tell you anything as to the goodness of that trend. The question of the Ought cannot be answered by the question of the Is. And in this respect, that was a very sound reaction. Now, before I turn to some concluding remarks about Comte, I would like to see whether I have made these points clear regarding Comte's teaching . . .[14]

What is directly interesting to us as students of political philosophy is, to repeat, Comte's critique of prepositivistic political philosophy, which he calls metaphysical political philosophy, and therefore I enumerated these points. The general impression one gets from that is that this is a criticism directed above all against the political philosophy of Hobbes and Rousseau and similar thinkers, and whether to some extent by implication it is of course also meant to be a criticism of Plato and Aristotle—if you think of the structure of Aristotle's *Politics*, especially in the more practical parts of the *Politics*, say, book 6 especially, where he raises the question how to establish, to set up a democracy, an oligarchy, and so on, the emphasis is on what voluntary action of men can bring about. Needless to say, Aristotle teaches all the time that you cannot set up a democracy if the whole situation is not suitable for democracy, and the same applies of course to oligarchy, and monarchy, and whatever else you might think of. But the emphasis on what can be done by man, by political action, is much more powerful in Aristotle—even in Aristotle—than in Comte, where the chief expectation is from what will take place spontaneously, as he called it, especially through the spread of the scientific spirit. Yes, Mr. . . . ?

STUDENT: If these states are supposed to be in a certain historical order, does he explain why, for instance, Aristotle and Plato, as metaphysical philosophers, came before the Middle Ages?

LS: No. That is, I wanted to bring this up. This is one darkness, this is not clear.

STUDENT: Does Comte have any speculations as to what happens after the positive age? Or *is* there an "after" the positive age? Is there a decay, or—

LS: Nothing. Silence. Characteristic of nineteenth-century progressivism, forgetting about the thereafter, in both senses of "there." Yes?

STUDENT: What is the character of the natural laws that . . . ? Are these specific behavioral laws?

LS: Yes, absolutely behavioral laws, not normative laws. One of the—

SAME STUDENT: I meant, does he look merely for some general principles as . . . of man?

LS: No, we have one example: the ineptitude of the female sex. That's a natural law. If you try to establish the equality of the sexes, you act against the natural law and the whole thing won't work. That's one example, but I suppose you could also say the abolition of private property, or even perhaps progressive income tax, is against the natural law. I would assume that.

SAME STUDENT: How are these laws established?

LS: By scientific methods. Comte has made it clear, however, to begin with, that in social matters, the ordinary experience of mankind, common sense, is quite trustworthy. And that can lead to difficulties. Yes?

STUDENT: If the development of history in stages is inevitable, what is the justification for Comte's writing his book? Can he influence things at all, or why is he writing it?

LS: Well, to some extent, yes, because the transitional stage, with all its miseries, will last longer than if people know what is the situation. They're in a crisis, and this would be admitted by some people, I am sure. Now what is the crisis, what is the root of the crisis? Even the insight that nothing fundamental can be done about it is of course an intellectual solution of the practical problem, is it not? Think of Vietnam[15] today. Let us assume that someone comes to the conclusion: nothing can be done, just hanging on. In other words, the crisis will go on for the possible future. That is still a practically important theoretical observation, is it not?

SAME STUDENT: Well, you said earlier that Comte even went so far as to say that individuals' acts were the product of the development of history in stages. If that were carried to the full extent, doesn't it mean that what anybody does—

LS: No, I suppose Comte would say that maybe if I don't do that, in fifty years, quite a few people will see without my help that this is a problem, and might adjust themselves, and advise others to adjust themselves. Two hundred years from now it wouldn't make, perhaps, any difference. But in the meantime it would make a lot of difference, whether they . . . Yes?

STUDENT: Is it proper for us to ask for evidence for some of his statements, like greater intelligence makes for greater sociability? Or is that just a first principle on which he—

LS: No, no. Well, he argues that out to some extent, that if people are more thoughtful, look into things more closely, then they will see that their responsibility extends further than if they had not done so. There is something to that, is it not true? I mean, if someone says: I don't care, that is not my business, and then you show him that his well-being depends on these and these public affairs being done properly, then he would act in a more enlightened manner, less narrowly egoistic than in the first case. He does not solve entirely the problem, because there can be a kind of egoism advanced, promoted by intelligence, I know that. But generally speaking, as was shown also by the last statements which I quoted, Comte is surely guilty of a very great optimism, and the strange thing is that he accuses the theologians and the metaphysicians of optimism. You know what optimism means originally: that this world is the best of all possible worlds. Now if someone says that social conditions are in every epoch as perfect as possible—if this is not optimism, it is hard to say what it is. In other words, that is not a reasonable kind of discussion: Are you an optimist or a pessimist? One would have to specify it properly.

Well then, I will turn and make a few critical considerations regarding Comte. I was happy to see that some of the points which I wanted to make have already been anticipated by some of you.

Now the core of Comte's teaching is the law of the three stages, as successive stages. Can one understand the history of the world, or at least the history of the West, in terms of that law? For example, if you take the development from Plato to Archimedes (and here we have in between the Stoics, who had some influence on Roman law, some social influence), this would seem to be metaphysical rather than theological, and yet it was succeeded by the clearly theological Middle Ages. This is a minor difficulty for Comte. But more important, his prediction of the victory of the positive spirit: in the foreseeable future, only the positive spirit will possess public power. He doesn't mean that there will not be individuals who think in either metaphysical or theological terms; that would be of no interest to him. But what about the "isms" which raise their ugly heads after Comte, in the twentieth century especially? Communism and fascism—clearly something like metaphysical politics from the point of view of Comte.

But on the other hand, if you think of such facts as the Supreme Court decision regarding desegregation, based on the findings of social science,[16] this would not have been possible a hundred years ago, whereas a Supreme Court decision based on metaphysical or theological considerations is, I believe, today unthinkable. This is one of the things which show some element of truth in what Comte meant. Yes?

STUDENT: I was thinking that the "isms" we have experienced in the twentieth century, communism and fascism, laid claim to validity partially on a scientific basis.

LS: Yes, but Comte could say with some plausibility that the old metaphysicians also claimed to be scientific, and were not.

SAME STUDENT: Oh, I see.

LS: Therefore, they are in fact metaphysical and not—as has often been said, of course, of communism especially—metaphysical and not positive.

Now to come somewhat closer to the core of his teaching, Comte's political solution: the rule of the men of science, the new power spiritual. This is based on the premise that ideas or opinions govern the world. From this it follows that the men of science will have the moral authority in the future which the clergy possessed in the Middle Ages, but the situation, I believe, is somewhat different, because in the Middle Ages, the temporal rulers were checked not only by the power spiritual but also by their armed subjects. What about the subjects of the captains of industry? The workers, peasants, and so on, remain stuck. And above all, in the medieval order, there were very great sanctions in the afterlife on obedience or disobedience to the power spiritual. There is no equivalent for that in the rule of the scientists. They do not have this power over the souls of their subjects as the clergy had. Comte overestimates the power of reason or of ideas. And this is very strange, because he insists on the secondary character of reason, as compared with the passions, especially the selfish passions. From this point of view one can see why Marx could have a much deeper social influence already in the nineteenth century than Comte, because Marx did not overestimate the power of ideas or reason.

Comte is clearly antidemocratic, and his notion of government shows this very clearly. The notion of the sovereignty of the people, which emerged especially in Rousseau, in the context of metaphysical politics, is for him an absurdity. His antidemocratic stand is based on his belief in the incompetence of the masses, and he puts his trust in the men at the top, the captains of banks and industry, controlled in a way by the men of science. The social organization tends ever more to divide labor in accordance with the characteristics of each individual, regardless of whether these characteristics are congenital or due to education and social position. Now here the question of justice arises. Is an inferiority due to inferior education, inferior social position, something which it is necessary to admit, or can this not be changed by a social action? And you know the tremendous importance which this thought had in the time after Comte.

The stabilization, the order, for which Comte longed was brought about after his time by democracy. And democracy existed at that time only in this country, and there was a great European thinker who informed Europe about this country and the likely future of Europe to be seen in America. That was Tocqueville. Tocqueville was more foreseeing of these things, in this respect more prophetic, than Comte. I do not say that a man must give right prophecies in order to be wise, but if he insists on prediction of the future as the sign of wisdom, as Comte does, to be a false predictor is fatal. In other words, stabilization was brought about not by science but by democracy. To this one might raise this objection: Is not the victory of democracy fundamentally the same as the victory of science? Dewey said that the method of democracy is the method of intelligence, and the method of intelligence is of course the method of science: Ergo, there is a fundamental harmony between science and democracy. Now this is a very long question. But that it is a question is shown by the fact that within democracy the question arises: Democracy or rule of experts, technocracy? And the technocracy is in a way closer to what Comte meant than the democracy. And so the technocrats would be strictly specialists, and the men who he believed should be the rulers could not be mere specialists, that goes without saying.

We must note the contrast between his positivism, his alleged sobriety based on knowledge of laws, of behavioral laws, practical laws, and his amazing utopianism. Now let us look a bit more closely at this point. Science as Comte understands it deals only with the How, not with the Why. For example, it is perfectly satisfied with the law of gravitation, the Newtonian law, without going into the question of what *is* gravitation, the innermost nature of it. As he also puts it, the question of the Where and Whither are not raised and answered by science, only the question of How. Yet these questions not answered by science remain, that is to say, the questions which theology and metaphysics try to answer. Even if we grant that theology and metaphysics do not supply knowledge, they take men's deepest concerns seriously and do not starve them, as science as understood by Comte does. What is most important to men is not dealt with by science. This experience, the ever-increasing awareness, has led to what has been called the flight from scientific reason. Science may progress indefinitely, but the more it progresses, the more it becomes aware of its essential limitations, the more that science itself teaches that

"I cannot teach you wisdom." And what is the use of all expertise without wisdom?

So in other words, Comte was in this respect too—to use his phrase—optimistic that science could truly take the place and fulfill the social and human function that surely theology filled, and to some extent even metaphysics. According to Comte, the fundamental error in theology and metaphysics consisted in making man the key to the understanding of everything: gods understood in the light of man; teleological explanation of nature, as it were all nature is willing and purposeful, also in the light of . . . According to Comte, the fundamental science is mathematics, *the* nonteleological science. His hierarchy of the sciences implies that there is no essential difference between men and brutes: psychology a part of zoology. Yet is not mathematics a creation of the human mind, the social mind, and not of the brutish mind? Science is essentially of human, not brutish, origin. Can science be understood as the product of the sub-human, directly or indirectly? Is man not then truly the key, if not in a very simplistic manner? Finally, regarding his religion of humanity, based on the awareness of a religious sanction, it is clear that this religion of humanity is an ersatz religion. I suppose you know this German term *ersatz*, which was coined in the First World War when Germany was blockaded and there had to be some substitute for coffee and cocoa, and perhaps even bread. *Ersatz* means substitute, but it has this especially nasty meaning which it acquired in Germany at that time. Now an ersatz religion is a substitute religion with which you could perhaps be satisfied in an extreme pinch, but which is surely not the right thing. The question would be: Can men who are heirs to the biblical tradition worship something that is not eternal?

Now I will read to you one quite revealing passage: "The actual march of our individual development from infancy to maturity."[17] And the same is also true on a large scale: there is also such a march of the human race from infancy to maturity. Well, if we look at the individual, we know that if he lives long enough, there will also be a stage of old age, not to say senility, and eventually death. What about the old age of the human race, to say nothing of its death? Here we see—this point came up in the discussion—here we see again his "optimism," so strange because his major objection to theology and metaphysics is frequently expressed by the assertion that they are fundamentally optimistic. Now the reaction to this kind of optimism (Comte and all that) came very soon in the second half of the nineteenth century, because this was exactly the heyday of "pessimism," which was connected primarily with the name of Schopenhauer but which had other famous representatives—Melville, in this country—and which was the counterwave to these unsupported hopes. And it is clear that what remained of Comte up to the present day was the clarity about the fundamental difference between the modern scientific approach and all earlier approaches; and then the second concern is that this has an enormous social influence, at least via technology, which no one can deny. But any further assertion regarding the positive spirit which Comte makes is unsupported, has proven to be unsupported.

Now with this I conclude my remarks about Comte. We will now turn to the post-Comtean transformation of positivism, to come to our present problem. And the most important development, as far as we as social scientists are concerned, is the stripping of science, in particular social science, of all right to pass value judgments. This change took place a long time after Comte's death and had nothing directly to do with him. For Comte there was no question: he taught a morality, i.e., an Ought, without any feeling that in doing so he ceased to be a scientist, this altruistic teaching. He spoke of progress all the time, and clearly, if you speak of progress scientifically, you presuppose that you know these and these and these are values, to use this language. It was no question for Comte, but this became a question towards the end of the nineteenth century, and it has now, after that, become completely victorious in the Western world: the view that social science as science cannot pass any value judgment. Now if this is so, clearly political philosophy as concerned with good or just government is an impossibility. It can be a matter of preaching, but it has no place in academic halls because there we are dedicated to science. To this issue I would like to devote the next lecture.

3   Positivism after Comte

Simmel

LEO STRAUSS: At the end of the last meeting one of the students raised a difficulty, an objection to my critical remarks about Comte. Now let me first repeat my statement, which he had in mind: Science in Comte's meaning deals only with the How of phenomena, not with the Why. Yet the questions regarding the Why, the Where, and Whither remain, that is to say, the questions which theology and metaphysics try to answer. Even if we grant that theology and metaphysics do not supply knowledge, they take care of men's deepest concerns and take them seriously, and they do not starve them. Hence what is most important to man is not dealt with by science, and this leads or can lead to the flight from scientific reason. Now the objection was this: But theology and metaphysics are untrue; hence they are in no way a threat to science. Was this not the point you made?

STUDENT: Yes.

LS: Well, the difficulty is this: positivism cannot say that the answers which theology and metaphysics give are untrue. It cannot go beyond saying that they go beyond the competence of science, that they are scientifically baseless. But that is not the same as untrue. This is a very serious difficulty. Now positivists in our age, and partly even Comte himself, have tried to find this way out, by saying that theology and metaphysics are not indeed untrue but their propositions are meaningless. Meaningless. That is in a way worse than untrue. For in order to be meaningful, a proposition must be susceptible of being validated or invalidated by scientific means, which the proposition, for example, "God exists" is not. Ultimately they must be susceptible of being validated or invalidated by sense perception, by observation. But the question arises: Is all experience sense experience? Is there not such a thing as religious experience? There is a book by William James on *The Varieties of Religious Experience*, which would give you food for thought.[1] Some people are, as Max

Weber said of himself, "religiously unmusical," but this means of course that they are for this very reason incompetent judges: just as an ordinarily unmusical man is a bad judge of music, a religiously unmusical man is a bad judge of religion. So positivism would need a kind of what we can call negative metaphysics in order to take care of theology and metaphysics, but, being positivism, it is incapable of developing such a negative metaphysics.

There is another point which one must consider. The primary view of the truth, which is still very powerful in Comte, is that truth is the adequation of the intellect and the thing, *adaequatio intellectus et rei,* or, in other words, that knowledge reproduces being as it is. There are certain difficulties here. In the very beginning of the modern development, say, in the seventeenth century, Locke made this distinction, already on the basis of Galileo and Descartes, between primary and secondary qualities: the primary qualities, extension and impenetrability; the secondary qualities, colors, sounds, and other sense qualities. And the latter were understood to be only subjective: green, shrill, or whatever you might take. This was generally understood. But then the question arises: What about the primary qualities themselves? So the thing itself consists of the primary qualities alone. The things as understood by physics: Are these the things as they are in themselves? Are they not theoretical constructs, i.e., human constructs, things relative to man in contradistinction to the things in themselves? The conclusion from this line of argument was this: science gives us only knowledge of the phenomenal, or what is relative to man; of the absolute, it does not give us any knowledge. This field remains open for a nonscientific or trans-scientific metaphysics. The very insight into the relativity of scientific knowledge causes the longing for absolute knowledge. The only school in our age which still maintains this old simpleminded view that truth is the adequation of intellect and the thing is orthodox Marxism-Leninism. The issue came to a head in Lenin's criticism of Mach, an Austrian physicist and philosopher, who had questioned this view that knowledge is knowledge of the things in themselves.[2] This school was called empirico-criticism, for some reason, and Lenin's criticism of empirico-criticism is very interesting to read.[3] He tries to uphold the simple, old-fashioned view that to know things means to know them as they are in themselves and not merely relative to man. And whether Lenin was victorious in that fight, that would be a long question to decide. Of course it was the older view, Aristotelian and so on. But in our age, on the basis of modern science, this phenomenalistic view, as it is sometimes called, has proven to be more powerful. This is an additional reason why the longings for metaphysics continue to exist and to be quite powerful, side by side with science. This difficulty is by no means solved. That would be my answer to your question. Good.

Now to turn to positivism as it appears after Comte, there are two differences which are of crucial importance. The first is this. Whereas for Comte science, positive science, is only common sense carried through, common sense universalized, for present-day positivism it is understood that there is a radical difference between science and common sense. An important step for this change was the emergence of non-Euclidean geometry, already in Comte's lifetime, but Comte apparently was not aware of it. Science is not the prolongation of common sense but its radical transformation. The world as seen by physics, by the physicist, is not the true world; it is a different world which has immense uses, but we have no right to say that it is the true world in contradistinction to the phenomenal world.

The second point is of much greater practical importance in the social sciences: in order to be scientific, social science, or science in general, must strip its subjects of all value predicates. And this applies of course especially to social science. In other words, not only the sense qualities (blue, green, or whatever have you) but also the value qualities are strictly, radically, subjective and have no place in science, even more so than the sense qualities because at least there is a universal agreement among all normal men that this is brown or that is green, but as to whether something is good or bad, there is a very wide disagreement among men. The starting point of this doctrine is at first glance the distinction between the Is and the Ought. Is-statements, that this or that *is* so, and ought-statements, that this or that *ought to be* so, have no logical connection with each other. It is not possible to infer from the fact that something *is* that it *ought* to be nor, vice versa, to infer from the fact that something ought to be that it is. To infer from the Is to the Ought means to be a conformist of the worst order—whatever is, is good—and to infer from the Ought to the Is is wishful thinking. Up to this point this is of course absolutely sound.

So this distinction between the Is and the Ought, which is a very difficult distinction, is somehow in a way immediately intelligible to everyone today. But the distinction between the Is and the Ought is not decisive for the present-day position, because this distinction was made by Kant above all, or by Hume, for that matter, and neither Kant nor Hume said it is not possible to make objective value judgments. On the contrary. So

POSITIVISM AFTER COMTE 51

the characteristic premise of present-day social science does not support this distinction, but the additional assertion that there is *no knowledge* of the Ought in any manner, shape, or form, while there *is* knowledge of the Is. This is a peculiarity of present-day social science, because there was a thing throughout the ages called skepticism, which denied the possibility of objective value judgments, but it denied also the possibility of Is-statements: there is no knowledge of the truth. Present-day social science is not skeptical at all. It admits the possibility of science but it denies the possibility of objective value judgments.

What I said implied another premise. Is/Ought is the first stage. Now by the Ought we ordinarily understand some moral things, duties. But this is extended beyond the sphere of morality, and that is implied in the term "value." For example, if I say something is beautiful, there is no Ought in any way involved, and yet it is a value judgment. So value includes the good and the beautiful and, if there is another sphere of values, that in addition. It is much larger. Ultimate values, it is asserted, are irreducible to any Is and hence indemonstrable. And furthermore, there are many (if only two, but more than that) ultimate values, which are incompatible with one another, because if they were not incompatible with one another, then there would be no difficulty. But since they are incompatible, the question is: Which to choose? This question cannot be rationally settled. And they are *ultimate* values because a given value—I won't define what a value is, following the positivists themselves—if I have a given value, it may be possible to reduce it to a higher value, to a more fundamental value, so that value A would follow logically from value B. So value A is no problem in itself; the problem is only value B, from which value A is derived.

Still, it is asserted that science is not completely baffled by the existence of values: science can handle them, in a manner. It can analyze them, it can describe them, it can clarify their meanings. Let us assume someone would say: My value is political liberty. Well, the social scientist can take cognizance of that, and he can explain what this individual understood by political liberty, and distinguish it perhaps from other meanings of political liberty, without however being able to say which is the superior meaning, or whether political liberty in itself is valuable. This is beyond its competence. Furthermore, social science can do the following thing: if the values function as ends, science can establish which means are required for the actualization of these ends, which includes the possibility that science might be able to show that certain ends cannot be actualized at all, and to that extent it refutes this end or this value as a possible end. Science can furthermore try to establish correlations between values and human types—social, racial, or what have you, for example, showing that lower-middle-class people as a rule go in for value A, upper-middle-class people go in for value B, and so on. This is a relation between values and facts, values and Is, without in any way of course establishing therewith the value of the values. If a lower-middle-class man who by virtue of his social class position could be expected to cherish value A—but he can only be expected to do that. If he is a loner, a Lone Ranger, and says No, I prefer the upper-class value, that is his business. He is not obliged, obviously, to follow the value of his class.

Now the fact-value distinction is meant as a logical distinction. What does this mean? What is the relevant meaning of this statement here? A psychological connection between a value and a given human type, for example, is irrelevant for the discussion of a value. For—and here we come to the meaning of the distinction between logic and psychology—psychology deals with the genesis of human thoughts. The validity of human thoughts is something entirely different, beyond the competence of psychology. The nondistinction between genesis and validity is said to be the error of something called psychologism. The proposition itself and its validity must be decided entirely in nonpsychological terms, i.e., in terms other than the genesis. So if a man would say that slitting men's throats and drinking their blood is good (there may be such a view), he cannot be criticized on the ground that this proposition stems from insanity, because that is only the question of the genesis of the proposition and has nothing to do with the question of its validity. We have to take the proposition by itself, in isolation. That is another important indication of this view.

Now this view is at present the official doctrine, by which I mean the large majority, perhaps the overwhelming majority, of social scientists—especially in this country, but also in a large part of Europe—holds to this view; and therefore everyone is compelled to familiarize themselves with it and to take a stand toward it. This view emerged in the last decade of the nineteenth century in Germany, but it became accepted in this country only after World War I, and only in the last two or three decades has it become unqualifiedly predominant. Now in order to get some inkling of this view I will read you a statement first by Albert Einstein, the famous physicist. I quote: "If someone approves as a goal the extirpation of the human race from the earth, one cannot refute such a viewpoint on rational grounds."⁴ That is to say, on nonrational grounds, meaning: I don't like it. Of course you can say that, but that is clearly not a refutation; it is only putting one preference against another. You see also that Einstein says it is not refutable on *rational* grounds. Now Einstein was a physicist, and if he would have said "on physical grounds," maybe he is right. He would surely be more competent to say that than I. But he doesn't say "on scientific grounds"; he says, "on rational grounds," identifying tacitly rational and scientific. This we note only in passing. Now let us consider this example, perhaps, in order to enter this subject matter. We have heard a different slogan in more recent times, "Better dead than Red," which agrees partly with this view, in relation to the H-bomb, which Einstein probably had in mind. But what is the difference between "Better dead than Red" and Einstein's proposition? There is a very striking difference, from the point of view of rationality.

STUDENT: The word "better" in there means there is a good and bad implied.

LS: Well, yes, I do think of that, but we can state it perhaps a bit more exactly. In the second case a reason is given, whereas Einstein's man doesn't give any reason, he only says: I like the extirpation of the human race. The other man says: No, no, I do not want the extirpation of the human race, but I am absolutely opposed to communism, and if the world should become communist I am in favor of last-minute war which may indeed have this consequence of death. Einstein does not even attempt to give a reason, and he calls this "rational." What could the reason be for a man to say: I wish the extirpation of the human race? Well, he might think that men are such abominable creatures that they should be extirpated. Prior to investigation, that is of course possible, but naturally it would apply to the speaker himself, yes? And one could say: Would it not be more sensible of him to commit suicide [laughter] and let the others decide for themselves!

Now let us take another example. The Nazis said that not the human race should be extirpated, but the Jews should be extirpated. Why? They were much more rational than Einstein. They said: It is good for Germany. So they gave a reason. I'm not concerned with whether the reasons are good or bad, I note the fact that the Nazis were in this respect more rational than the great physicist Einstein. They gave a reason. Now what is implied in that? That destroying human beings just for the sake of destroying them, or even destroying anything for the sake of destroying it, killing for the sake of killing—"for kicks," as some juveniles, I believe, say—there is something savage, inhuman in that. When you read the *Iliad* and see the manner in which Achilles treats the corpse, mind you, of Hector in a very beastly manner, the horror of the poet is quite clearly visible in that. Here we have an example. This is a way in which human feeling goes. Something in us, we do not know what, but something in us as human beings disapproves of destruction for destruction's sake, killing for killing's sake. We are perfectly open to the possibility that some killings may be good, but cause must be shown why it should be good. Perhaps there is a connection between being a human being and humanity. The etymological connection is known to every one of you because *humanus* is Latin for human. Perhaps there is a connection between being a human being and humanity, between being a human being, i.e., the Is, and the Ought of humanity. This is only a very general and provisional example.

We can also take this into consideration: Why are people empirically opposed, even if they are old and willing to die, and tired of life, why are they generally speaking opposed to the extirpation of the human race without any reason? I believe it is this, mostly: people have children, and they think that what is good for old people is not necessarily good for the children. They think of these children. Via their children, these tired men have a stake in the future. And even if they do not have children, they regard themselves as members of society, say, the United States, which they wish to have a future. One would have to take this into consideration in order to form a judgment on Einstein's bald thesis.

Now what is the character of the reasoning we use in discussing such a proposition? We did not inquire regarding absolute values, for no reference was made in the statement itself to absolute values. Why should we open this question? An unsupported, practical proposal was made. We asked for support, as we would even if it were a very minor thing, say, that we should have reading periods only of two weeks instead of four weeks. You would say: Why? Now this kind of argument, in a very limited way demanded by the situation, may be called dialectical argument in the original sense: we argue out the case on the basis of what is necessarily implied in it. We can also state it differently. What Einstein did was to identify science with reason. Is there no other reason? Is there not, for instance, practical reason, which has a different character from scientific reason? The reasoning used by Einstein, if you can call this reasoning, is characterized by the fact that it disregards the context in which this proposal is made, the inevitable human context. One can call this kind of reasoning, strictly speaking, abstract insofar as it disregards context.

Now the fact-value distinction is at present generally accepted as evident. Such propositions like those of Einstein are, as the mathematicians today say, elementary. You learn this in the first grade. This of course does not prove the truth of this distinction, for this precisely is the character of prejudice, that something is very evident: How could you ever doubt of it? It may be perfectly questioned. The power of this view merely proves that there are very powerful psychological incentives toward that view. The status of the fact-value distinction cannot be compared to that of a very sophisticated theory in physics, for example, the very understanding of which requires a high degree of competence, say, Einstein's own theory of relativity. Or take Copernicus's theory, centuries before: that was also once paradoxical, and yet accepted and remained. Because the fact-value distinction is not a sophisticated theory, it is extremely simple: the mere thesis can be grasped by the meanest capacities, as Hobbes would say, in a single sitting.[5] It is a very recent doctrine. When you think, for example, of John Dewey, who was a very powerful influence in this country for more than one generation, he still did not yet accept it. The first statement of it occurred, as I said, in Germany, in a book by a philosopher-sociologist, Georg Simmel, *Introduction to Moral Science (Einleitung in die Moralwissenschaft)*, 1892.[6] Now what Simmel does in this book, as he says in the preface, is to give a historical and psychological study of moral principles—a "historical-psychological study." And he calls this pursuit "positive ethics" ("positive" here in the sense of Comte), which treats, as he puts it, "good and evil as equally indifferent subjects of a merely genetic knowledge."[7] It looks at good and bad as a meteorologist would look at good weather and bad weather: with complete indifference. I will read to you a few more passages:

> What is called normative science [as ethics was traditionally thought to be—LS] is in fact only science of the normative. Science itself does not establish or prove norms, but merely explains norms and their correlations. For science always raises only causal, not teleological questions [the question, this norm, what is its cause, that it is accepted in this or that society—LS] and norms and purposes may as well as anything else be the subject of scientific inquiries, but cannot be the essence of science itself.[8]

In other words, science itself cannot be normative, it can only deal with norms.

The pure and ideal scientific problem is this: Given these purposes and conditions, what must we do in order to realize those purposes, while considering these conditions? Only a moral legislator, a practical revolutionary in moral matters, can say simply, while setting up moral, ultimate goals in a dogmatic manner, "this ought to be!" [no scientist as scientist can—LS] for the ultimate setting up of a rule is a fact which silences criticism [however atrocious that rule may be, it silences criticism. Ethics can set up only hypothetical imperatives, in Kant's sense, not categorical ones—LS].[9]

Now a categorical imperative is one which says: Thou shalt do this and that. The Ten Commandments are categorical imperatives. A hypothetical imperative is this: If you want to drink this soup, you must use a can opener. "You must use a can opener" is hypothetical, if you want to have that soup in the can.

I quote another sentence: "value is nothing objective,[10] but arises only in the subjective process of preferring."[11] I must confess, in my earlier browsings in Simmel's book, I did not become aware of the fact that Simmel truly has this view already perfectly. What prevented me from seeing it was this: Here a man makes a complete break with the whole tradition of ethics in all its forms, without any apparent awareness of the immensity, of the enormous character, of this change. And this I believe is not possible. I believe this is not possible. Take this example, the one fundamental reason which Simmel gives: science is causal, not teleological. Now that was an old story since the seventeenth century. The greatest and most outspoken enemy of all teleology was a man called Spinoza. And what is the title of Spinoza's chief work? *Ethics*, and *normative* ethics. So the distinction between causal and teleological thinking cannot possibly be the sufficient reason for this view of a value-free social science.

I believe, or I suspect, that no epoch-making change in human thought takes place without awareness of it. In other words, there may be great economic changes, for all I know, which take place without any men being aware of it except after it has happened. But in human thought, I believe that is not possible. Now how can we understand this great, radical change in the character of the study of man, which is represented by Simmel's book, and Simmel's not being aware of the profound character of the change? Now Simmel was preceded by Nietzsche—Nietzsche, who died probably four years before Simmel's book appeared. Now Nietzsche regarded Schopenhauer as his teacher. Simmel himself later wrote a book on Schopenhauer and Nietzsche. Now Schopenhauer had said that all philosophers agree as to the content of morality. As he phrased it: Don't hurt anyone, but rather try to help everyone as much as you can. This simple, ordinary morality—there is agreement among all thinking men, Schopenhauer thought. The only difference, and that is very great, among the philosophers concerns the ground on which we believe these things to be our duty. Now this caused Nietzsche's violent reaction. I will read to you one statement: "It is a correct judgment of scholars that men believed at all times to know what is good and bad, praiseworthy and blameworthy; but it is a prejudice of scholars that we know it now better than any time."[12] In other words, there is no knowledge of good and bad. No knowledge of good and bad. Nietzsche goes beyond that. Ultimately, all so-called knowledge of good and bad is based on acts of evaluation, not necessarily of the individual, but of a whole nation, or a group, and so on. But Nietzsche goes much beyond it. Nietzsche says that ultimately all knowledge, all science, rests on such acts of evaluation and is in this sense subjective. Now what Simmel did, we see in the light of Nietzsche more clearly. He made a compromise between Nietzsche's revolution (of which Nietzsche himself was fully aware that it was a revolution) and positivism. In other words, he still accepted the positivistic view of the objectivity of science, and combined it with Nietzsche's view of the non-objectivity of values.

One more point which is important in Simmel, and to some extent even also later, is the issue, the conflict with which Simmel was most immediately concerned, which was that between an aristocratic ethics as it partly existed or lingered on in Germany at that time (Prussia), and the socialistic ethics at the other pole. The key point that appears very clearly from the book as a whole: this conflict between these two kinds of ethics cannot be settled by rational means. Social science has to be neutral between these two kinds of morality, just as physics is metaphysically neutral between spiritualism and materialism, a neutrality of which I have spoken before. So from this point of view, more recent developments in the social sciences seem to continue only the tendency of modern science towards such a neutrality, but a neutrality now extended beyond metaphysics to ethics. Before I turn to a critical consideration of this view, with which I suppose you are all familiar, I would like to find out whether I have made myself clear regarding the character of the thesis.

STUDENT: I wonder if you could go over once more your point that Simmel makes this compromise between Nietzsche and positivism.

LS: Nietzsche's eventual thesis is that at the bottom of all human convictions there are acts of evaluating, of setting up of values, so that, for example, modern physics, theoretical physics, itself rests on such an evaluation and not only because science is based on the acceptance of the value of truth—this you could say of every form of science—but a very specific evaluation which . . . the problem. Now Simmel rejected that. He accepted the authoritative character of modern science without any hesitation, but as far as the moral things are concerned, he accepted Nietzsche's view. So it is a kind of compromise between Nietzsche and the then-prevailing view. Yes?

STUDENT: In your explanation of Simmel, you said that you couldn't understand how such a radical break could be made in the tradition of philosophy without his comprehending it. Now do you think that—

LS: Well, when you read what he says about these matters, and this enormous book of more than six hundred pages in two volumes, it does not in any way make the impression of being a revolutionary book. When you read later on the statements of Max Weber, they are much more revolutionary in their substance, although Weber himself says it is nothing new, because this was already a kind of settled opinion in certain academic circles in Germany by Max Weber's time. But Weber is overwhelmed, as it were, by this state of things, that certain things which were hitherto regarded as knowable are now admitted to be not knowable at all.

SAME STUDENT: In other words, you didn't mean that simply stating the fact that Simmel combined Nietzsche with positivism should take away our shock at seeing him lay these things down.

LS: No, no. There was no pedagogy or soft-sell, no, no. And I believe it becomes intelligible when one presupposes that this book appeared in a country which had been hammered for at least a decade by Nietzsche's immoralism. "Immoralism" is a word which Nietzsche himself used, and which meant surely this: There is no knowledge of good and evil possible. It meant more than that, but this it also meant. Yes?

STUDENT: Could you explain Nietzsche's position a little bit more? Did he believe there was no knowledge of the good and the bad, that all scholars had been mistaken on this in the past?

LS: Well, of course this was naturally implied, because hitherto ethics had been a normative science, and not only the doctrines of the so-called Idealists but the British utilitarians. That is of course a normative doctrine: the greatest happiness of the greatest number. But Simmel does not convey to the reader an awareness on his part of the fact that this is a complete change in the character of man's study of man, that what hitherto was taken for granted by everyone, a normative science, ceases to be. I mean, there were of course some preparations for that—Marxism, to some extent. But Marxism in its attack on bourgeois morality of course appealed to another, truer sense of justice, as it thought. No one could say that Marxism is simply nonnormative and ethically neutral in the way in which this present-day social science claims to be ethically neutral. This, I must say, was the reason why I was not inclined to credit Simmel with that, whereas Max Weber, whose essays on this subject appeared about a decade later, originally—Weber is filled with a kind of passion to which he gives very powerful expression due to this new insight. He doesn't claim any originality, he says it is known to the logicians; but Weber was the first who *preached* it, as it were, so that it became after Weber a matter of intellectual integrity whether you will use value judgments in scientific considerations or not. Weber's articles are translated into English, and I remember in former times they were read in the College here in the social science courses. I do not know what they do now, but I suppose some of you have read them. The most famous of these things is his lecture on "Science as a Vocation," which gives this view a very powerful expression. And I think if you can read it, you should read that. Yes?

STUDENT: Who was the writer who developed the idea that scientific knowledge somehow is superior to common sense? How did Comte's idea that commonsense knowledge was scientific knowledge come to be overthrown?

LS: Well, you can say the other view, the contempt for common sense, was a much more powerful thing in modern times. If you read Descartes's *Meditations* and see what happens there to common sense, that was a more powerful—. In Comte, his relative sympathy with common sense had very much to do with his peculiar political or social preferences, with a certain conservative inclination. It was an exception of him. Yes?

STUDENT: Mr. Strauss, you said that this movement, trying to be able to speak of values in a causative sense—from which discipline, from which area would the necessary universals for a causal analysis be supplied? You seem to have rejected psychology as a source.

LS: Oh, no. Max Weber thought very little[13] of academic psychology, and he thought the psychology you need for the study of social phenomena is the kind of psychology you practice by playing bridge—you know, you have a certain estimate of the fellows with whom you play—and the refinements of academic psychology are of no value. But generally speaking, the discrediting of psychological questions regarding questions of validity[14] has nothing to do with a contempt for psychology.

SAME STUDENT: I was asking a very narrow question: How do these people see a causal aspiration in terms of value as possible?

LS: Not in terms of values. At most, in terms of people's believing in values. There is a great difference. So if people believe, say, in the Christian values, this will affect their action, of course. And you have to take this into consideration without taking the Christian values as in themselves good or bad. This is beyond the competence of social science. But the prevailing view in this school is this, which is also the prevailing view in this country: multicausal. There is Marxism, which says that ultimately you must understand all social phenomena in terms of the relations of production. And Weber wrote long books in order to show that while in some respects that is quite helpful, there is also the other causation. Well, his famous study on Puritanism and the spirit of capitalism is meant to show that the religious motivation had here a crucial effect on economics, on economic action.[15] I think that this is the view now generally prevailing. They call it multicausal: there is no universal rule as to what has priority in a given situation. That depends. In a certain situation one might be able to show that the decisive causation originated in economic things; in other cases, it may have been religious, or may be due to size, whatever it may be.

SAME STUDENT: A further question: This then leaves room open within the social sciences for disagreement on what *the* cause of a particular act is? Some may want to attribute it to religious feeling, the other to an economic—

LS: You know, they would say that is a factual question, and I believe they might very well say, without getting into any trouble on that score, that in a given case you cannot find out unambiguously that this or that was the cause. You must leave it open. There is no difficulty in that. So the key point is: only social science gives causal explanations, and cannot possibly engage in evaluations.

Now let us consider this position critically. Simmel had spoken of the indifference to good and evil, however good or evil may be understood. No consideration of good or evil can be permitted to enter social science. Nothing is intrinsically good or bad, intrinsically high or low, healthy or unhealthy: any preference is as good as any other or as bad as any other. Science itself is, of course—that is the natural implication—science itself is not intrinsically higher than prostitution, only some people prefer science and others the other. [Laughter] To the extent to which we are sensitive to good and evil, however understood, we lack the objectivity of social scientists. The necessary condition is moral obtuseness, in any sense of the word. Social science thus understood, if it is consistent (which it very rarely is), inevitably fosters moral obtuseness.

The question arises: Can one understand values, whichever they may be, without being moved by them, without one's horizon being changed by such understanding, so that our very science, our very hypothesis formation and so on, is affected by our understanding of values? People use the word "empathy," and surely in order to understand something you must have empathy with it. Even a criminal judge, and perhaps he more than anybody else, must have empathy with the criminal in order to see what speaks in favor of the criminal. Even with racketeers. And we as social scientists, if we have to deal with that unsavory subject, must have that empathy because this can be rightly expected. From time to time you read works of political historians (I will not give an example) in favor of some hero who was of course at his time attacked by another party, without the historian even making the slightest effort, for a second, to look for one moment at the hero from the hero's enemy's point of view. Perhaps the enemy had a point, maybe it was not an important point but a point which one should surely consider. That is a very poor historian—that is a party book, a party pamphlet, and not a historical work. So even, as I say, the racketeers, we have to understand them. Now if we do that, then the values of the racketeers coexist in our mind with the non-racketeer values. There is conflict within us to that extent between the square values— the square's values—and the crooked values. Is it merely blind preference in us which makes us prefer, after due consideration, the square values? Does it make sense to say of a man who is prepared to destroy thousands and thousands of men—drugs, for example—merely in order to have the maximum of sensual pleasures: Does it make sense to say of such a man that he is a *good* man? If there is an absolute relativity of values, then of course he could be said to be a good man. We sense something of what goodness is; the racketeer does not. He is blind to it; he is incompetent to judge because of his unawareness of that. He is at least as incompetent to judge of the issue as a blind man is incompetent to judge of pictures or of colors.

Some people argue that social science thus understood is not morally irrelevant. For instance, it can show that certain ends are impossible to achieve, and therefore it gives us moral guidance: Abandon this end which cannot be achieved. But as has been said somewhere in Goethe's *Faust*: "Him I love who desires the impossible."[16] To desire only the possible— rationality is a value like any other. Or if you say that the matter is that everyone wants to succeed, that is a question: Do all men wish to succeed? Are not some people desiring to fail—tragic natures, as some people say? It is also said that social science can show that certain ends are based on objectively untrue premises. For example, the Nazi theory. But again, this helps very little because the question arises: Why should a man choose truth? Why not myth, which supplies power in one way or another? Truth is a value like any other. Social science cannot show of course that social science itself is good, because that would be a value judgment. Yet you hear from time to time this view: whatever end a man may choose, he needs clarity about the means. And this clarity about the means is supplied by social science, that is to say, while all ends are arbitrary, social science is not, because you need it for whichever end you want. But there is this difficulty, of course. If this were so, there would be one objectively valid value judgment: that social science is good, and this is contrary to the premise of the whole position.

The fundamental questions, the most important questions, concern the ends, because the means depend entirely on the ends. Social science is incompetent regarding the ends. Social science cannot give us guidance regarding the most important things; hence the flight from scientific reason. Just as in the case of the Why as distinguished from the How, which keeps alive the concern for theology and metaphysics despite the ever-increasing progress of science, and this is true in a more direct way in the case of the value judgments. Now let me explain this a bit more fully.[17]

... desire which arises in man and for which he is not responsible, and that for which a man takes the responsibility. So let us say then that a value is more appropriately defined as the object of conscientious choice; hence the range of values depends on the answer to the factual question of what a value is. Many things which are values on the basis of the crude view according to which a value is an object of desire are not values on the basis of the less crude view. So a different answer to a factual question answers a value question. Take as a simple example the difference between a coward and a conscientious objector. Both don't want to go into the army, but obviously for very different reasons: the coward simply fears death and wounds and discomfort, but the conscientious objector is willing to die for his objection. This distinction is a factually necessary distinction and implies a value distinction, as the conscientious objector, however wrong he may be, is a much more respectable human being than the mere coward.

Now let us apply this to the question of the goodness of science. Science may be an object of desire, like a cake, but it may also be an object of choice, of conscientious choice. Even in the latter case, science is not chosen because it is intrinsically good, objectively good—such things do not exist, according to the hypothesis. It can only be chosen in an act of choice which is not guided or enlightened by the insight into its goodness. This act of choosing science cannot be justified by science. It cannot even be understood by science, for scientific understanding presupposes that we have chosen science already. The fundamental phenomenon, more fundamental than all science, is the abyss of choice. One way to overcome that abyss is the choice of science. A psychological explanation of this fundamental choice of course comes too late: it presupposes the choice of science.

Another consideration: science is susceptible of infinite progress. That is essential to the present view of science. This implies that reality is such that it cannot be understood in a finite process; otherwise science could not be essentially infinite. In other words, reality is unobtrusively and irretrievably mysterious. This mysteriousness of reality and this abyss of choice, they somehow belong together. These are, one can say, the starting points of existentialism over against positivism in our age. Now it is essential for the claim of present-day social science to be amoral—morally in no way committed. Yet if we proceed empirically, we observe that most social scientists take a very definite moral position, even a political position. That is so. Is this a mere coincidence? For example, generally speaking, social scientists do not take the same moral-political position which many physicians take. I mean, the American Political Science Association has a different line than the AMA,[18] which is I think a simple sociological fact. But in the case of the AMA we have no direct interest, but in the case of the APSA we do. Now what is this peculiar position? We can say liberalism, in the wide sense in which the old-fashioned liberalism of Milton Friedman of our economics department as well as the New Deal liberalism go together.[19]

Now what does this position mean? What is this liberalism? I would say, a permissive egalitarianism. There is a certain difficulty within permissive egalitarianism, because there may be a possible conflict between permissiveness and egalitarianism. For example, to what extent should one be permissive toward nonegalitarian tendencies? That is a well-known difficulty. Egalitarianism is, I think, clear. Permissive. Think of such questions as homosexuality, the whole thing of the Kinsey Report,[20] and the whole attitude toward penal law which now prevails. Now, is there a connection between permissive egalitarianism, the prevalent posture of present-day social scientists, and the very principle of social science as previously defined? The social science position implies that all values are equal, naturally: if they were not equal, there would be an objective reason for preferring value A to value B, and so on. So all values are equal; that is to say, the principles of actions are equal. Now for any man of common sense, it follows that if all values are equal or all desires are equal, they ought to be *treated* as equal. If you treat equal things differently, then you act in a grossly unfair manner. In other words, it is very hard to avoid this step from the Is to the Ought. Well, naturally there is one limitation for every man of common sense: they ought to be treated as equal within the limits of the possible, so the man who has the value of slitting people's throats and drinking their blood—this wouldn't work very well together with the values of most other people, who strongly object to someone doing that to them. There is a conflict of values, but how can such a conflict be rationally settled? Precisely given the equality of everyone around, the only just way of settling the conflict is to let the majority have it. The majority are absolutely opposed to these throat slitters, for example, and therefore we have laws making this a forbidden action, and so on. So I think there is a deep connection between the social science, the allegedly strictly logical, methodological teaching regarding the equality of all values, and the substantive morality for which most social scientists today stand up.

Now let us have first an exchange about this subject, the question being the effect of value-free social science on morality and the connection with that. Yes?

STUDENT: You said before that there must be very strong psychological inducements to believe modern-day positivism. Would you care to comment on what these might be?

LS: That is a very long question, but what I have in mind fundamentally is that this social science as it exists now is the heir of a long tradition which was still normative: think utilitarianism. By virtue of this heritage, of this tradition, the inclinations are in a certain direction. I said many years ago already: Scratch a present-day American relativist, as they call them, and you will find a utilitarian. There is this proverb: "Scratch the Russian and you will find the Tatar," *Grattez le Russe et vous verrez le Tatar.*

And in this sense: Take off the thin varnish of this methodological doctrine and you will find a simple straightforward utilitarian. One reason why especially Max Weber, and to some extent also Simmel, developed their doctrines was their insight into the grave difficulties in which utilitarianism became entangled and, wholly independently of the socialism question, the very great difficulty to define what the greatest happiness of the greatest number means—although, in a crude way, what Bentham and his successors meant was of course clear: Better food, better housing, better care for health of the large mass of the population. And in this respect nothing has changed. I've thought of that. Yes?

STUDENT: Let's suppose that we are social scientists who are asked to join the next administration, and we are called in to counsel the governor or the president or what have you. And he's not going to ask us: What would be good policy? He's going to say: What do the people want? So the point being that it strikes me that as a theoretical objection, your objection to modern social science is valid, but it has little practical consequence, because the agency that decides what values should be the public values are not philosopher-kings but are the sentiments of the people.

LS: That is as it should be in a democracy, but it is not quite so simple. That may be true most of the time, but what is true most of the time may not be true in the most important cases. Some of you may remember what happened in 1945, when President Truman, in accordance with the sentiment of probably 99.9 percent of the American people, demobilized the American forces in Europe: The boys must come home. The consequence was that the boys had to go back again to Europe a few years later. In other words, one could say that precisely in a democracy, it is the duty of the government to look somewhat further ahead than the average citizen does and, if I am not mistaken, that was the underlying idea of representative democracy, i.e., that the people do not govern themselves but are governed by men supposed to be more far-seeing than the people at large. This I would say. Now in addition, practical political questions are of such immense complexity that most of them would be in themselves indifferent to the theoretical or moral position a man takes, because they have become truly merely technical questions in this manner. But still, at one point or another, and you can never tell in advance at which point, the question of principles will arise. Yes?

STUDENT: Earlier, one of your criticisms of the social scientist taking a perfectly objective view as regards the criminal and the noncriminal was to say that the criminal is as blind to moral things as the sightless person is to the beauty of paintings. I was just wondering how far you would take this analogy, whether you want to imply that moral values are objects of perception in the same way that colors in paintings are, or—

LS: They obviously cannot be objects of sense perception. But there could conceivably be another kind of perception. When you speak of a perceptive man, someone who senses in a way when someone makes a tactless remark—does it not happen?—and he senses it in a way as strongly, although it is very hard to say how this sensing takes place, as when one senses a color or a sound. Does this fact not exist? Have you never seen people either expressing sentiments which impressed you as very noble, or others expressing sentiments which are very base? You sense that nobility on the one hand, and the baseness on the other. I mean, the analysis of what this sensing means is very difficult, but nevertheless there is a kind of direct awareness which we have and which surely we would not have if we did not have a certain upbringing, so that a baby or a very young child might not have it at all. Yes?

SAME STUDENT: Certainly for most people you could say that if he didn't see that a certain sort of action would hurt another person or, not if he didn't see it, but if he saw that it would hurt another person and said "So what?," we would call him morally blind or something like this. But wouldn't you say that for some people, at least, most of these moral judgments are capable of being based on a more rational ground, or perhaps—

LS: Yes, but it is not necessary that the individual should be able to state these grounds. Well, take a simple case: You talk to a man and you see he is incapable of any consideration other than what will be conducive to his earning money. Have you seen such people? I mean, there are such people. And you see he is completely incapable of any other consideration: that something might be good for the country, or something might be good from any other, broader point of view, they are completely unable to do that. This can surely be spelled out in the form of a proposition: Money is the highest good. And this, if it is stated in the form of a proposition, you can of course go into it rationally and ask the questions: Why do we have money? What is the function, the purpose of money? And does not the understanding of the purpose of money show you that money cannot possibly be the greatest good? Then you find that this is not a very profound and far-fetched thing. People sometimes say of another man: Well, he's amassing money, but he cannot take it with him. You may have heard that expression. There is something very profound implied in that; this can be spelled out. I am sure that these things can and must be spelled out to have their full evidence, but it is not necessary for us in daily life to have it fully spelled out. Our shock about a man of atrocious meanness is of course based on some reasonings which we are not necessarily able to fully develop at the moment and perhaps have never taken the trouble to develop, and yet we can say of the man who has this narrowness that he sees only the value of money, and of another, who sees also the value, say, of genuine friendship—I would say that the second man is surely a wider man, a more competent man in human matters than the first. This I would say without going into any deeper question. And to that extent, we can leave it at this simple question of human competence. I fully agree with you that these things must be spelled out, and the only way to spell them out is to say what the purpose of a certain line of action—if not of a whole way of life—is, and see whether it makes sense to say for any man that this is the highest good. For any man. Yes?

STUDENT: Could not one say, in criticism of your criticism of positivism, that just like an inarticulate police chief who can't explain penal theory very well but can run a very good department, these modern-day positivists are not very deep or articulate, and they can be easily destroyed, but what they produce under that seeming theory is significant? And so really you're attacking a straw man, and not the real substance of their work.

LS: Very well, it could be. But I would say this: there is a great difference between a police chief—especially in a smaller place, because here we have Orlando Wilson, he's a professor himself [laughter]; and professors, university people, academicians, they are supposed to *know* what they are doing, to be able to give a theoretical account of what they do.[21] A police chief may be excellent, he may have an unfailing smell of who is a crook and who is not, and he may be wholly unable to give an account of that; and that's very good, because no defendant will be punished on the police chief's merely saying so. There must be proof, naturally, and therefore it is immensely helpful if you have men who have such wonderful instincts. But in science, in all rational pursuits, these kinds of instincts are not sufficient. And in addition, it is truly a question whether the political views generally favored by the general run of political scientists, of this kind of political scientist, are good. That is a question.

SAME STUDENT: Well, to your first point, can't one answer: Well, that happens to be a characteristic of American people, that they're not very theoretical, and political scientists are American people, as de Tocqueville described them, so they have that defect, but that's the price of a little democracy. But on the second point—

LS: Yes, that is something—this I could say: If they did not raise claims as theoreticians, I would entirely agree with you. But they raise these claims.

SAME STUDENT: I don't see which ones you're referring to, but the ones I have seen never raised that claim. That's why they weren't worth studying in the first place.

LS: Well, of course it would be very indelicate to mention names. [Laughter] But let us take a man who is, I believe, now regarded as *the* greatest, most influential American political scientist: that's Harold Lass- well.[22] He surely raises a claim to be a theorist, and he has said these things more than once. I mean, this doctrine exists and is powerfully represented by a whole literature, in all kinds of books, pamphlets, and courses, and must therefore be faced. That must be done.

SAME STUDENT: So once you've faced it, even if you've won the battle, you still have to deal with their work, with their production, with their publications, as—

LS: No, I believe it is not so negligible because this would, I believe, also show in the so-called empirical studies which they make. Because the value of an empirical study does not depend entirely upon whether it is exactly done according to all prescriptions of scientific logic; it depends also upon the relevance of the study. This depends on the values.

SAME STUDENT: Well, take a look at the great advance we have since Sigmund Freud's day, to take just one example—the curing or bringing back to competence people who are mentally incompetent.

LS: Yes, that is an infinite question into which I cannot go, because the question arises immediately: Are not these kinds of incompetencies a product of the same society which produced Freud? This raises a ques- tion, whether the incompetencies which existed a hundred years ago— could they have been taken care of adequately by Freud? That is a moot question. That is a long question, we cannot take this for granted. And one could also say some other things about that. All right.

STUDENT: It seems that a radical social scientist might grant that facts are value-constituted, and that the selection of his material proceeds more or less from a bias, from an evaluative bias of some kind. And what I'm asking is, is your criticism directed more to their effects in practical, everyday political life, or to their methodology?

LS: Well, one surely cannot disregard what the implications of their doctrine are, if it is taken seriously. If we do not take it seriously, as our friend just said, well, that is all right, but we must reckon with the possibility that it is taken seriously, what its social or moral effect is. But as for the question which you raise, that is complicated. I mean, what is generally admitted by the men who work in these things is this: that the distinction between relevance and irrelevance presupposes values. I mean, what is important and unimportant, what is relevant and irrelevant, presupposes values. So if a man writes a study on this particular subject rather than on that, an empirical study, there is a value involved. But what they say is this: That is uninteresting because what we are concerned with is that *after* he has chosen his subject, no evaluation enters there, so if he says that X is the cause of Y, there is no evaluation which enters here. The difficulty is rather this: whether there are not certain subjects, scholarly subjects, which are constituted by value judgments and which do not make sense without them. Take this example, which I take also from Max Weber. Max Weber asserted—I am not interested in whether it is right or wrong, it is only an example—that Puritanism had a bad effect, a deleterious effect, on music in England. Now this proposition is of any interest only because of certain assumptions: (a) that Puritanism is a form of religion which is very high; and (b) that there was music of high order in England before, which was destroyed under the influence of Puritanism. The highness of Puritanism and the lowness of the music coming from Puritanism are essential for the phrasing of the question, because if there were, say, a low and mean superstition which issued in the production of very low and mean music, that's a different phenomenon. The value judgments are essential to the definition, to the scholarly definition, of the subject matter. Now I will take this up next time, when I will discuss the question of whether it is possible to understand social phenomena without making value judgments, so in other words, disregarding entirely the practical question of what the effect of this kind of social science on moral evaluations is, but whether it is possible as a purely theoretical pursuit. I believe you had a question, and I was deflected by these other students.

MS. BARNETT: Yes. There are branches of the social sciences ... which say that the last assumption they make is that their propositions are falsifiable in principle. Now if you have this kind of social scientist, someone operating in this country, even though his reason for choosing the study and the evaluations he makes may be questionable, it is possible the *data itself*—going back to . . .'s question—is acceptable and can be used later on; it seems that the problem, as someone in the back pointed out, is that if you're trying to use the social scientist as . . . or someone who goes ahead and assumes that certain values are better than other values . . . how would you act, if you wanted to get policy from either kind of study? Because one kind of value is not communicable. For example, if a human being is not competent to understand a certain value or disagrees with it, it seems that when you get down to the basic assumption, there's just a disagreement and that's all you can say, whereas on the other kind of study, when you get to the basic assumption you can say: Well, I have falsified a principle here. You can falsify. You sense that there's a difference here that leads to action. Or not-action.

LS: Yes, but this was a very long statement, and would you do me a favor and write it up and hand it in to me next time at the beginning of the lecture? Please do that, because I would have to ask you to repeat it and it is rather late now.

4 Value-Free Social Science

Weber

LEO STRAUSS: Now, you were the one with—here is this question:[1] "Karl Popper claims that science can be separated from nonscience on nonverificationist principles, and agrees that the verificationist separation is untenable. If this claim is true, it would mean that a value-free social science was possible." Well, in the first place I must say: What does "verificationist" mean? No, honestly, I do not know. I simply do not know what it means, and therefore I do not see the connection between this assertion and the possibility or impossibility of a value-free science in general, or social science in particular. Could you explain to us what it means?

MS. BARNETT: Well, verificationists simply say, if someone presents a proposition—"All crows are black" is the standard one—if someone presents a proposition, and a verificationist were asked: "How do you know?" This, according to the Popperian, leads to an infinite regress. And he says that at the end of this infinite regress, according to their philosophy, is their answer, which is: Well, I don't know, but I will only ask questions that are in principle falsifiable.

LS: I see. Well, does it not amount to this, ultimately: that the attempt to reject certain questions as meaningless, as distinguished from untrue, begs the question? You know, when the question is raised, these so-called metaphysical questions regarding the Whither and the Where, as Comte puts it—and they cannot be answered by science, admittedly. And then the question arises: But are these not the most important concerns of man, and is therefore science not of a very limited value? Then one can try to get rid of this difficulty by saying these questions cannot be answered by science, but for this very reason they are meaningless questions. So you see, then you have solved the problem by definition, i.e., completely arbitrarily. Popper rejects that, probably. And what he means by this, "science can be separated from nonscience on nonverificationist principles," I simply do not know and therefore I cannot answer your question. Perhaps you will spell it out for us next time? It will do you well.

MS. BARNETT: Well, it's a long—a five-hundred-page book.

LS: Yes, but still the main point should be—I mean, I know Popper's position in a general way from some of his publications, but I could not—

MS. BARNETT: . . .

LS: I know, Popper takes the ordinary view, or the ordinary positivistic view, but he is more careful than some of the other writers of this kind around. But the difficulty in Popper comes in rather another way: that he tries to establish his position, his frankly value position, i.e., not scientific position, regarding permissive egalitarianism by attacking the men opposed to it, such people as Plato, Hegel, etc. But in doing that he proceeds in a most unscholarly manner, i.e., in a most unscientific manner, and therefore there is something very awkward if someone whose principle is science is unable to behave scientifically when it counts. This is my objection to Popper.

MS. BARNETT: Is this *ad hominem?*

LS: In a way, sure, it is a mere accident. But I believe the question is whether there is not a deeper necessity for that, I mean, whether the lacking concern for understanding these positions is not due to the fundamental certainty that this—say, Plato—that this *cannot* be true as Plato meant it, because Plato meant it as scientifically or objectively true. He doesn't take the necessary trouble of studying it. That is a bit more complex. Let us disregard Karl Popper altogether, since the relevant point to which you referred has not become clear to me, and I suppose to no one else. Or is there someone who knows these things of Popper and would like to take them up?

MS. BARNETT: Do you mean, what he means by "verificationist"?

LS: Yes, what this issue is, "science can be separated from nonscience on nonverificationist principles."

MS. BARNETT: Oh, I see. Well, he would call Comte a verificationist in that, in the end, if you were to ask Comte the question "How do you know this?," Comte would have to say: I know this by common sense or by empirical studies. So this, to Karl Popper, is verificationist and this leads to an infinite regress. That's what he means by "verification."

LS: And where do we begin, then? I mean, how do we avoid that infinite regress?

MS. BARNETT: Well, according to him, you avoid it by saying at the end: Well, I don't know. All I can say is that it can be falsifiable. Any propositions that are not falsifiable he won't deal with. He'll only deal with propositions that are falsifiable, so he'll say to the person that he's talking with: Well, help me falsify it.

LS: But without saying that nothing—

MS. BARNETT: He believes that most theories and propositions are false indeed, and that science proceeds by falsifying these theories. But what he'll say is: I don't know, and it remains to be falsified.

LS: Well, I suggest that you give us a somewhat more detailed report about it. Unfortunately, I do not have the time now to read it. Good.

Now I have spoken of the crucial change which positivism has undergone after Comte: the realization that science or reason is unable to substantiate value judgments. Social science cannot settle conflicts between fundamentally different preferences. When considering Comte, we saw that science must leave open the questions raised by theology and metaphysics—in Comte's formulation, the questions regarding the Why as distinguished from the How—and that this fact endangers the claim of science to be *the* guide of men, a claim which Comte raises on behalf of science, and endangers the claim of science to take the place formerly occupied by theology and metaphysics. That claim of science to be the guide is still more endangered, of course, in the moment in which science becomes value-free, because we may conceivably turn our backs to the question of the Why or Where and Whither but we cannot well turn our backs to the question of how we should live, how we should act.

Now the practical consequence of this exinanition of science is what has been called the flight from scientific reason to something else, whatever that may be, which claims to give men guidance. I think that is a fact, but it is concealed from one by the following state of affairs, a state of affairs which creates the delusion that a value-free social science can nevertheless guide us. Now take the simple example supplied by the present situation, the last elections. President Johnson's program is based on certain values, which from the point of view of social science are as good or as bad as any others, say, they are as good or as bad as those of Senator Goldwater.[2] But only the values cherished by Johnson have a sufficiently powerful political appeal, as was shown by the election—or are in step with the times: the argument that Senator Goldwater has horse-and-buggy values and therefore values of no real interest. Now if we broaden the spectrum somewhat and go much beyond the United States, we have seen that fascism has failed completely, and of Marxism one can very well say that while it has been conspicuously successful in some respects, it is theoretically or scientifically wrong. The great conservative statesmen in our age, Churchill and de Gaulle, failed in the decisive point. Churchill had said: "I have not become His Majesty's prime minister in order to supervise the liquidation of the British Empire," and de Gaulle said similar things about Algeria. And look what has happened.[3]

In brief, to summarize this kind of thing which you all know: merely factual considerations of what is possible, and politically possible *now*, decide in favor of what is now called the liberal line. That means, however, that science, value-free science, decides in favor of liberalism. This is one important part in our present situation. And from this point of view, the social science relativism regarding the values is a purely scholastic or academic affair which has no practical meaning. It is perfectly possible to take this view. But we must see the question is only this: Granted that this is the wave of the future, and therefore the question of whether it is good or bad cannot arise because you cannot do anything against the wave of the future, the question is whether this difficulty does not raise its ugly head in another way.

Now I would like first to read to you an old passage, which you will see has some relevance, but perhaps not sufficient relevance. Very briefly, what many people think today is this: We know where the development goes. The nuclear war is an insanity, and unless some insane individual like Hitler comes[4] to power somewhere, there will not be a nuclear war. This will be avoided. Surely the Russian system will become more liberal, demands for consumer goods will make themselves felt, and, on the other hand, the West will become more socialistic. And we can see that even China will eventually mollify, because this will not always ... And so there is a development in front of us which is both obviously possible, and perhaps more than possible, and in addition absolutely sensible. There is no problem, no fundamental problem.

Now the first passage which I will read to you is from Nietzsche's *Zarathustra*, near the beginning. Zarathustra addresses the multitude:

"One must still have chaos in oneself to be able to give birth to a dancing star ... Behold, I show you the *last man* ...

"No shepherd and one herd! Everybody wants the same, everybody is the same: whoever feels different goes voluntarily into a madhouse ...

"'We have invented happiness,' say the last men, and they blink."[5]

Now this is Nietzsche's formula for what looks so very different in the communists', especially in Marx's own, presentation. Nietzsche says, although he didn't know Marx—disgraceful, that he didn't know him—he says as it were that what Marx regards as his final state of the communist society, as the society of the highest culture: *this* is what you in fact will get. Now we all know that there is some little element of truth in what Nietzsche says. Some things which we know from our time make it worse. For example, he says those who feel different go into a lunatic asylum. We know that is not necessary, we just go to a psychiatrist, we don't have to take this extreme step. But in other respects, Nietzsche doubtless exaggerates from every point of view.

I would like to read you a statement by a present-day sociologist, an American sociologist, who is very far from the extremism of Nietzsche. This is Professor Nathan Glazer.[6] In a discussion which is not printed but which I am sure he would permit me to use, he speaks of the most successful revolution of our age, "the organizational revolution, or the scientific revolution," and its implications. Through this revolution the gap between "the intellectuals," "the radical and liberal critics," on the one hand, and the organizations "representing the status quo" (say, the War Department) has been closed or at least very much narrowed. The reason was that the intellectuals proved to possess "new techniques for making organizations more efficient." One might say that in proportion as the scientists drew all conclusions from their basic premise, which is the assertion that science is limited to "factual" assertions as distinguished from "value" assertions, they lost the right to be radical critics of institutions and became the willing servants of any institutions. Does it not make sense? I mean, in order to be a radical critic, you have to have values which you can defend intellectually. Yet, strangely, the cooperation of scientists and men of affairs (including generals) has affected the "values" of the latter, so that one begins to wonder whether there is not a preestablished harmony between the allegedly value-free science and the liberal values. Be this as it may, the question which troubles Professor Glazer is whether the society rendered possible by the cooperation of the scientists and the managers—the society guaranteeing to everyone "simple justice and simple freedom"—can be regarded as a good society. I quote: "Both conservatives or reactionaries, on the one hand, and intellectuals and radicals and anarchists on the other, often come together in opposition to what we might call establishment Liberalism."

Both the reactionary and the intellectual question the claim of the welfare state—"the whole organization, the machine for doing good"—to be the good society. Glazer sees only one way out: "to improve the organization" by setting up "the great organization" or "the big organization" or "the determining center of allocation," which is enabled to direct all other organizations because it "will have far more information and will make much better diagnoses" than anyone else can. Hence it will be "the good *big* society." But this is a solution not for Mr. Glazer. Alongside it, he predicts "there will be developing good *small* societies," composed "of reactionaries and anarchists and radical intellectuals."[7] But he is not sure whether "the organization will be tolerant enough to let them be," nor whether "they will be clever enough to evade it."

This is a statement of the problem with which you are all familiar, namely, that this solution, which seems to be so self-evident and demanded by "simple justice and simple freedom," will not necessarily lead to what is ordinarily known as conformism, the destruction of all human originality. That is of course what Nietzsche meant when he spoke of that star in the *Zarathustra.* So in other words, however plausible the view that "Look around! For a serious and sober man, there is no question, we know what is coming and no one can object to it, no one can complain about it," yet if one thinks a little bit deeper, one sees that it is not so, and therefore the value question arises again.

Now last time I began a discussion of the value-free social science, and I would like now to continue that. I would now like to raise the question: Is it possible to understand social phenomena without evaluating? I do not deny that you can understand some social phenomena without evaluating them; that is not the point. But when we speak of social science we think of course of all possible subjects of social science, and the question is, therefore: Is it possible to understand all social phenomena without at any time evaluating? In other words, I am not concerned now with the practical consequence. I take it for granted that social science is a merely theoretical science. Can it fulfill its theoretical function of understanding social phenomena without evaluating?

Now the general answer would be no, because social phenomena are all of a purposeful character, and therefore they as it were demand to be judged in terms of the purpose which they are meant to serve. This kind of immanent evaluation, as we might call it, namely, Given this purpose, does it fulfill the purpose? is inevitable. The question arises whether the immanent evaluation does not necessarily turn into an absolute evaluation, and not for an accidental reason. For example, let us start from a very obvious fact: the analysis of the last election. It is absolutely impossible to say anything relevant about the last election without speaking of the ineptness of certain men in the running and the noninept-ness of others. This value judgment—if you don't use that, you don't say anything—Senator Goldwater stepped on every toe, one can say, and on the other hand, the handling of the Bobby Baker case was too obviously clever.[8] I mean, these are value judgments, whether we like it or not. But these merely immanent evaluations take on an absolute significance for the very simple reason that the beings judged are not merely running for president—or maybe generals, or dogcatchers, what does it matter—but they are all *human beings*! While it is entirely voluntary, in a sense, whether you run for president or general or dogcatcher or some other kind of catcher, it is not voluntary for you to be a human being. You are subject to the standard implied in that without any possibility of avoiding it. The beings judged are men, and there are virtues and vices of men. A man who regards war as unqualifiedly bad must make a distinction never-theless between a good and a bad general if he writes military history, but regarding war as thoroughly bad, he must mean the distinction between a good and bad general like the distinction between a good and bad thief, because here too we have a distinction. But nevertheless, if he is not completely narrow, he must see a difference between the cause to which the thief applies his resourcefulness and the cause to which the good general applies his resourcefulness, or rather the absence of a cause in the one case, in the case of the thief, and the presence of a cause in the other.

Fundamentally, one can state this as follows. We are concerned with political things. What is political? A hard question. But we can answer it etymologically or, if you please, from the point of view of an earlier age. "Political" is a derivative from the Greek word *polis*, the nearest equivalent to which is probably "commonwealth," the English word "commonwealth." Now a commonwealth has a purpose—it is controversial what that purpose is, but that it is meant to fulfill a purpose is granted. The standards for judging political things are inherent in political things as political things for this very reason. There are very great difficulties here, and it suffices to think of the difference between Aristotle and Locke re-garding the purpose of civil society or of the commonwealth. But that on which Aristotle and Locke agree is very frequently sufficient for political judgment. We do not always have to raise the most fundamental questions; we can remain sometimes in a more limited horizon. Judgments in this sphere are solid enough, despite the fact that they remain within

an area surrounded by darkness. As Aristotle in his wisdom puts it occasionally: "to speak politically and crudely."⁹ To speak politically means
to speak crudely, not to make very refined distinctions which have no
political relevance.

An example: when Plato presents, in the first book of the *Republic*, this
old gentleman Cephalus, I think everyone likes that very nice old man
and everyone would wish to have such a grandfather. He is very nice, educated, reasonably delicate, and in addition also reasonably wealthy, which
is always a good quality for a grandfather to have. [Laughter] Now then,
when you read more carefully and follow Plato's presentation and therewith begin to use the x-rays with which Plato looks through Cephalus,
we come to see that this wonderful gentleman has a very seamy side. Now
Plato analyzes that—I mean, he still makes him a perfectly nice man for
all practical purposes, but *only* for all practical purposes. [Laughter] Now
Plato has a theory of what he does, namely, that true virtue as distinguished from this more superficial virtue requires a conversion, a conversion of the whole man, and this conversion Cephalus has never undergone. Plato speaks of that at the end of the *Republic*: the nice gentleman
brought up well and decently who yet chooses at the beginning of the
next life the life of a tyrant, meaning the most unjust life, precisely because
he has not undergone this conversion which according to Plato can be
brought about only by philosophy.¹⁰

Now let us take a very simple example. A man, a sociologist, writes a
sociology of art, (a) in general or (b) in particular. And then someone reads
it and sees that the paintings, or whatever it is which he has discussed, are
all trash. There is some impossibility in that. He should have called it a
sociology of trash, say, of the 1920s, and not sociology of art. But what is
that distinction between art and trash but a value distinction? A sense of
quality, as art historians say, is a prerequisite for being a competent student of art and therefore also a sociologist of art. Similar things apply to
all other parts of the social sciences. Let us take another case which surely
falls within the province of any special social science and therefore of political science in particular. As you know, political scientists, once they have
reached a certain age, are supposed to publish. As the maxim goes: "Publish or perish." Now, they publish [laughter], naturally, because they prefer
life to death. But then after they have published, something will happen
which is ultimately as important as the publication—an old hand tells
you that—namely, there will be a review. And if the poor fellow cannot
bring his publications together with a series of reviews which are favor-

able, he may be worse off than if he had not published at all. Now in these reviews we find such statements as "perceptive," "penetrating," "imaginative," "deep," "broad," etc., and very rightly, because these words indicate the standards with which a scientist or scholar is meant to comply. Naturally, not everyone can apply them properly (that is the great difficulty regarding the objectivity of reviews, and for that matter of science altogether), because you need judgment. And someone might find a certain observation very profound which is in fact very shallow. There is no protection and no guarantee for that; this vicious circle cannot be overcome. And needless to say, this is one of the great secrets of university life, because all appointments are made on the assumption that the appointers are competent. And how is competence to be judged? Ultimately by very external criteria: you have published, you can lecture, and so on and so on. Very difficult. But I am not concerned with this question now. I am concerned only with this. When people make these statements on scholarly productions, they mean, as value-free social scientists say, only this: if scholarship, then good scholarship. But why *scholarship*? So in other words, this is a merely immanent evaluation. I choose, for God knows what reason but surely not for rational reasons, scholarship, and then, if I have chosen it, then I am subject to the immanent standards. But this is simply not true to the facts, because when we look at such statements or make such statements, we observe that we admire these qualities *simply*. If we see that someone is perceptive, we mean more than: Since he has chosen to be a scholar, he ought to be perceptive. We mean more: there is a quality of a human being that will show also in entirely different fields of endeavor than scholarship. And the principle, again, to repeat: every human phenomenon and every human being is subject to being judged in terms of what is a good human being—and good in the widest sense, not only moral in the narrow sense of the term. A man may be a good man in the moral sense of the word without being perceptive, perhaps, but we mean a good man in the full sense of all human virtues and vices.

Now to come back to the question of how a social science would look which would completely avoid value judgments: I would like to illustrate this by an example. Social science must of course use concepts, articulate its subject matter in the light of concepts. One very famous one, found or invented by Max Weber (Max Weber being the most outstanding representative of the fact-value distinction), is the distinction between the various kinds of authority: rational, traditional, and charismatic. Let me take another, more recent example, not as important but still revealing: for some time, people used, especially at the Hoover Library in Stanford,[11] the distinction between the democratic and the authoritarian personality: strictly value-free. But if you read that, you saw that it was very value-loaded. The democratic personality was obviously a nice man, and the authoritarian was just an ogre! [Laughter] Not for one moment did they make the attempt to see that there could be an authoritarian personality, say, a father or grandfather, old-style, who might be quite annoying from time to time but who could also be very good as a guide for young people, and so on and so forth. But the Max Weber case is much more interesting.

Now I will read to you from the English translation of Max Weber's *Theory of Social and Economic Organization*, translated by Henderson and Talcott Parsons.

The term "charisma" will be applied to a certain quality of an individual personality by virtue of which he is set apart from ordinary men and treated as endowed with supernatural, superhuman, or at least specifically exceptional powers or qualities. These are as such not accessible to the ordinary person, but are regarded as of divine origin [of course, social scientists cannot say whether they are or are not of divine origin, but they are regarded as of divine origin—LS] or as exemplary, and on the basis of them the individual concerned is treated as a leader. In primitive circumstances this peculiar kind of deference is paid to prophets, to people with a reputation for therapeutic or legal wisdom, to leaders in the hunt, and heroes in war. It is very often thought of as resting on magical powers. How the quality in question would be ultimately judged from any ethical, aesthetical, or other such point of view is naturally entirely indifferent for purposes of definition [because the social scientist doesn't judge from an ethical or aesthetic point of view—LS].

What alone is important is how the individual is actually regarded by those subject to charismatic authority, by his "followers" or "disciples."

For present purposes it will be necessary to treat a variety of different types as being endowed with charisma in this sense. It includes the state of a "berserker" whose spells of maniac passion have, apparently wrongly, sometimes been attributed to the use of drugs. In Medieval Byzantium a group of people endowed with this type of charismatic war-like passion were maintained as a kind of weapon. It includes the "shaman," the kind of magician who in the pure type is subject to epileptoid seizures as a means of falling into trances. Another type is that of Joseph Smith, the founder of Mormonism, who, however, cannot be classified in this way with absolute certainty since there is a possibility that he was a very sophisticated type of deliberate swindler.[12]

Now what do you say to that? To the honor or dishonor of Max Weber, I have to say that this passage is mistranslated. Parsons apparently hadn't understood at that time what Weber's value-free social science was. Weber says, in effect, that *it doesn't make any difference* whether he was a swindler or not. In other words, the difference between a fake charisma and true charisma is already a value judgment and therefore has no place in social science. But one can rightly say that while it is a bad translation, it implies a sound criticism: the question must be raised, and for the very simple reason that social science, if it is to be worth its salt, can never leave it at finding out how an authority is *regarded* by its followers. If a society is subject to a fundamental delusion and regards legal fictions as literally true, then it is the first duty of the social scientist to say that these people were fooled about the character of the authority to which they were subject—the minimal critical duty of social science. Max Weber himself called the kind of constitutional monarchy which existed in Germany until 1918 sham constitutionalism. In other words, he said: This is not a truly constitutional monarchy, but a barely disguised absolute monarchy. I will not go now into the substantive truth of this assertion; the main point is that such distinctions are of course necessary for the social scientist to make: Is this a genuine constitutional government or only a sham? The kind of authority in a given group is to be determined by what the people concerned regard as authority. But it is impossible to leave it at that. That means literally passing the buck to people who may very well be less competent than the intelligent social scientist to judge whether the authority under question is genuine or a sham.

In addition, this whole doctrine of the kinds of authority suffers, I think, from a very grave defect. Naturally Weber didn't know anything of Hitler, although Hitler would really have to be classified as a charismatic leader in Weber's sense. But would this be sufficient? Would this be adequate, fundamentally adequate? Is it not in every case necessary, apart from these formal characteristics, to ask, regarding political legitimacy, as regards the cause which is the basis even of the claim of the charismatic leader? Hitler was elected and had this tremendous intra-German success, not merely because he had immense rhetorical and demagogic and other gifts of this kind, but also on the basis of what he stood for, what he called National Socialism. Can you disregard that when you speak of what legitimacy meant at that time in Germany? Without this cause, all his charisma would not have been helpful to him.

I would like to add another point here, namely—and this has been observed by more than one reader of Weber—that in Weber's theory of charisma, rational, and traditional authority, there is a value judgment implied, although obscure. Of course, Weber did not start with phenomena like Joseph Smith and so on. He took this conception from Christianity, and especially from a certain Protestant lawyer, Sohm.[13] Weber used the expression "the routinization of charisma," by which he implies that the original leader, who has this profound impact on people because of his particular gifts—on this basis the social order cannot last for any length of time, and there must be some substitute for it: the routinization of charisma. And according to Weber, this has taken place especially in the Christian Church, when Jesus and the Apostles were followed by the organized Church. But the very term "routinization," whatever Weber might say, implies a value judgment: routine versus charisma.

A last point which I would like to mention in this connection is this. The value judgments which are strictly forbidden by the ruling doctrine: they may not enter the front door, they come in by the back door. Because there is one discipline (not necessarily belonging to social science but affecting it very plainly) called psychiatry, and here the distinction between well-adjusted and ill-adjusted people enters, which is naturally understood and meant as a value judgment, whatever the pedantic and strict methodologies of the social sciences might say in a given case. I would say the only difference between such a value judgment as "well-adjusted" and "ill-adjusted," compared with "good" and "bad," is that it is very poor because there are perhaps situations in which it is good to be ill-adjusted. I mean, if a child comes from an abominable home, the worse he is adjusted to that home, the better for him, even if he has to go through quite some troubles. So it is a very narrow, unthought-through thing. Incidentally, I happen to know of one psychiatrist at least who claims that the distinction between adjusted and ill-adjusted, or sane and insane people, is also not scientific, because it is a value judgment and must be treated as such because what is sanity and insanity is differently understood in different cultures, and therefore we must even avoid that. Ultimately this would of course lead also to the abandonment of the distinction between healthy and sick in medicine or in biology. There will be an occasion to come back to this later. I'll turn now to another consideration which has to do with the question of value-free social science.

Value-free social science is distinguished from, and ultimately op-posed to, prescientific political understanding, what we loosely call com-mon sense, because common sense dealing with political or social matters of course evaluates all the time. Value-free social science questions com-mon sense and therewith follows a great tradition. The famous example: Copernicus's refutation of common sense. Here we see how poor com-mon sense is compared with the scientific approach, and what worked so well in astronomy, physics, etc., must also be done in the social sciences. Common sense evaluates. For common sense, the judgments "X has been in politics for forty years" and "X is a corrupt politician" have the same cognitive status. I mean, there is no logical difference from a common-sense point of view. Now the radical questioning of common sense is of course not the work of men like Copernicus, but above all by Descartes, Descartes who begins the whole philosophic-scientific enterprise with his universal doubt. Literally understood, he must doubt of everything. And something of this doubt is still visible in present-day social science when people want to have scientific proof for every assertion. Of course, this cannot be taken quite literally. For example, that there are presidential elections every four years: if a political scientist makes this assertion, no proof will be demanded from him. This is equally well known to com-mon sense and to scientific political science. The important point here is this (it is a simple example): that by being used in science, the statement, or the truth, or whatever you call it, does not undergo any change what-soever. So common sense is capable of knowing the truth. This example shows even that science depends on commonsense knowledge. That de-pendence can be shown most simply, and also universally, by the following consideration.

Political science deals with certain activities of human beings. As such, it presupposes that we have awareness of human beings as human be-ings, to state it simply, that we are able to tell human beings from other beings—from trees, dogs, stars, or what have you. Now when a sociolo-gist in a sociology department or, for that matter, a political scientist in a political science department is sent out with questionnaires to ask people about how they think about this or that subject, very detailed statements, and in the ideal case, so that not the slightest possibility of a misunder-standing by the poor student is possible, very well. But one thing they are not told: how to tell a human being from a nonhuman being, how to know that they should ask this being here and not this one, and how to distinguish them. Well, they learned this of course in their seminars.

[Laughter] No! They didn't learn it in their seminars. They didn't learn it in the college, not in high school, and not in elementary school. Where did they learn it? How did they learn it? I don't know. Most of us would say: I don't know. But we all know that we know it.

Now this little thing on which the whole enterprise absolutely depends is not scientifically known, and yet, as I said, it is the basis of the whole enterprise. Political science stands and falls by the truth of the prescientific awareness of political things. The question arises, of course: How are we aware of that truth? How do we become aware of this fundamental distinction to which I referred, between man and nonman? Do we in fact become aware of something, or is this not rather a convention of sorts, embodied in our language, and by learning language we become initiated into that convention?

Now this question of how we know that, there is a name for this kind of question, which I'm sure you have heard, that's an *epistemological* question, a question regarding the theory of knowledge. And this is a very important and highly respected part of modern philosophy. There is, however, one difficulty. Every epistemology, of whichever persuasion, presupposes the truth of empirical statements. We try to understand how it is possible that such a thing as perceiving things or perceiving people is possible. There are all kinds of theories about it, yet our perceiving things and people is more manifest and more reliable than any theory of knowledge, any explanation of how our perceiving things and people is possible. The truth of any theory of knowledge depends on its ability to give an adequate account of that perception presupposed to be true. It depends on its ability to give an adequate account of this fundamental reliance which we have. When I say, "I see here a young man," and perhaps give a more detailed description, there is no question about it that we are all in this room, 122. The fact that we know that is more evident, more manifest, more reliable, than any explanation of it, because any explanation presupposes that we are, and that we know we are, now in room 122.

I use the word "reliance," which is the literal translation (and in this case the best translation, I think) of the Platonic expression for the strange state of things that we know without knowing necessarily how or why we know. When Plato describes the various form of knowing, in the famous discussion in the sixth and seventh books of the *Republic*,[14] there is one stage which he calls in one version sense perception, which has here a wide meaning, like our knowing that we are here, for example. And he calls it, in the parallel, reliance—this, our sense of knowledge of things and people, has the character of such a fundamental reliance. What Plato implies can be stated as follows: We are in the midst of things. We cannot begin with a clean slate, using only perfectly clear and distinct concepts. We cannot begin at the beginning, but we must try to ascend to the beginning. In other words, in dealing with human things, at any rate, we are in an entirely different situation than the mathematicians are, who do begin and may begin at the beginning. We cannot do that. There is an interesting illustration of this state of things. Spinoza was perhaps the first philosopher who tried to present a whole philosophic doctrine in mathematical form, in a book called *Ethics Demonstrated in a Geometric Manner*, beginning with axioms, postulates, etc., as Euclid had done, and especially dealing with man—the book is after all called *Ethics*. And then there is suddenly an axiom somewhere, or a postulate, which runs as follows: *Homo cogitat*, man thinks, man is a thinking being.[15] He never defines man. Never defines man. This is not a mere accident. This is the essential difficulty of beginning in this manner. Now before I go on, let me first see whether I have made myself clear up to this point.[16]

STUDENT: The problem is that value-free social science doesn't strike me as being conscious fundamentally of having a theoretic function, whereas I think the political science which begins in common sense is more conscious of fundamentally having a theoretic function. I mean, I know that value-free social science has something that it calls theory—

LS: Well, but the theory, I think, is implied in the claim that it is a science in the same way in which physics, chemistry, biology are sciences, and therefore the general notion of science which has developed in the modern centuries is their theory of science, which has to be somewhat modified (perhaps one should say rather as economics is a science, as biology and so forth). No, common sense has of course no theory as such, naturally. That is a point. But common sense can *lead* to a theory. I will discuss this later on, when I come to speak of Aristotle.[17] But in itself, common sense has no theory.

SAME STUDENT: That's correct. But the problem that I'm trying to get at is that I think the theory, the value-free social sciences theory, is practically oriented. Because when you hear a value-free social scientist talking theoretically or abstractly, they always take their bearings from practical problems.

LS: Well, this is not necessary, because a practical statement would have this character: If you want to have this and this thing, if you want to achieve this end, you must use these and these means. But you can turn this into a theoretical statement by calling the means the causes and the end the effect. Then the practical statement is transformed into a theoretical statement. Therefore, whether the practical intention is very noticeable in many cases in value-free social science is ultimately irrelevant for the fundamentally theoretical character of present-day social science. I cannot go now into this question. This is perhaps one of the deepest differences, that traditionally political science, as you know, was regarded as a practical science, not a theoretical science, and this change from a practical to a theoretical science which took place roughly in the seventeenth century is a thing which we have to consider later in this course. Yes?

STUDENT: You mentioned for example that the knowledge that the election of a president takes place every four years in the United States is ascertainable both through common sense and through scientific methods. Now I'm wondering whether "commonsense" knowledge doesn't really depend on empirical verification in the sense that we can look back and see that every four years an election has taken place. In other words, doesn't common sense in this case, and perhaps in more cases than this, rest on empirically verifiable circumstances? For example, if a man were coming from another country, with no knowledge of the history of the United States, and he came to the United States this past year and saw the presidency, how Johnson succeeded Kennedy, his common sense wouldn't tell him that an election would occur every four years. So doesn't this common sense rest on empirically verifiable propositions?

LS: Sure. That is perfectly true, although it is not sufficient, but as far as it goes, it is all right. But the question is this. The positivists, especially the strict ones, would say that the empirically verifiable statements are the preserve of science. To go somewhat deeper: we all constantly make empirical statements. When I say, "We are now in room 122," it is obviously an empirical statement. But there is a difference between empirical statements and empiricistical statements—you know, between ordinary empirical statements, as men make them at all times, they've always made them, and statements complying with certain canons demanded by an empiricistic theory of knowledge. This is what it would amount to ultimately. But take the example which I gave: You are a human being; that [LS taps on the table] is not a human being. It is obviously an empirical statement. We wouldn't question its validity for one moment. But when you imply, in a way, that you cannot be certain that it's true unless you know how perception takes place and what gives it its validity, then the whole is changed. It may very well lead to the view—did you ever hear of that?—called solipsism, that strictly speaking you can only say: I have a perception of these and these colors, sounds, etc., which are patterned, and this particular pattern I call a human being, and I have no right to say that this human being *is* by himself. Have you never heard of that? And according to a very powerful school now, if one wants to be strict, one cannot go beyond solipsism. This is an example of the radical change which the word "empirical" undergoes when it is taken over by certain kinds of epistemological theories. Surely, there is no question that commonsense statements are empirical statements; whether this is true of all commonsense statements is another matter. Mr. Levy, you wanted to say something.

MR. LEVY: The value-free social scientist … does not express his opinion as to what *he* thought was good and bad, but what he was analyzing or studying. You have said that to understand the commonwealth, you have to understand what the commonwealth stands for, what its purpose is.

LS: Ya.

MR. LEVY: If we all agree with this, and we should, why can't the value-free social scientist remain value-free and still say: The American purpose is X, Y, Z; the Russian purpose is A, B, C; the British purpose is C, D, E, and I will study the politics of America, Russia, and—

LS: I do not deny that within a limited sphere you may do that. But I believe that in the long run, you cannot avoid the question of what the relative merit of these various definitions of the purpose are, unless you are completely uninterested in the subject. Well, then you shouldn't be a political scientist, I would say. But if you are interested in that, you are compelled to worry. Maybe you do not reach a result, but your worrying about it makes you nevertheless a better political scientist than if you did not worry about it and simply said: Well, let these fools have their prejudices, whichever they like, and I don't care about that. Your understanding even of what these people say can be deeper or shallower, obviously, and this means already to enter into the discussion, to become involved in that dialectics going on within each side as well as between the two sides. I have nothing against starting in the most modest manner—that is always wise to do, but I believe you will be dragged into that when you begin there. The lady—yes?

MS. BARNETT: If I understand what you said just now, it's a matter of determining what is the province of what political science in truth should now study, and then it becomes a conflict of views as to whether we can ascertain the knowledge of absolute values. And when you haven't resolved the foundations of science, and—

LS: But I didn't speak of absolute values, but take this question—

MS. BARNETT: But that's implicitly what you're saying.

LS: I do not—

MS. BARNETT: When you discussed Weber, you said that he could not help but make value judgments, and that his claim to not make value judgments was invalid. But the point of whether, in Weberian terms, something is true charisma, or not true charisma—one, you can't make such a statement, because the way Weber defines legitimacy is the way the people perceive it, and so there is no charisma separate from that.

LS: Ya, I know that. But the fact that Talcott Parsons mistranslated Weber—for which of course Weber is in no way responsible—indicates the problem. I mean, Weber says, whether this charismatic leader is a charlatan, a swindler, or genuinely convinced is wholly indifferent, provided the followers don't notice it. But still I ask, must the social scientist not be critical regarding the opinions which followers have of their leader? In many cases, they may not have sufficient evidence to answer the question, but must they not at least raise the question of whether the authority believed in is actually of that kind in which it is believed? I gave the simple example that constitutional monarchy can be sham constitutional monarchy. And the same: Can there not be a distinction between a genuine charismatic leader, what Hegel called a world-historical hero who identifies himself with a great cause, and a clever swindler?

MS. BARNETT: True. But to determine the difference, that doesn't mean to make a value judgment—

LS: Oh, yes, it makes a value—

MS. BARNETT: You don't say one is good and the other is bad. You say he fits correctly into the category or he does not.

LS: No, not quite, because what I stated before, perhaps in too general terms to be understood, is this: That these so-called immanent value judgments, for example, "good general" or "bad general"—that can be objectively found out, because one knows a bit about which kind of qualities a general must have and does have, and it is not an *absolute* value judgment, because why should there be generals—i.e., why is not war altogether bad, and therefore generals as bad as thieves? Then you can also make a distinction between good and bad thieves. But the question arises: Is it possible to stop there, at this immanent judgment? Is there not a necessity, if you say of a man—now what was the example? A fake, and a genuinely dedicated, inspired man, you say "this is only for purely theoretical purposes," it goes beyond that, you cannot arbitrarily put a stop to that. And the fundamental reason—I tried to say it in this form, because we are dealing in all cases with human beings, whereas it is arbitrary or voluntary whether a man is a general, or a thief, a painter, or whatever it may be, it is not voluntary for any human being to be a human being. Yes?

MS. BARNETT: But to make an arbitrary stop—you can't—the man who attempts to make an arbitrary stop is doing that because he believes that the certainty of his knowledge ends at that point.

LS: Yes, all right—

MS. BARNETT: So then a conflict results in whether we can have absolute values.

LS: Surely, if he believes that, he must stop. But his belief may be erroneous.

MS. BARNETT: So that's the disagreement—

LS: That is the issue—

MS. BARNETT: The absolute values the scientist ...

LS: The word "absolute values" has so many connotations, which are in my opinion wholly superfluous, and therefore I would not like to use it, but let us take it in this way. When I say, He is a first-rate general with these and these qualities, I mean a very outstanding man, the greatest general around, whatever it may be. We can find out about these things a bit in a commonsensical manner, or even if we know nothing about strategy, by a certain sensible belief in authority. For example, knowing that Montgomery is admitted to be a very good general (the British), we can find out who Montgomery regarded as top generals; this can help us a bit.[18] But I do not want to go into this question. The main point is that these limited, conditional judgments, like "If general, he's good," mean more, turn out to be more, than these if-statements, because the qualities ascribed, at least some of them, are qualities which we call virtues, distinctions, excellences, of human beings.[19] And there we cannot simply say: If you like that, you may, but if you don't, don't. Because these excellences have this character: that if we realize them, if we are open to them, we cannot but respect or admire them.

There are many questions. All right. I should really have someone, a kind of chairman.

STUDENT: Well, I'm wondering whether this just applies in one direction. It seems to me that the argument so far would lead to the conclusion that the factual judgments that have been made by the social scientist in his effort to leave out values are things that must be taken into consideration and are judgments based on values. In other words, you can't ignore whether or not a particular man has the qualities that he is reputed to have in making a judgment about him. It's not only whether or not these qualities are good or bad if you're making an evaluation, but also whether or not he has them, so that the factual part is necessary for the judgments that we must make of human beings. Is the discussion meant to apply also in the other direction, that somehow the social scientist's task, to the limited extent that he's set it for himself, necessarily needs value judgments to become involved in it?

LS: I believe so. I mean, there is a possibility of arbitrarily limiting oneself. There are some kinds of questions in which no value judgments arise. For example, in mere statistics, in most cases no value questions would arise. That is possible. But we are now concerned with the question whether you can define the scope of social science as a whole, of all the questions relevant for social science, in such a way that value judgments are strictly forbidden. That's the question. A man may, for example, abstain from making value judgments for reasons of modesty, sensible modesty, because the case is extremely complex and he doesn't dare to judge. But he would misunderstand himself if he didn't see that this restraint implies that he is on his way towards a value judgment and he knows he has not yet the sufficient equipment, factual or other, in order to pass a value judgment.

SAME STUDENT: In that case, then, there's no disagreement over the fact that the two realms may be different in their nature, and the kind of proof that is appropriate to them or to which they are susceptible may be different, but the point of argument is that the modern social scientist is going from the fact of difference into the fact of not being able to pay any attention to [it]. And would it be correct to say that *because* these questions must be raised, they must be the concern of the social scientist anyway, even though they're of a different nature from the ones—

LS: No, that is exactly what I deny. In an arbitrary manner, it can be done, but if we are concerned with purposive things, we have not only to know the purpose, but the things demand to be judged in terms of the purpose. And this requires that you take the purpose seriously and see even whether it is a sound or unsound purpose. It belongs to that, you cannot separate that. And the great question is whether a value-free social science does not, by its arbitrary limitation, necessarily lead to misinterpretation.

I once discussed the case, a famous case, of Max Weber's theory of the origin of the capitalist spirit.[20] I'm speaking now from memory. It is roughly this. Weber's thesis can be stated as follows: Calvinism is a most important cause of the capitalist spirit. You have heard of that in college, I'm sure. Now when you read Weber more carefully and don't leave it at this general statement, you see what he in effect means is that a certain *corruption* of Calvinism led to the capitalist spirit. That is something very different from simply saying Calvinism. In Calvin's language, which Weber naturally would not use, it would mean: Owing to a carnal, or fleshly, understanding of a spiritual teaching, Calvinism led under certain conditions to the emergence of the capitalist spirit. Here you see that by the omission of the value judgment—the corruption of Calvinism, say, a lower form, a degraded form, of Calvinism—he arrived at a factually untrue judgment. As Tawney put it, the Calvinism which became capitalist was a Calvinism which had made its peace with the world, i.e., which had become entirely worldly, which is another way of saying that it was not the real stuff.[21] Now these are not ultimate value judgments, because the question is here left open whether Calvinism is *the* true religion, or the true interpretation of Christianity, or whatever, but within these limits we must judge. And that happens to us all the time. In many cases we are unable to judge, no doubt. I mean, I, for example, would be wholly unable to judge of musical things—well, I naturally don't judge them. But in other cases, if you are a social scientist, you must judge.

STUDENT: Is it not possible to say that Calvinist spiritual belief was corrupted without saying that this is a good thing or a bad thing? It's the same question, but we keep coming back to it.

LS: Yes, but don't you see that in doing that, you cannot go on to a more interesting or a broader question except after having made value judgments. That is the point. Just as you cannot go on in medicine before you have made the value judgment: This is a corruption of the liver. And then you ask how that corruption was introduced, by alcohol or whatever it may be. That is the point. Therefore, I hesitate to speak of absolute value judgments—these are questions which arise in a proper manner, so that one is properly prepared for seeing them or understanding them only after a very long effort. Why not proceed in a truly empirical manner, in a way in which we know our bearings, and ascend, step by step, and not simply say from the beginning: Cut these kinds of things out because there are value judgments involved—because in this particular, limited way, you can be sure of your ground, and if you are not, you shouldn't make them. Yes?

STUDENT: Going back to the question of the distinction between common sense and science: Is the essence of what you have said in this respect that common sense and science both rest on the same epistemology?

LS: No. Common sense rests on *no* epistemology. Science, whether it knows it or not, rests on an epistemology. In most cases I believe scientists know that. There is this great change, this radical change in philosophy connected with the name of Descartes, the great mathematician and physicist, which is at the bottom of modern science. Strictly speaking, there is no epistemology before modern times. But surely common sense doesn't have that. The posture of common sense is that which we all have in ordinary life: Are you sure that this was X who hit Y? Of course I am sure: I was there, I have seen it. Well, even in that case errors are possible, as we all know. But still, common sense also knows the ways in which these things can and must be checked. I mean, all judicial procedure is based on some commonsense awareness of how such statements of a witness, for example, have to be checked. That has nothing to do with epistemology.

SAME STUDENT: Yet isn't common sense based on empirically verifiable propositions? That is, a commonsense proposition is one that can be verified empirically.

LS: Ya, but what does this mean? For example, if you have the statement: This is a human being, to whom I can address my questionnaire, and this is not a human being. What does it mean, that this is empirically verifiable? The one will not say hello when I say hello? [Laughter] This is an empirical proof that the one is a human being, the other is not?

SAME STUDENT: What I'm saying is that, yes, it does raise questions of epistemology, and because science says that we accept only statements which can be verified empirically, it's resting on the same—

LS: Ya, to that extent. But you see that the divergence of common sense and science comes out in such simple things. Common sense tells us that the sun is rising in the east and setting in the west, that the earth is standing and the sun is moving. Then Copernicus came, and there came infinitely greater complications later, especially in our century. Common sense has been proven wrong. What does common sense say about heaven which can stand up after the invention of the telescope? What about the enormous worlds opened up by the microscope, which are wholly inaccessible to common sense as common sense? It would be more helpful to say: Common sense is unarmed reason—I mean not armed with telescope and microscope—and science is armed reason. Now if you state it in this way, the question arises: Are there not spheres where unarmed reason is at least as good as armed? (You know what I mean by "armed"; that is not the best word, but you understand me.) For example, in our relations with human beings, in our understanding of them, in our handling of them, we are not helped in any way by telescope and microscope. If you don't believe me, read *Gulliver's Travels*, where, when he was in Brobdingnag, he looked in a way through a microscope and saw the people of enormous size and other things of this kind. This, I believe, is in a more practical way the issue. And this also shows the limitations of this analogy: since the natural sciences have led us to a much deeper understanding of extra-human nature than we possessed formerly, the application of the same approach and of the same methods to human things must bring about a similar progress, a radical progress and improvement of our knowledge of human things and of human affairs.

STUDENT: You said that social science must ascend to the beginning, and mathematics, we can start at the beginning, and you gave as an example of this Spinoza's sentence about—

LS: "Man."

SAME STUDENT: —about "Man thinks" and that there was an undefined term, being "man." But I always thought there were undefined terms at the beginning of mathematics also, so I don't see the relevance of that.

LS: Yes, but Spinoza defines all the terms at the beginning. I mean, must you not define a point, a line, a plane, a sphere, at the beginning?

SAME STUDENT: You're saying that "point" was defined? I thought that "point" was an undefined term.

LS: Well then, *stigmē*. Euclid begins, if I remember well, with the definition of "point." At any rate, here the key point is this: that *the* chief subject of the *Ethics*, or at least of three-fifths of the book, is man and human things, and it is not said what man is. Of course, Spinoza tries to do it by simply saying that man has this peculiar quality of cogitation; and by making clear what cogitation is, then we understand from this way what man is. That's the way in which he does this.

STUDENT: I think the distinction to which most of us are accustomed as a premise of at least contemporary social scientists is not simply the distinction between armed and unarmed common sense, but rather the distinction between sense perceptions, along with the aids which sense perception employs, such as microscopes and telescopes on the one hand, and on the other hand, what are said to be nonempirically verifiable statements, such as questions of moral and aesthetic goodness.

LS: That is the reason why I was a bit hesitant to leave it at the identification of science and common sense, because for common sense this distinction doesn't exist. I gave this example: "X is so-and-so many years in politics." Empirical statement. "X is corrupt." Empirical statement, yes? From the point of view of common sense, there is no question. How do they know that he is corrupt? Because they have seen him acting corruptly: empirical. That this is excluded in a certain manner—of course, the social scientist, I suppose, would say that you can speak of X as corrupt, but strictly speaking you have to use "corrupt" in quotation marks in order to explain that this is a popular expression which, when it is used by a social scientist, does not have the simply condemning meaning which it has in ordinary political life.

SAME STUDENT: But if I understand your argument correctly, what you are saying is that although it is true that science concedes that certain parts of our common sense are true without question, i.e., sense perceptions, by the very act of splitting up common sense into sense perceptions and perceptions of moral and aesthetic qualities, science is denying the primacy of common sense, and only after having set up this arbitrary distinction is it then going to concede part of the sphere of common sense back to it, and by that act it's—

LS: Ya, but there are representatives of this view who would not go so far and would question that because—well, look at this very simple thing. Common sense speaks of *things*. When we speak commonsensically of sense perception, we do not mean mere sense data. If I say I see a cow, that is not merely the sense data. I mean, if I analyze exactly what is on my retina and so on and so on, and what I know by any other senses and put this together, that is not the same thing which I mean when I say I see the cow; and therefore there is a difficulty already here in sense perception. Sense perception, as ordinarily understood, means the perception of things and people. But from the scientific point of view, the question is: What is really sensually perceived? Not merely sense data? And then the great question arises: How can we come from the sense data to the thing—I mean that peculiar pattern which is constructed in some way or other out of the sense data? This question then arises, and then we see that has something to do with language. And then language of course differs from culture to culture and from nation to nation. And then the question arises: Should there not be a truly objective language which is free from all the vagaries of the empirical languages? The extreme answer to that is of course to have mathematics as the true, universal, and objec-

95

tive language. Now this whole issue is involved in the question of common sense and science. Yes?

STUDENT: Well, couldn't a more sophisticated social scientist just not stand so strongly on this point of being value-free but still try to buttress this original argument that's the basis of the distinction of what's sensually perceivable and what is . . . and ultimately make everything empirically verifiable, by saying something like: When we say we are looking at a human being, or when we say we are in room 122, for example, we are obviously saying something more than just "I have an opinion that" or "I believe that." And when we say a man is corrupt, the question arises whether we are merely stating an opinion or, again, stating something more.

LS: Ya, sure—

SAME STUDENT: Now the more sophisticated scientist, not the person trying to uphold this value-free-ness, might say: Well, just as you would say that saying that so-and-so is a human ultimately depends upon a certain convention that grows up in any language, that that language depends ultimately on our having received certain perceptions, on being able to organize perceptions, let's say, or on certain other contingencies; similarly, the fact that somebody's corrupt, the fact that somebody's good or bad, would also depend upon certain perceptions, causing them pleasure and pain and things like that. And again, the best way to find out that so-and-so is corrupt, just as the best way to find out that so-and-so is human, is to hold surveys, for example, to see just what the concepts are in certain societies—

LS: No. All right, what the concepts are, but the judgments are a different thing. So the concept of corruption prevalent in a society may very well lead to the conclusion of a sufficiently discerning man that A is corrupt. But the general opinion about that A may be that he is uncorrupt, because they are not sufficiently discerning. That would be another difficulty. But apart from that, I think one would have to raise the question, one could not avoid it: Is the conception of corruption which is prevailing in a society a sound or an unsound one? After all, we want not merely to find out what the society thinks and does, but also what kind of a society it is, and that has very much to do with how deep and thought-through and sensible its views on such matters as corruption are. I'm sorry, I must now stop. We will continue this discussion next time and, I hope, finish it.

5 Strauss's Responses to Contemporary Defenses of the Fact-Value Distinction

LEO STRAUSS: [In progress] . . . we take to be nothing, like air. And I meant by this, in the first place, the fact-value distinction as now accepted in social science. It is true, the fact-value distinction is made explicit and conscious, but what is not made explicit is that it constitutes a problem. And in the second place, this enlargement of our horizon, or this greater clarity about the situation: that we should at least learn to consider the possibility that something taken for granted generally, at least, may not be true. There is an old-fashioned word for this kind of thing, the word "prejudice." There may be true prejudices, but as long as it is a prejudice, you cannot know whether it is true or not. To indicate this character of the view in question, I remind you of a few facts to which I have referred occasionally. Simmel,[1] who began this kind of thing, linked the fact-value distinction up with the fact that science is causal and not teleological, and hence it can deal only with facts and not with values. But science was causal from its very inception in the seventeenth century; it was opposed to the teleological science of Aristotle, and yet no one ever dreamt until the end of the nineteenth century that the causal science must issue in a value-free social science. Or, to take another example, some people take it for granted that the basis of the fact-value distinction is the distinction between Is and Ought. But the distinction between Is and Ought is much older; the distinction between Is and Ought does not imply that there is no possibility of knowledge of the Ought. So the specific condition is not only the distinction between Is and Ought but the alleged or real realization that there cannot be any knowledge of the Ought. The distinction between facts and values arose about seventy-five years ago and became quasi-all-powerful only after World War I. It has come into being, and therefore it may perish again, and not merely because of human inability to keep to that high level; it may also be due to an inherent defect of that doctrine. Fundamentally, I do not wish to convey more than this simple enlargement of horizon.

Now before I go on, I would like to say a few words about the question raised by Miss Barnett regarding Popper, Popper's distinction between verificationist and falsificationist theories of science. I read that statement, I am grateful to you. Let me read to you a few statements, and what I have to say is very brief.

> Popper claims that there is no appeal to any standard of rationality that must be accepted a priori. Since justificationists [namely, the ordinary positivists—LS] have at least one infallible element in their arsenal of criticism, or in other words have the standard of rationality that is accepted a priori, they must succumb to the I.R.A. [which is the infinite regress argument—LS], and choose an arbitrary starting point. Popper claims he does not choose an arbitrary starting point, obviously.

Now how does he proceed?

> Popper's answer to the "How do you know?" question is: "I don't know, I guess." He may further add: "I try to turn my guesses into criticizable ones, e.g., potentially falsifiable, so that they may be replaced by, not knowledge, but by improved guesses." Thus the demarcation between science and nonscience for Popper is fallibilism based on the falsifiability criterion. [In other words, any statement which cannot be falsified by scientific methods simply falls without the province of science, but if it is falsifiable in principle, then it falls within the province of science.—LS] Of course, a skeptic can still ask: "How do you know that you improve your guesses by falsifying your first guess?" But the answer is easy: "I guess."

That's it. Now whether that is a satisfactory account of knowledge in general and of science in particular is a long question into which we do not have to go here. I would say of that only this: it is hard to abolish the distinction between knowing and guessing, without which we cannot possibly take our bearings. I guess Mr. X is in his room, then I go into his room and then I *see* he is in it: I do no longer guess, I *know*. A theory which excludes the distinction between knowing and guessing would seem to be radically imperfect. Now when making this remark I make one qualification: I have not looked at Popper proper, and you or your teachers may have misinterpreted him, that I cannot exclude. I can only speak about what I have seen.

But this is not our question. The whole issue is not relevant to what we are discussing. What we are concerned about is this: whatever Popper may say, he still means (and in this respect there is no difference between him and the other positivists, including Comte) that science is limited to a certain kind of question, while it cannot answer another kind of question. This remains unchanged. And he does not commit this question-begging folly to say that the questions which science cannot answer are meaningless questions. That would be extremely simple: then science would have the monopoly of all meaningful questions, and that would be fine. That he does not do. And this is, by the way, the issue between him and the more common brand of positivists. The questions traditionally answered by theology and metaphysics—the questions of Why, in Comte's formulation, and the questions of value—remain and are outside the domain of science. Science cannot even assert that science is good, because that would be a value judgment.

Now this fact, that questions of the utmost importance, the most important questions remain wholly outside of the realm of science, leads and has led to what has been called the flight from scientific reason toward theology or metaphysics. We shall see later that there is or there is thought to be an alternative towards which one can escape from scientific reason, or must escape, different from theology and metaphysics. But before I take up this question I would like to complete my discussion of this question of the fact-value distinction.

I will proceed in the following manner. I will discuss briefly some criticisms of the argument which I have advanced in the last few lectures. The most detailed and serious criticism, I found in a book by Arnold Brecht, *Political Theory: The Foundations of Twentieth-Century Political Thought*, Princeton, 1959. This is a very solid and respectable book. It does not keep its promise to deal with the foundations of twentieth-century political thought—you would think of things like liberal democracy, and communism, and fascism, and other things of the same nature—but it is a strictly methodological book. So what he means by "political thought" is the thought you find in political science departments, not in the political arena. But this error is easily corrected: if you look at the table of contents, you see immediately that this is a strictly academic and not a political book, a book dealing with political matters as such.

Now I will read a few points. He calls the position which I describe

"Scientific Value Relativism," putting the three words in capitals, in order to make quite clear that this is an entity by itself, and he says the following thing.

> Most revolters against Scientific Value Relativism [the usage is interesting: Scientific Value Relativism is the established thing, and therefore those who disagree with that are revolters—LS] describe it incorrectly. They do so in good faith, of course, but for that reason the more passionately. The commonest misrepresentation is to arouse the impression that "scientific" relativists are "philosophical" relativists who teach that there *is* nothing of absolute value and that all values *are* equal—a dogma that could be upheld scientifically only by someone who was not alone personally disinclined to believe in God but was positively convinced that there was none, and more than that, who thought that the nonreality of God could be scientifically demonstrated.[2]
>
> . . . Strauss says that Weber "assumed as a matter of course that there is no hierarchy of values: all values are of the same rank," and Voegelin, that Weber "treated all values as equal." Now, Weber taught nothing of the kind, and he could not have done so, because in the first place he was not of the opinion that the absence of a hierarchy of values, and that includes the nonreality of God, could be scientifically ascertained; and in the second, the very point of his work was that values are unequal according to their different origins, implications, and consequences, and also because of their different ideal meaning.[3] [In other words, the value "freedom" has a very different meaning from the value "piety"; hence they are unequal.— LS] He did not treat values as "equal," but merely their validity as "equally undemonstrable" beyond the demonstrable consequences [i.e., if you choose value A, you are bound to choose something else—LS]. He did not even treat all values this way but only "ultimate" values; for he recognized of course that each value can be judged scientifically as to its consistency with, and its usefulness for the attainment of, some allegedly ulterior value.[4]

Now I can only say this. The key point which Brecht makes is that it is wrong to say that the positivists regard values as equal: they regard them only as equally undemonstrable. This distinction would make sense only if social science had any other criteria than demonstrability and indemonstrability. For instance, all revealed religions regard each other as equally indemonstrable, but not therefore as equal, because they possess relevant criteria other than demonstrability and indemonstrability for preferring one's own position to that of the other religions. There is no other possibility; i.e., for social science positivism, there is no criterion whatever for regarding one value as preferable to another or as higher than another. The moment you say that the value, say, guiding a biblical prophet or guiding Socrates is higher than that of any member of the Cosa Nostra, then you have committed a value judgment. I think Brecht only tries to evade the issue by not facing that. On the contrary, I think that the belief in the equality of all values is, as I stated on a former occasion, the hidden reason why so many of the social-science positivists are democrats of a certain kind: if all values are equal, then each value, or each man's value, should have the same right to be considered in the formation of government policy as that of somebody else.

> Strauss, likewise, sees inconsistency in the fact that relativists cannot help using value judgments themselves. If they were consistent, he says,[5] relativists in describing concentration camps would not be permitted to speak of "cruelty" because this includes a value judgment; they could merely describe the acts actually committed, in a factual manner.[6]

Factual manner: in other words, you describe the various acts of torture in the way in which you would describe some chemical reaction or something.

> Nor would historians be permitted to speak of "morality," "religion," "art," or "civilization," when interpreting the thoughts of peoples or tribes that are unaware of such notions or use them differently, or of "prostitutes," or of "epigones."[7] Wittily[8] he enumerates many value-impregnated expressions Weber used in his own historical papers, such as "grand figures," "laxity," "absolutely unartistic," "ingenious," "crude and abstruse notions," and "impressive achievement."
>
> These illustrations only go to show that Weber's own interpretation of his methodology was very different from Strauss's. No scientific relativist would condemn words like cruelty, civilization, prostitution, or, for that matter, crime or slums, wherever they are used within a clear frame of reference as descriptive in accordance with known standards—

Now he underlines: "*as long as these standards are not themselves at issue*"— i.e., if everyone concerned takes it for granted that crime must be fought, then we use the word "crime" and there is no difficulty. "Whenever the latter is the case"—whenever the standards are at issue—

> then indeed, according to Scientific Value Relativism, is it scientifically not correct to continue using one's own standards as though their absolute validity had been proven. Then the scientist must first analyze meaning and implication of the different standards within the possibility of science[9]—possibilities that, as we have seen, are by no means so limited as to exclude scientific contributions.[10]

It means that science is capable of showing that certain values are not realizable in the circumstances, etc. I would reply to this as follows. On the very basis of relativism, the standards are necessarily at issue. Whether they are at issue between two particular social scientists who happen to agree as to the badness of slums or corruption is wholly uninteresting; that is merely a subjective fact. From the point of view of social science, the standards are necessarily at issue, since all value judgments are rationally questioned. So the strict social scientist ought to use value-impregnated expressions, such as "corruption," "cruelty," only in quotation marks, meaning what the vulgar call cruelty, but which we would have to call X, Y, Z, if at all. Those expressions imply that the things in question are bad. When you speak of prostitution, you mean something bad, and then you have to coin a new word. We are calling it, say, free love of a certain kind: free love which, however, is perfectly compatible with remuneration, let me put it this way. [Laughter] Yes, well, that would be still better; then no one could blame you.

I heard once the following argument in favor of corruption in New York City on that basis, namely, that the conventional judgment of these people is so unfair, because these corrupt politicians gave great help to poor immigrants. The only way in which these poor fellows could get some hearing for their rightful claims was to find corrupt politicians. Now what is this? That is of course not a refutation of the ordinary view of corruption; it is an argument showing that what is regarded prima facie as simply bad is in fact, in the circumstances, a lesser evil. These are all value judgments. No one, if he speaks of any of these things, will say that these things condemned as such are under all circumstances bad. No one can defend corruption as such, namely, the misuse of public power for one's private purposes. In other words, it is impossible to say that corruption is a subjective value judgment. I will come back to a similar issue later. Let me say a few more remarks, because in an appendix, he comes back to this question. In the first section, when he discussed my criticism, he spoke of "misrepresentations" in the heading, making it clear that it is not deliberate. Now he calls it "misunderstandings."

> Strauss resumed his objections in another paper.[11] The relativists hold, he asserts, that "civilization is not intrinsically superior to cannibalism"; hence, speech for the cause of civilization will be to the relativist "not rational discourse, but mere 'propaganda,' a propaganda confronted by the equally legitimate and perhaps more effective 'propaganda' in favor of cannibalism." Relativists teach, he further contends, that "the absolute truth of value systems, such as Plato's, has been refuted unqualifiedly, with finality, absolutely," and he contrasts the "apparent humility" of relativists with their "hidden arrogance," considering all people "provincial and narrow" except themselves.[12] [What I meant was that they regard all these people like Plato and so on as provincial and narrow because they were the slaves of value systems accepted by their society, whereas they are completely free from such biases.—LS]
>
> This squarely put challenge is particularly helpful if it is neither ignored nor ridiculed [which he thinks would be the natural reaction of any sensible man—LS] [laughter] but met in equally forthright language. And it can be met. For each of Strauss' statements is in conflict with the facts, insofar as Scientific Value Relativism is concerned. First of all, where and when has a scientific relativist ever asserted as a fact that civilization *is not* superior to cannibalism? Such apodictic negative statements would be quite contrary to the principles of Scientific Method.

I can only say, if the scientific relativists [LS chuckles] did not assert it, then they simply keep silent about what they mean. But I do not even have to go so far. Look at the use of the terms "culture" and "civilization" in present-day anthropology: there are cultures which are cannibalistic, and are they treated as in any way inferior by the social scientist to noncannibalistic cultures? Of course not. Now let me go on.

> The only question that could be raised by some pedantic relativist or for the matter of methodological argument is, What is the scientific *evidence* for the superiority of non-cannibalistic civilization? [Now, I would say this: In a matter of such importance, one cannot be pedantic enough.—LS] How about civilizations that abhor the eating of cattle or hogs?

Well, to which I would say: Here Brecht seems to say that the question of the eating of cattle and hogs has the same status as the question of the eating of human beings, which I think is a grave thing. [Laughter]

> But here too Dr. Strauss would have no valid point. Scientific Value Relativism, although not satisfied with easy references to intuition [that's a dig—LS] [great laughter], is at no loss to show the superiority of noncannibalism, once "superiority" is defined, as it generally is, in terms other than selfish satisfaction of personal or tribal passions and with references to humanity.[13] Even if the term "superior," in the proposition "Noncannibalism is superior to cannibalism,"[14] were used in a strictly selfish sense (which Strauss certainly would not do) Scientific Method would not be at the end of its resources; the long-run superiority of one pattern of behavior over another can often be demonstrated even when the question is solely that of personal satisfaction.[15]

Well, take the case of drugs, where every doctor can prove to you that you have momentary satisfaction from the drugs, but in the long run, damage. But listen to the main point. He regards it at least as possible that social science is able to prove the superiority of noncannibalism (a) on nonselfish, (b) on selfish, grounds, i.e., on the basis of all possible grounds, because that seems to be a complete disjunction, selfish and nonselfish. That would mean, in plain English, that social science can prove the superiority of noncannibalism to cannibalism, i.e., social science can establish at least one value judgment. The whole position would be destroyed if this were true. Let me see. There is I think one more point here.

> On the other hand, Scientific Value Relativism may indeed be too humble to offer a *scientific* decision on a question like this: whether the captain of a marooned crew ought to be condemned if he permitted his men to eat the flesh of other men killed in battle or by accident, when this was the only alternative to starving.[16]

I think also a very interesting case. Why did he choose this example of the starving men in this particular situation, in preference to an example of men eating human flesh while they have other food in abundance? I think I understand it perfectly: because the latter would be a much graver case than the former. These people have at least the excuse that this was the only way in which they could possibly survive, and there might even be a deeper one, because it is assumed they are on public duty. It all depends that they remain there to watch the enemy, and therefore they have to survive for their country, and therefore this may be defended. In other words, social science can legitimate the condemnation of what we may call frivolous cannibalism, a cannibalism not demanded practically by the situation.

Now I turn to another discussion which in a way leads further or leads to a deeper stratum, and that is in the book by Ernest Nagel, *The Structure of Science*, 1961, page 491, following. After having quoted a passage from my study on *Natural Right and History*, he continues.[17]

> We shall not attempt a detailed assessment of this complex argument, for a discussion of the numerous issues it raises would take us far afield. However, three claims made in the course of the argument will be admitted without further comment as indisputably correct: that a large number of characterizations sometimes assumed to be purely factual descriptions of social phenomena do indeed formulate a type of value judgment; that it is often difficult, and in any case usually inconvenient in practice, to distinguish between the purely factual and the "evaluative" contents of many terms employed in the social sciences; and that values are commonly attached to means and not only to ends. However, these admissions do not entail the conclusion that, in a manner unique to the study of purposive human behavior, fact and value are fused beyond the possibility of distinguishing between them. On the contrary, as we shall try to show, the claim that there is such a fusion of fact and value[18] and that a value-free social science is therefore inherently absurd, confounds two quite different senses of the term "value judgment": the sense in which a value judgment expresses *approval or disapproval* either of some moral (or social) ideal, or of some action (or institution) because of a commitment to such an ideal; and the sense in which a value judgment expresses *an estimate* of the degree to which some commonly recognized (and more or less clearly defined) type of action, object, or institution is embodied in a given instance.[19]

Now Nagel calls, in the sequel, the latter kind of value judgments, which he admits are indispensable, characterizing value judgments, and he distinguishes them from *appraising* value judgments.

STUDENT: Could you give the definition again, please?

LS: There are appraising value judgments that say "this is intrinsically wrong"—the distinction is not very clear, as you will see—and the other, the characterizing, doesn't speak of intrinsic goodness. This is my formulation, by the way, not his. You say "prostitution"—you characterize it as prostitution. Now he gives the following example: a given animal has anemia. Factual, and at the same time evaluative, to the extent that anemia is understood to be a defect. But according to Nagel, this characterizing value judgment does not mean that anemia is an undesirable condition; this would be an appraising value judgment. But the question I raise is this: Does he not admit that anemia is a defect? And this is, I think, the crucial point.

Now let me take another example. Nagel cannot deny that it is possible sometimes to make the characterizing value judgment "X is a crook." It is quite clear that "crook" is not very well defined, but in some cases the situation is so clear that everyone would admit that it's . . . Now he would then say this does not necessarily mean that X is undesirable—that would be an appraising one. And I can easily see that it doesn't follow; it may be highly desirable, for example, as a stool pigeon. But in giving this illustration, I show already the intelligible context within which we make value judgments, and within which we qualify them. But if I say "X is a crook," it surely means that he is despicable. Now whether this is a good reason for you never to speak to him, never to meet him, that is a practical question, in the normal sense. That is left open, naturally. I mean, if you are Orlando Wilson, it may be your duty to talk to him. And there may be other reasons: he may be a very near relative and you cannot avoid him without harming your nearest and dearest, and so on. But this is possibly the meaning of the distinction between characterizing and appraising. The key point, it seems to me, he admits: that characterizing value judgments, as he calls them, are inevitable. Now let me see how he continues that.

> It would be absurd to deny that in characterizing various actions as mercenary, cruel, or deceitful, sociologists are frequently (although perhaps not always wittingly) [what a satire—LS] asserting appraising as well as characterizing value judgments. [In other words, they say not only "he has a defect, a human defect," but also "it is undesirable that there is this kind of thing"—LS.]
>
> Terms like "mercenary," "cruel," or "deceitful" as commonly used have a widely recognized pejorative overtone. Accordingly, anyone who employs such terms to characterize human behavior can normally be assumed to be stating his disapprobation of that behavior (or his approbation, should he

use terms like "nonmercenary," "kindly," "truthful"), and not simply characterizing it.

Now here the question of course is this: The social scientists who use these terms, do they merely give in to a temptation—you know, we are brought up in this way, that we think in these terms—or is there a necessity for that?

> However, although many (but certainly not all) ostensibly characterizing statements asserted by social scientists undoubtedly express commitments to various (not always compatible) values, a number of "purely descriptive" terms as used by natural scientists in certain contexts sometimes also have an unmistakably appraising value connotation [not merely characterizing—LS]. Thus, the claim that a social scientist is making appraising value judgments when he characterizes respondents to questionnaires as uninformed, deceitful, or irrational [this was an entirely fictitious example which I used, because I have never heard that pollsters ever do that—LS] can be matched by the equally sound claim that a physicist is also making such judgments when he describes a particular chronometer as inaccurate, a pump as inefficient, or a supporting platform as unstable. Like the social scientist in this example, the physicist is characterizing certain objects in his field of research; but, also like the social scientist, he is in addition expressing his disapproval of the characteristics he is ascribing to those subjects.[20]

Now it is clear that in the case of artifacts like chronometers and so on, it is impossible not to judge whether they work or don't and to make this characterizing value judgment which in most circumstances becomes an appraising value judgment. But again, we must make a minor qualification: this may not be the last word. Think, for example, of a broken chair: it might be preferred to a chair in perfect working order, if that broken chair happens to be an heirloom, or perhaps some other quality, it goes without saying. But a broken chair is still a defective chair, although in a given situation a broken chair may be preferable to a chair which is intact.

Well, these are the points which I wanted to bring up, and I must say I was grateful to Dr. Nagel for admitting at least this much, which would have been admitted by everyone thirty or forty years ago, but today creates a difficulty.

Now I think it is best if I take this up right away, although I thought first of taking it up in a different context. Nagel's position as a whole is a positivist position as it is familiar from many, many contemporary books. I would like to discuss with you one question here. The fundamental question for all physical sciences, and of course also for social science, is the question of causality. After all, explanation, correlations, one set of events functions of another set of events, etc.—we used to call this, in the old-fashioned form, causality. Now what is causality? He quotes an author, and he seems to agree with it: "'Whenever you come across an *incomplete or disturbed system*, try to the best of your ability to *amplify it to one undisturbed whole*, looking for the *supplement* first among things known, near and far. If the desired supplement is not found among them, search for it among *things unknown*.'"[21]

This is a kind of operative definition of causality. Now what is the fundamental question here? "What is the upshot of the discussion[22] of the logical status of the principle of causality? Is the principle an empirical generalization"—obviously not—"an a priori truth"—excluded by positivism as such—"a concealed definition"—which would be merely tautological—"a convention that may be accepted or not as one pleases?"[23] The principle is a maxim, a maxim of research.

> But if the principle is a maxim, is it a rule that may be followed or ignored at all?[24] Is it merely an arbitrary matter what general goals are pursued by theoretical science in its development? It is undoubtedly only a contingent historical fact that the enterprise known as "science" does aim at achieving the type of explanations prescribed by the principle of causality;[25] for it is logically possible that in their efforts at mastering their environments men might have aimed at something quite different. Accordingly, the goals men adopt in the pursuit of knowledge are *logically* arbitrary.
>
> And that applies to the principle of causality itself. Nevertheless, the actual pursuit of theoretical science in modern times is directed toward certain goals, one of which is formulated by the principle of causality. Indeed, the phrase "theoretical science" appears to be so generally used that an enterprise not controlled by those objectives would presumably not be subsumed under this label. It is at least plausible, therefore, to claim that the acceptance of the principle of causality as a maxim of inquiry is an *analytical consequence* of what is commonly meant by "theoretical science"[26] [whether theoretical science is a pursuit which acts on this maxim—LS]. In any event, one can readily grant that, when the principle assumes this special form,[27] so that it prescribes the adoption of a particular type of

state-description by every theory, the principle might be abandoned in various areas of investigation. But it is difficult to understand how it would be possible for modern theoretical science to surrender the general ideal expressed by the principle without becoming therefore[28] transformed into something incomparably different from what that enterprise actually is [i.e., it would cease to be theoretical science, in the hitherto meaning of the term—LS].[29]

This key principle is logically arbitrary. Other principles could have been chosen. It is historically contingent. That was chosen, say, in the seventeenth century; something else could have been chosen, other principles were chosen in other ages. Men have chosen—*chosen*—this particular kind of intellectual orientation; they might have chosen others. And this choice is not susceptible of any legitimation, because if you say, "But this is the only way in which we could have made this tremendous progress in medicine, etc., etc.," then the answer is of course open: "Well, what about the thermonuclear bomb and other things which are also consequences of that?"

More generally stated, if modern science supplies very great benefits to the human race, as no one denies, it also endangers the human race. On this basis, the question cannot be settled. There is no possibility of saying that the abandonment of this kind of science would be a relapse into barbarism, as everyone would have said in the nineteenth century and the early twentieth century. Logic deals with this particular kind of science, but this is only a particular kind of science, there are *n* others. Therefore, logic would have to be integrated into a larger whole which deals with all these fundamentally different forms in which men can take their bearings, and what is that most comprehensive study which deals with all possible forms of orientation? There is an ordinary name for that.

STUDENT: "Philosophy"?

LS: No, that's misleading; it's too general. Intellectual history. Intellectual history would be that broader consideration of which logic, as the study of present-day scientific thought, would find a part.

Now in more general terms, positivism, the view that science, modern science, is the only genuine form of knowledge, leads eventually into historicism, and that is the subject to which I will turn now. And historicism is to that extent the deeper position, the philosophically more serious position, because it is aware, it takes seriously, the implications which positivism does not. Positivism, one could say, still carries on the old notion of science going back to Plato and other people, that science is the actualization of a high perfection of man as a rational animal, knowledge of *the* truth. And yet it can no longer maintain this Platonic assertion, as we saw from the quotations from Popper, for instance, when he says it is only a kind of guessing, of a relatively controllable form of guessing as distinguished from uncontrollable guessing, and no longer any reference to knowledge and truth.

In a different way, in Nagel the fundamental and characteristic principle of modern science is a certain understanding of causality which is logically arbitrary. And the justification which would have been given for it, and is perhaps still given to it today by some more or less backward people—the enormous progress of natural science made possible by this interpretation of causality becomes doubtful when progress itself becomes doubtful. And it must become doubtful if value judgments cease to have intrinsic validity. Mr. Glenn?

MR. GLENN: I can understand how there could be different kinds of science. But Nagel doesn't say that, I don't believe. He says, I think, that in their efforts at mastering their environments men could have chosen other methods, other kinds of science, and I don't see how that could be.

LS: He says it is logically arbitrary. That means there are logically alternatives, which were not chosen. But furthermore, it is historically contingent. That refers us back to the decisive moment in the seventeenth century when this kind of science emerged. But there were some kinds of science before: there was Greek science, there was Babylonian science, there was perhaps even a kind of sorcery, and alchemy, and all these kinds of things based on an entirely different notion, which don't work in the way in which modern science works, but perhaps they work in another way as a form of satisfaction of human needs. That would need a long study.

MR. GLENN: Yes, but from the little that I know of Greek science, for example, I don't believe that we would characterize Greek science as trying to control the environment, but rather as trying to understand it—

LS: Yes, but then it would be very simple. Modern science differs from all other sciences by the fact that it tries to control the environment. Then there would be nothing quite so arbitrary about it. But he does not directly link up causality with control of the environment. I suppose one reason being that he doesn't believe that is the primary function of modern science, to control the environment.

STUDENT: A point of information: would most present-day writers on scientific method and so on agree with Nagel that the principle of causality is logically arbitrary?

LS: Well, usually they are not as honest, or don't go so far in the discussion as Nagel does. Reichenbach, for example, he is one of the more common sort of positivist.[30] I read his discussion of causality some years ago. This did not even go so far. Simply: it works, and we assume it will work in the future. That's all. He[31] faces this difficulty.

Now I could also state what I was trying to convey by this quotation as follows. I referred last time to the ultimate dependence of science on common sense. But this might be sufficient as an argument against positivism, but it is of no help to political philosophy, with which we are here concerned, for the following reason. For political philosophy, according to its primary meaning, is the quest for *the* just or *the* good political order, but common sense is historically variable. And so political philosophy remains exposed to this much more serious difficulty: that it is built on historically changeable ground, and therefore can never be able to answer the question of *the* just or *the* good political order. One can state this also as follows. In order to be true, a proposition must be meaningful. "Abracadabra is mabracadabra" cannot possibly be true because it is not a meaningful proposition. But what is and what is not meaningful depends on the specific historical situation: time, culture, nation, class. Hence, owing to this dependence of truth on meaningfulness, there cannot be universally valid truth. If science depends on common sense, and common sense is essentially historical, scientific truth cannot be universally valid—which is tacitly admitted by Nagel, insofar as all scientific truths are based on the use of the principles of causality as logically arbitrary and historically contingent principles. To this one can easily object and say: Look at the factual universality of mathematics and natural science in the modern world. This mathematics and science may be of Western origin, but they are obviously accessible to all men who are sufficiently gifted, wherever they are. This does not go to the root of the matter, but I limit myself only to one point. Do we have the same universality in the humanities, and in the more interesting parts of the social sciences? There is no necessary conclusion from the natural sciences to the sciences of man, for the very simple reason that there may be an essential difference between the human and the subhuman. And natural science, this immensely successful enterprise, deals with the subhuman, and perhaps something radically different appears when we come up to man.

Now I would like now to—I mean, after having repeated this statement that positivism, for reasons I have not sufficiently explained but which have to do with the fact that the original understanding of science has been abandoned, namely, that science is the perfection of human nature—and this was so to say the rock on which science was built. Now when this was abandoned, in connection with the abandonment of the view that there are such things as perfections of natures, then eventually made it questionable: What is the basis of science?[32] Why is science good? Some answers were given in modern times by people who rejected the teleological conception of nature, for example, Bacon and Hobbes: science is for the sake of power, for the sake of human well-being. This has great difficulties even prior to the emergence of modern weapons because scientists frequently did not recognize what they were doing in this definition. I mean, mathematicians passionately concerned with these amazing riddles of the theory of numbers, for example, or concerned with the fantastic order or disorder of prime numbers—there is no essential relation of what they are doing to the benefit of the human race. "Science for the sake of science" is a view still present in many mathematicians and also physicists, but of course the mathematicians and physicists may go on, they are not professionally obliged, as it were, to give an account of why they do what they do beyond the fact that it is generally regarded as a respectable thing. But the fundamental question of science—"Why science?"—has become questionable. And this questioning leads under modern conditions to historicism. I will now try to explain that.

Now let me first use a definition because, as is always the case, positivism and historicism shade into each other and the pure cases of positivism and historicism are extremely rare. Only this much: that they both at present rule the Western world in the way in which Marxism rules the communist world—only, because of the fundamental divergence between the two, there is of course considerable freedom of argument which cannot exist if you have a single monolithic doctrine monolithically interpreted by the government.

Now positivism, we may say, asserts that all values are subjective, while scientific truth is objective. Historicism says, in the clear case, that the distinction between facts and values is not tenable. The categories of theoretical understanding are inseparable from the principles of evaluation. At any rate, not only values but science too is in a radical sense subjective. All human thought and action rests ultimately on premises which differ from age to age or from culture to culture, none of which can be said to be superior to any other. If this is so—and I remind you of what I said in connection with Nagel's argument regarding causality—the consequence is that you have to turn from—I mean, for the fundamental consider- ations, from scientific considerations, including those of political or social science, to those of fundamental history. History deals with the funda- mental questions—of course, intellectual history.

Now in order to understand the problem of historicism, one must first get this clear in one's mind, that this is a very novel phenomenon. In the ordinary presentation, you find remarks about Plato's philosophy of his- tory. *Ça n'existe pas*: that doesn't exist. You couldn't translate this into Greek, except into modern Greek. There are some people who say that the Greeks did not have that, but the origin is to be found in the Bible, in the Old Testament. But the trouble is that there is no Old Testament word for history. There is none. The Hebrew word for history is *historia*, of which you see that it is the Greek or the Latin word which has been taken over in modern times. It doesn't exist. Let us consider briefly the status of what we call history in classical times. The word "history," *histo- ria*, exists in the wide meaning, first, of inquiry. Therefore, natural history in the old sense of the term, which the oldest ones among you may have come across in your childhood, that natural history was the description of animals: you know, lions, and tigers, and also animals nearer home. That was called natural history—and also description of plants, etc. History means inquiry and of course also the results of inquiry. But apparently early on it took on this peculiar meaning: inquiry with *other human be- ings*. Now it is obvious that if you inquire about a hedgehog, you don't necessarily need other human beings, you look for yourself. But there are other things where you cannot find out what was except by inquiring with other human beings, living or dead. Dead: you look at their papers, and eyewitnesses you would like to have. Then it came to mean the inquiry into the deeds and sufferings of political societies and their members, and also the presentation of the results of such inquiries. So Herodotus's book could be called a history, it being an account of the results of what he has found out.

In modern times, to make this clear from the beginning, when people speak of the philosophy of history, they very frequently mean in contra- distinction, say, to philosophy of nature. There is a dimension of reality called nature, while philosophy deals with *kinds* of beings and therefore never thinks with proper names. Aristotle says therefore that poetry is more philosophic than history because a poet, say, when he presents to us Achilles, lets us see in Achilles, *Man*. The historian is not supposed to do this. He is supposed to tell us about Achilles: *this* individual, with these particular deeds and sufferings. Poetry is therefore more philosophic. That is Aristotle's statement.[33]

There is a most striking example of this which you find in Thomas Aquinas's *Summa*, in the first question, the second article, where he discusses the question whether theology, what he calls sacred doctrine, is a science.[34] The objection is that science doesn't deal with individuals, *singularia*. But theology does deal with individuals, for example, with the deeds of Abraham, Isaac, and Jacob: beings indicated by proper names. Hence theology is not a science. Thomas replies as follows: The individuals are not the principal subject in theology but are only used as models of lives, as we do that also in moral science, as Aristotle also would in the *Ethics* occasionally give some examples of men. In considering the question of justice, or of magnanimity, he might use occasionally an example of a well-known magnanimous or just man to illustrate, but the theme is the universal.

Political philosophy, when it emerged, dealt with justice, with the just order which is possible, and it did not hesitate to use history as a storehouse of examples, naturally. But it was in no way a historical discipline. The just order was called or could be called what is by nature right, and this notion of what is by nature right developed later in the notion of the natural law, which was conceived of as binding all men as men. As such, it must be duly promulgated: everyone must be able to know it; otherwise he cannot obey it. Now whether the natural law is or is not always duly promulgated depends on how man was at the beginning. That is the crucial test case. If man at the beginning was Adam and Eve, created perfect, there was no difficulty in seeing why they should know the natural law. But if man at the beginning was imperfect—the examples used in the seventeenth century would be the North American Indians or so—there is no reason to suppose that they would have been capable of understanding such a law. And this was a view accepted by the "progressive thinkers," in quotation marks, of the seventeenth and eighteenth century, the men who formed the modern tradition. Man has an imperfect beginning, a beginning in which he cannot know the natural law, in which he cannot know what is by nature right. There is a development of man from a state in which he was incapable of understanding the natural law towards a state in which he is now. The whole work of Vico, for example, is based on this point.[35] Rousseau's *Discourse on the Origin of Inequality* is also a very important document, called by him a history of man, *the* history of man, meaning not anecdotes, more or less exciting, but the fundamental fact of man is that man is essentially a developing being, or, as Rousseau called it, perfectibility is of his essence. Here *the* true political teaching of Rousseau regarding the just society has become available only now, 1756 or thereabouts. *It could not have been known earlier.*

Now this thought, which is so elementary for us, we can say was wholly absent from the earlier tradition. Rousseau implies that his political philosophy differs more or less from the teaching of all his predecessors. Excuse me if I emphasize these trivial things, but a very great problem is implied in that. In fact, every great political philosopher did this—that is, he said: Here I present the political truth. And that has nothing to do with modesty or immodesty, but he implies it is of course different from that of others. Why else should he write a new book? Take Locke, a man who was rather self-effacing compared with other political philosophers, and as such he refers and defers to authorities: "the judicious Hooker," Richard Hooker. But on one occasion at least he says, after having quoted Hooker, "But I moreover affirm,"[36] i.e., Hooker was right 99 percent but not 100 percent; otherwise there would have been no reason for Locke to write his *Treatise*.

So in other words, the simple, elementary thing: that many great political philosophers teach very different things about the just order. One can say we have no political philosophy, but only political philosoph*ies*. There is not one edifice impressing us by its unanimity, so to say, or quasi-unanimity, as modern science in a way does, where there is at least some notion of the identity of method if not necessarily of teaching. But here we have an anarchy. This of course could not have escaped men at earlier ages. But what was the conclusion which earlier men drew from it? Those who were duly impressed by it became skeptics and said: Well, this is obviously an enterprise beyond human power for one reason or another; it is not a feasible thing. But the political philosophers themselves were not deterred by that scandalous state of their own pursuit. On the other hand, they did not pay particular attention to it. I mean, they knew it, but they did not pay attention to it. And the very strange thing is that after Rousseau, or after Vico, this fact had to be faced for the first time: How can the variety of political philosophies be reconciled with its truth, with the possibility of political philosophy? Is this variety merely a disgraceful fact, or does it make sense? And now the observation by virtue of which it proved to make sense is this. Everyone can see, when he reads Aristotle's *Politics*, say, on the one hand, and Locke's *Civil Government* on the other, that either Aristotle is right and then Locke is wrong, or vice versa. Of course, they may both be wrong, but they are surely incompatible. There is chaos: *n* political philosophers—twenty, forty—a Babel of disharmonious sounds. And then someone made this observation: there is no disharmony; there is perfect harmony, if you consider the context. Aristotle is concerned with the Greek city, Locke is concerned with the British state around 1688, and if you take these obvious facts into consideration, then the conflict disappears. They do not contradict each other, because they speak in a way about different things. I suppose this is so elementary that it is taught—not even explicitly taught, but taken for granted—in the general civilization courses. Generally stated: doctrines are functions of times. Yes?

STUDENT: Could you give us an idea of who said that?

LS: I will gradually come to that. (This is a minor rhetorical device, for which you must forgive me.) Here is what I wrote down, literally: Now the first great thinker who paid proper attention to this state of affairs was Hegel. This problem was in the air prior to him. The last section of Kant's *Critique of Pure Reason*—it is very brief, four pages in the *Critique*—has the strange title "The History of Pure Reason."[37] Wholly unimaginable in earlier thought that pure reason itself could have a history. And Kant meant it with many qualifications, but still, that he could speak of that was a sign of the times. In Hegel's words, the individual—and he meant by that not only thoughtless individuals, but the most thoughtful men, the philosophers—is the son of his time, and not in the way in which he shaves or wears clothes, but in his highest and most sublime and abstruse thoughts. This was corrected somewhat later by Nietzsche, but fundamentally in agreement with Hegel, that the philosopher is the stepson of his time, i.e., is not in step with his time. But this of course means that what he teaches all belongs to the time nevertheless.

Now Hegel, who had seen that the individual is the son of his time, thought as little as any of his predecessors that his political philosophy is true only for his time. In other words, Hegel had realized that Aristotle was right for his time, Locke for his, and each of the others for his. But as for Hegel, he was as "naive" as these earlier thinkers had been when presenting the true teaching. Now this couldn't be, that would be wholly unintelligible. Hegel justified the absoluteness of his political philosophy, contrasted with the nonabsoluteness of the earlier philosophies, by this consideration: Each philosophy belongs to a moment in time, but there is an absolute moment, and the philosophy which belongs to the absolute moment is the absolute philosophy. [Mild laughter] Yes, it sounds funny. But we will have occasion later on to see whether this is not absolutely inevitable, something of this kind, once you take the question of history seriously in this way. Now the official reasoning of Hegel can be stated as follows. Hegel wrote in the early nineteenth century, when Germany surely was a Christian country. All his addressees were Christians, and naturally they took it for granted that Christianity is the true religion or, as Hegel calls it, the absolute religion. And for Christianity there is of course an absolute moment: resurrection. And just as there is an absolute moment in Christianity, there is an absolute moment in history, in profane history, for the following reason. Christianity appeared first in a wholly pagan world, the Roman Empire, in radical opposition to that pagan empire. Then expansion of Christianity in the Roman Empire, the migrations: a Christian order, a Christian world, emerges in the Middle Ages. Here you have Christianity, not separated outside of the world of politics, but informing it. Yet in informing it in that way, there is a fundamental distinction between the Christian proper, the spiritual, and the temporal, shown especially in the distinction between the power spiritual and the power temporal, but also in the distinction between clergy and laymen, and other dualisms.

Now Hegel was not only a Christian but also a Lutheran, a Protestant; and therefore he took it for granted that Protestantism was by far superior to Catholicism. What did Protestantism do? It abolished this dualism: it secularized not only the monasteries, it secularized Christianity. Every Christian is a priest: universal priesthood. Now this secularization of Christianity meant according to Hegel that the world, the *saeculum*, became Christianized fully. The secularization of Christianity is the Christianization of the world. And this culminates—again, I repeat what Hegel says—in the Enlightenment, the great movement following the Reformation and the religious wars. The Enlightenment, according to Hegel's interpretation, only takes the last step in this secularization of Christianity or the Christianization of the world, and that culminates in an event which at first glance seems to be *simply* anti-Christian: the French Revolution. But for Hegel that was not so; Hegel regarded the French Revolution as a quite terrible thing but nevertheless as fundamentally progressive, because it was the first time that, at least on European soil, in an old country, the rights of man became the foundation of civil society explicitly in a formula which you surely have heard very frequently: the dignity of man, every man, based on the biblical view that man is created in the image of God. That is a biblical heritage. The secularization of that—that it became politically effective, the basis of all legislation of a new order—this is a consequence of the French Revolution. Of course Hegel saw that the French Revolution had one fundamental defect: it did not show the possibility of government. Proof: the Terror. And therefore, what came after the Revolution—Napoleon's work, the *Code Napoléon* and the Napoleonic order, which indeed did not last—nonetheless supplied the outlines of what Hegel thought is the rational state: a state based on the recognition of the rights of man, but where government is not simply derivative from the will of the mass of citizens. How it did this in detail is of no interest. I only wanted to make clear this crucial point: that for Hegel, with the establishment of the rational state (of course not yet everywhere, but that is a question of a few generations, that is uninteresting), the fundamental question is now solved. The question of the just state, finally solved, and *it could not have been solved* earlier, namely, prior to the radical secularization of Christianity. History is completed. Only because this is the case can one say that the historical process is rational. How could we know that it is rational, if we did not know its completeness? It might be rational up to a certain point, but we wouldn't know until later. Good.

One point I think I should mention. In other words, men now—say, around 1830—live on the peak. However great the achievements of some earlier thinkers and societies may have been, they are fundamentally defective because the decisive truth has not been known. And the philosophic, theoretical truth and its knowledge are bound up with the actualization of the practically or politically right order. You see, when an earlier thinker, say, Descartes, presented his doctrine about the vortices and so forth, there was no relation whatever to the question of whether the most desirable political society was established. But here in Hegel's case the previous solution of the practical or political problem by the actual establishment of the just order is the condition for the completion of theory, of theoretical knowledge. One can explain this as follows. Theory, philosophy, has to do, as one loosely says, with all reality. But how can it do that if reality is incomplete? As long as reality is incomplete, philosophy must be incomplete. Only after reality is completed by the establishment of the just society can philosophy as a study of reality be complete. The difficulty, which appears within Hegel, is indicated by one expression which Hegel uses. He says that the owl of Minerva, of the goddess of wisdom, begins its flight in the dusk. The evening of mankind has arrived. The progressive process has been completed. This is just what our heart desires, but it means also that there are no longer any fundamental tasks for the human race. The night comes. Therefore the view which Spengler[38] has popularized in our century about the decline of the West, meaning the decline of all high culture, is a possible implication of Hegel's own thought. Hegel was the great beginning of this historicization, but historicism proper is a post-Hegelian phenomenon, and I will have to speak of it later. I think it would be better next time. We have a few minutes, which we can devote to an exchange of opinions. Yes?

STUDENT: Way back at the beginning of the lecture, you were speaking of Nagel's distinction between characterizing and appraising. Now if you say that something is anemic, you are judging it in terms of its own ends and constitution. If I say a human being is anemic, there is a standard by which a human being exists, and he deviates from this. I don't appraise, I don't say it is good that he's anemic or it's bad that he's anemic.

LS: Yes, sure. That's what he means.

SAME STUDENT: But somehow you said that this distinction wasn't really that clear, the distinction between appraising and characterizing.

LS: Yes, but still, this characterizing statement in such cases means that this thing, whether it is an animal or a chair, whatever it might be, is defective. Now from this in itself, no practical conclusions follow. Take the simple example of the broken chair which I prefer for some reason, but still I give a reason why I prefer the defective thing to the whole thing. Whereas if someone wants to have a horse—still simpler: A farmer says to a boy, Bring me a horse. And he brings him a lame mare, or he brings him a colt, four weeks old. Then the farmer says: I told you to bring me a horse! He meant, of course, a normal horse. Normal means also grown up. Therefore, a colt which is perfectly healthy in my assumption is nevertheless not a horse. You can say that is the simple starting point of Aristotle. When we go over a street, and we come too late because a lot of people prevent us, and all these beings which prevent us from walking quickly through the mass are children, or all of them are women, I think we would not simply say, "people prevented us," but we would say there was "a mass of children," or "a mass of women." So in other words, our ordinary language contains in itself a pointer towards the normal in the sense of the perfect. But don't think that "perfect" means something farfetched; it means "the complete." I think for this reason one cannot leave it at the distinction. I gave the example of the stool pigeon, which is clearly an undesirable human being, yet one who can be useful in certain contexts. Of course, we must not have a very schematic notion that here are the good things and here are the bad things (and it is in practice very hard to avoid the bad things, and even the bad human beings), but the distinction is nevertheless very necessary. Even if you use a crook, you must know that he is a crook; otherwise you will not have that benefit from him which [LS chuckles] you might reasonably expect. Yes?

STUDENT: When Nagel says that "X is a crook" doesn't imply that X is undesirable, does he understand that there might be other things about X which make it desirable, or does he say simply that being a crook isn't necessarily undesirable?

LS: Well, you see he does not go into that, that is the trouble. I mean, in all these matters, I believe examples and their discussion are so very important, because they open up the difficulty, and I think that will always show how many value judgments are implied all the time. The usual view is so offensive to me above all because of its schematic character.

SAME STUDENT: But I think we would have to say, interpreting Nagel, that when he says "X is a crook" does not imply that X is undesirable, what he means is not that you may want to use X for an ulterior motive; it means simply that being a crook, although the word itself has a negative connotation, is not in any real sense undesirable. Someone might say: Well, X is a crook, and therefore is desirable simply on the basis of—

LS: I think he goes somewhat beyond that, I do not know—I think he cannot leave it at that.

MR. BARBER: Mr. Strauss, could you clarify the connection between Nagel's judgment that the principle of causality is logically arbitrary and his position on the fact-value distinction?

LS: I believe that there is no direct connection between the two things.

MR. BARBER: Well then, why was it brought up?

LS: Well, I had a number of arguments regarding the fact-value distinction or social science positivism, and one of them was that positivism turns into historicism, and in the latter connection, I spoke of what he says about causality.

MR. BARBER: Then historicism, as I understood you . . . is regarded by Nagel as an alternative—

LS: Oh, no, no, no. In this respect he is extremely simple, and he rejects historicism and all considerations regarding historicism as wrong. No, no, he is not aware—I mean, that is exactly the point. He believes that nonhistoricist, positive science is absolutely well-protected against any historicist objection. I may take this up next time, what he has to say on this subject. He doesn't see any difficulty there. But what I wanted to show is that whether he sees any difficulty there or not, he is in fact exposed to them, as is shown by his remark on causality. Is this so hard to understand?

MR. BARBER: Yes, sir, it is.

LS: I am sorry, I do not see how I can—keep it in mind, and we'll try to clarify it next time. Mr. Glenn?

MR. GLENN: Mr. Strauss, the owl of Minerva is the symbol of wisdom or philosophy, is that correct?

LS: Well, no. Minerva is the goddess of wisdom. Pallas Athena, in Greek. The owl was her symbol, yes, and Hegel makes a subtle joke with that: just as the owl flies in the dusk, so wisdom, philosophy, self-consciousness, emerges when a culture has fulfilled itself and is about to go down.

MR. GLENN: Does he include both theoretical and practical wisdom there or—

LS: He doesn't make any distinction. Well, we will continue next week.

B. Historicism

6   Historicism as the More Serious Challenge to Political Philosophy

LEO STRAUSS: The death of Churchill[1] is a healthy reminder to academic students of political science of their limitations, the limitations of their craft.

The tyrant stood at the pinnacle of his power. The contrast between the indomitable and magnanimous statesman and the insane tyrant—this spectacle in its clear simplicity was one of the greatest lessons which men can learn, at any time. No less enlightening is the lesson conveyed by Churchill's failure, which is too great to be called tragedy. I mean the fact that Churchill's heroic action on behalf of human freedom against Hitler only contributed, through no fault of Churchill's, to increasing the threat to freedom which is posed by Stalin or his successors. Churchill did the utmost that a man could do to counter that threat—publicly and most visibly in Greece and in Fulton, Missouri.[2] Not a whit less important than his deeds and speeches are his writings, above all his *Marlborough*, the greatest historical work written in our century, an inexhaustible mine of political wisdom and understanding which should be required reading for every student of political science.[3]

The death of Churchill reminds us of the limitations of our craft and therewith of our duty. We have no higher duty and no more pressing duty than to remind ourselves and our students of political greatness, human greatness, of the peaks of human excellence. For we are supposed to train ourselves and others in seeing things as they are, and this means above all in seeing their greatness and their misery, their excellence and their vileness, their nobility and their baseness, and therefore never to mistake mediocrity, however brilliant, for true greatness. In our age this duty demands of us in the first place that we liberate ourselves from the supposition that value statements cannot be factual statements.

I turn now to the question Mr. Barber raised at the end of the last meeting, namely: Is there a connection between the distinction which

Nagel makes between appraising and characterizing value judgments and his view regarding the status of the principle of causality?

There is no immediate connection. The distinction between the two kinds of value judgments serves the purpose of defending value-free social science, within the limits to which it can be defended, in his view. What he says about the principle of causality shows that he is involuntarily succumbing to historicism. Nagel himself believes that positivism (the view which he defends) is in no way endangered by the problem of history. But his discussion of the principle of causality shows that he underestimates that danger.

I will show this at somewhat greater length. Let me remind you only of the simple starting point of historicism, the alleged fact that doctrines are functions of time, a historical situation. The question is whether this can be proven by history, by merely historical evidence. It cannot. Before you can establish that, you have first to prove that the doctrine in question is not tenable, because if it were the true doctrine, the relation to a particular time would be of no interest. Presupposed in this historical evidence is that these doctrines are all wrong, a presupposition which needs of course some form of proof before it can be accepted.

Now I would first like to discuss briefly, because of the interest which it has, Nagel's discussion of historicism, and of the view that all doctrines, of course not only those of political philosophy, are historically relative. Let us first see how he states the issue.

> Human behavior is undoubtedly modified by the complex of social institutions in which it develops, despite the fact that all human actions involve physical and physiological factors whose laws of operation are invariable in all societies. Even the way members of a social group satisfy basic biological needs—for instance, how they obtain their living or build their shelters—is not uniquely determined either by their biological inheritance or by the physical character of their geographic environment, for the influence of these factors on human action is mediated by existing technology and traditions[4] [that is to say, by historical factors—LS]. The possibility must certainly be admitted that nontrivial but reliably established laws about social phenomena will always have only a narrowly restricted generality.[5]

In other words, the claim of positivistic social science that the task of social science is to establish universally valid laws is questioned by the fact of the decisive importance of the variety of historical situations.

It is therefore clear that the "historically conditioned" character of social phenomena is no inherent obstacle to the formulation of comprehensive transcultural laws.[6] [In other words, he regards this objection as
unimportant.—LS] The relevance or the validity of a generalization for
social groups belonging to other societies may be quite uncertain. For example, the generalization (based on a study of American soldiers in World
War II) that better-educated men drafted into the armed forces of a nation show fewer psychosomatic symptoms than those with less education,
is quasi-general in the above sense[7] [meaning one cannot be certain that it
is simply general and not only quasi-general—LS]. The possibility must
be recognized[8] that in comparison with the variables employed in the past
in proposed transcultural laws [meaning that the laws suggested by political scientists or social science in general, that these laws are universally
valid—LS] the concepts required for this purpose may have to be much
more "abstract," may need to be separated by a greater "logical gap" from
the familiar notions used in the daily business of social life, and may neces-
sitate a mastery of far more complicated techniques for manipulating the
concepts in the analysis of the actual social phenomena.[9]

In other words, he means ordinarily in these proposed universally valid
laws, terms or concepts are used which are taken from modern Western society, and there is not necessarily a correlation to these concepts in
other societies. For you have to use much more abstract concepts, and the
question of course arises: Can we still recognize phenomena when we use
concepts of that extreme abstractness?

Now this much regarding the historicity of social phenomena. Here,
with some hesitation and qualifications, Nagel believes the notion of universally valid social laws is still defensible. But what about the historicity
of the concepts used, an issue to which he has already alluded? Now there
is a long quotation which I will read to you, and which he introduces as
follows:

A third form of this claim is the most radical of all. It differs from the
first variant mentioned above in maintaining that there is a necessary *logical* connection, and not merely a conclusive[10] or causal one, between the
"social perspective" of a student of human affairs and his standards of
competent social inquiry, and in consequence the influence of the special
value[11] to which he is committed because of his own social involvements is
not eliminable. This version of the claim is implicit in Hegel's account of

the "dialectical" nature of human history and is integral to much Marxist as well as non-Marxist philosophy that stresses the "historically relative" character of social thought. In any event, it is commonly based on the assumption that, since social institutions and their cultural products are constantly changing, the intellectual apparatus required for understanding them must also change; and every idea employed for this purpose is therefore adequate only for some particular stage in the development of human affairs [and in this sense historically dated—LS]. Accordingly, neither the substantive concepts adopted for classifying and interpreting social phenomena, nor the logical canons used for estimating the worth of such concepts, have a "timeless validity"; there is no analysis of social phenomena which is not the expression of some special social standpoint, or which does not reflect the interests and values dominant in some sector of the human scene at a certain stage of its history.

Now this view is fully familiar to you from the Marxists, but it differs from the Marxist position in that it denies that there is some group, like the proletariat, which has the absolutely privileged position of seeing things as they actually are. Each of these social-historical groups sees things in a certain perspective, and none of these perspectives can claim to be superior to any other.

In consequence, although a sound distinction can be made in the natural sciences between the origin of a man's views and their factual validity [between genesis and validity—LS] such a distinction allegedly cannot be made in social inquiry; and prominent exponents of "historical relativism" have therefore challenged the universal applicability[12] of the thesis that "the genesis of a proposition is under all circumstances irrelevant to its truth." [This thesis being the thesis by which positivism stands or falls.— LS] As one influential proponent of this position puts the matter [the man in question is Karl Mannheim—LS]: "The historical and social genesis of an idea would only be irrelevant to its ultimate validity if the temporal and social conditions of its emergence had no effect on its content and form. If this were the case, any two periods in the history of human knowledge would only be distinguished from one another by the fact that in the earlier period certain things were still unknown and certain errors still existed which, through later knowledge were completely corrected." [Roughly the view obtaining in the natural sciences.—LS] "This simple relationship between an earlier incomplete and a later complete period of knowledge may to a large extent be appropriate for the exact sciences.[13] For the history of the cultural sciences, however, the earlier stages are not quite so simply superseded by the later stages [say, in which Newtonian physics is superseded by nuclear physics—LS] and it is not so easily demonstrable that early errors have subsequently been corrected. Every epoch has its fundamentally new approach and its characteristic point of view, and consequently sees the 'same' object from a new perspective."[14]

And you cannot say that the new perspective is superior to the old one. But it is necessary for the people concerned; because of belonging to this kind of society, to this social group, they cannot help looking at things in this respect.

"The very principles, in the light of which knowledge is to be criticized, are themselves found to be socially and historically conditioned. Hence their application appears to be limited to given historical periods and the particular types of knowledge then prevalent."[15]

This view is known especially now under the title "sociology of knowledge." Now let us see how Nagel replies to that.

Even extreme exponents of the sociology of knowledge admit that most conclusions asserted in mathematics and natural science are neutral to differences in social perspective.[16]

In other words, a proletarian mathematician and a mathematician who is the prince would learn the same mathematics, and also whether they are Westerners or Easterners wouldn't make any difference. That is in a crude way also true. Nagel goes on: "Why cannot propositions about human affairs exhibit a similar neutrality"—why not? And then he adds the qualification which I, if I had this position, would regard as favorable—"at least in some cases?" Because the question arises: Are these not likely to be the trivial and uninteresting cases? But here comes the decisive point.

In the second place, the claim of these sociologists of knowledge[17] faces a serious and frequently noted dialectical difficulty—a difficulty that proponents of the claim have superseded[18] only by abandoning the substance of the claim. For let us ask what is the cognitive status of the thesis that a social perspective enters[19] into the content as well as the validation of every assertion about human affairs. Is this[20] meaningful and valid only for those who maintain it and who thus subscribe to certain values because of their distinctive social commitments? If so, no one with a different social perspective can properly understand it; its acceptance as valid is strictly limited to those who can do so, and social scientists who subscribe to a different set of values ought therefore dismiss it as a lot of empty talk.[21] Or is the thesis singularly exempt from the class of assertions to which it applies, so that its meaning and truth are not inherently related to the social perspectives of those who assert it? If so, it is not evident why the thesis is so exempt; but in any case, the thesis is then a conclusion of inquiry into human affairs that is[22] "objectively valid" in the usual sense of this phrase—and, if there is one such thesis,[23] it is not clear why there cannot be others as well.[24]

Well, one can say very simply that this thesis, that no universally valid knowledge of human affairs is possible, claims itself to be universally valid. And therefore there is something wrong. You can avoid this by all kinds of logical tricks, but ultimately this difficulty is a hard one. Therefore, on this ground, Nagel regards this difficulty as finished.

In a way I agree with him, but I believe he underestimates the danger of historicism. A universally valid social science must be based on historical knowledge. But all historical knowledge is selective, of course. Who could make use, in history, of every detail? Most of the details are lost, anyway, and there are no universally valid principles of selection. To take an example: when we read passages today in the '50s and '60s we are quite struck by the awful stories of the Terror and the Thaw, something which we have experienced in our age even without being, fortunately, immediately exposed to this terrible experience.[25] The experience opens us up to something to which we would not be open, at least not to the same degree, and this is the experience of men of a particular time. Or take the example which I discussed on a former occasion: Max Weber's distinction between the three principles of legitimacy, rational, traditional, and charismatic. This is related to the experiences of the nineteenth century, and therefore belongs to that age. In a different age, say, in 2100, an entirely different fundamental distinction might present itself, not on account of any progress of science, mind you, as it happens all the time in our society, but on account of changes in society, which one cannot possibly call progressive or the opposite, even the prohibition against value judgments.

Now Nagel does not discuss this issue at all; therefore he fails to discuss what is at issue. Without being aware of it, he is confronted by the problem in his discussion of science in general, not only social science, or history, but science in general, namely, in his discussion of causality. I remind you of what I read to you last time, that the principle of causality as understood by present-day natural science is logically arbitrary and historically contingent. At a certain moment, men, say, the founders of modern science, chose this understanding of causality in preference to any other, and this is ultimately not intelligible except as a contingent fact. Because as I said at that time, if one says that modern science leads to enormous practical possibilities and progress which would be impossible on the basis of any other understanding of causality, the question arises whether this criterion is objectively valid given the fact that modern science itself constitutes the problem. Or, more simply stated, to say that modern science is good is a value judgment which is forbidden by the demand of the new science.

I hope I have now cleared this up, Mr. Barber. Because the question, of course, in spite of what Nagel says, is that the difficulty is ultimately not only social science, or the sciences dependent directly on human society, but finally in the natural sciences and mathematics as well. I will gradually explain that.

I began to take up the question of historicism last time, and spoke especially of Hegel's great attempt at reconciling political philosophy in the traditional sense, i.e., the claim to present the true teaching regarding the just society, with the fact of historical variety of political philosophies. Now Hegel's general solution, as you may remember, was that the historical process is a rational process, a progressive process which leads to a peak, to an absolute time, to an absolute moment, in which the true doctrine, which will no longer be superseded by a truer doctrine, belongs to the absolute moment. Now here the difficulties do not yet arise. (Of course, they arise in this way, that you would have to examine whether Hegel's doctrine, his philosophy of right, is the sound and true doctrine or not. In other words, in this respect Hegel's philosophy would have to be criticized as any other political philosophy would have to be criticized.) The problem of history arises only afterwards, and in the following manner. These men[26] still accept the . . .[27] view that also is historical, i.e., belongs to a specific historical situation. Contrary to Hegel, they assert that history is unfinished and unfinishable. It can be finished externally by nuclear war, by catastrophe, but in itself it has no principle or end. And this historical process is not a rational process; it cannot be a rational process because it is not yet completed, and we do not know what will come afterwards. It is not progressive, because all standards with a view to which we assert progress or its opposite are themselves historical. "Every epoch is immediate to God," as Ranke, the famous German historian, wrote, i.e., every epoch is immediate to the truth.[28] It is not so that the last epoch, the final epoch, is more immediate to the truth than the early epochs.

This is today trivial. I mean, the equality of all ages and all cultures is a tacit premise of present-day social science. It is not any longer so called, but it is in fact the case. Think only of a similar case: All cultures are equal. That was popularized especially by Spengler, and when this was taken over by American anthropology, Ruth Benedict especially, it was applied to all cultures, not only to the six or seven high cultures to which Spengler had applied it.[29] What we know as truth differs from epoch to epoch. There is not *the* truth. We cannot help regarding certain things as truths, but we know that they will not be so regarded by a later age, or for that matter, by a past age. This fact, this historical relativism, is the most comprehensive knowledge at which we can arrive. In other words, the highest theme of human knowledge is the fact of the variety of *Weltanschauungen*, as the Germans say, of comprehensive views of the whole. You may remember what I said on the occasion of Nagel: we arrive at a logically arbitrary, historically contingent principle of causality. But you can also say: the way in which time or space is understood. And the sequence of these comprehensive views which underlie all science, in particular, this is the most comprehensive thing. Now this view gradually developed in the nineteenth century, and then, in the recent past, its problematic character was seen and faced for the first time by Nietzsche, in his essay "On the Use and Abuse of History," of which I have to say something.

According to Nietzsche, history teaches a truth that is deadly. It shows that culture is possible only if men are fully dedicated to principles of thought and action which they do not question and cannot question, which limit their horizons and thus enable them to have a character, a style, a culture. An unlimited horizon, so to speak, as the nineteenth-century and twentieth-century historians claim they have, can no longer be bound to one particular character and style. And the same is characteristic of the late nineteenth and early twentieth centuries: the restoration of earlier foreign styles—in architecture, for instance, introducing styles into a context in which they do not fit at all—was only a consequence of this fundamental defect. History shows us at the same time that the principles of thought and action do not possess the validity which they claim, that they do not deserve to be regarded as simply true. The only way out seems to be that one turn one's back on this lesson of history, this deathly lesson, that one choose life-giving delusions rather than deadly truth—in other words, that one fabricate a myth, an ideology. This has in the meantime become very popular, and you are all familiar with that.

But this way out is impossible for men of intellectual probity because it is a deliberate self-delusion, and this is to say nothing of the fact that a fabricated myth is not a genuine myth. The true solution comes to sight once one realizes the essential limitations of history, of objective history, and of objective knowledge in general. Objective history, which shows us the common coming-into-being and perishing of all cultures and *Weltanschauungen* and that they deserve to perish ultimately, suffices for destroying the illusion of the objective validity of any principle of thought and action. It does not suffice for opening up a genuine understanding of history. The objective, scientific historian cannot grasp the substance of the past, because he is a mere spectator, not dedicated or committed to any substantive principles of thought and action. And this is the consequence of his having realized that such principles have no objective validity. But committed men, as the men belonging to high culture, can only be understood by committed men, and not by neutral bystanders. An entirely different conclusion must be drawn from the realization of this objective truth, namely, that there is only a relative validity for all principles of thought and action. The different values respected in different epochs have no objective support, although they claim to be based on reason, and were claimed to be based on divine revelation at one time or another. But this was a delusion, that they had such support; in fact, they are human creations. They owe their being to a free human project that formed the horizons within which a culture was born. What man did in the past unconsciously and under the delusion of submitting to what is independent of his creative act, he must now do consciously, which is, one can say, the final solution. I read to you a statement which shows in a very impressive and clear way how Nietzsche viewed this. This is taken from *Zarathustra*, the first part, "Of the Thousand and One Goals."

And Zarathustra found no greater power on earth than good and evil [meaning men cannot live without notions of good and evil—LS].[30] No people could live without first esteeming; but if they want to preserve themselves, then they must not esteem as the neighbor esteems [because if they agreed in most important respects, then they would not preserve their own being—LS]. Much that was good to one people was scorn and infamy to another: thus I found it. Much I found called evil here, and decked out with purple honors there. Never did one neighbor understand the other: ever was his soul amazed at the neighbor's delusion and wickedness. [The tacit implication for the modern historian: *he* is not amazed. He takes it in his stride that there are *n* different notions of good and evil.—LS]

A tablet of the good hangs over every people [i.e., the value system appears to be independent—LS] ...

Verily, my brother, once you have recognized the need and land and sky and neighbor of a people, you may also guess the law of their overcomings, and why they climb to their hope on this ladder. [In other words, there is a partial possibility of understanding a people, namely, by considering their "need, land, sky and neighbor."—LS] ...

"To speak the truth and to handle bow and arrow well"—that seemed both dear and difficult to the people who gave my name to me[31] [the Persians—LS].

"To honor father and mother and to follow their will to the root of one's soul"—this was the tablet of overcoming that another people hung up over themselves and became powerful and eternal thereby [the Jews—LS].

"To practice loyalty and, for the sake of loyalty, to risk honor and blood even for evil and dangerous things"—with this teaching another people conquered themselves [the Germanic people—LS] ...

Change of values—that is a change of creators [namely, the values are all created, they are not in being by themselves—LS].

First, peoples were creators [he has given four examples—LS] and only in later times, individuals. Verily, the individual himself is still the most recent creation [a radical change has taken place—LS] ...

... the works of the lovers: "good" and "evil" are their names. [In other words, what Nietzsche means by "will to power" is the same as love and creativity.—LS]

... Tell me, who will throw a yoke over the thousand necks of this beast [a thousand different value systems—LS] ...

... humanity still lacks a goal—is humanity itself not still lacking too?[32]

So a universal goal, a goal for humanity, a goal which transcends historical particularity, becomes possible only after the historical insight into the historical relativity of all previous systems. This is what Nietzsche meant by "the transvaluation of all values." It is a radically new project, different from the former projects, not only in its content, but also in its mode, because it is based on the consciousness that this new goal is due to a human creation, whereas the older goals were all held to be based on objective supports. The transvaluation of all values entails the rejection of all earlier values, for they have become baseless by the realization of the baseless character of their claim by which they stand or fall, the claim to objective validity. But precisely the realization of the origin of all such principles makes possible a new creation that presupposes that realization and is in agreement with it, and therefore is intellectually honest. Yet it is not deducible from the historicist insight, for otherwise it would not be due to a creative act performed with intellectual probity. Now in Nietzsche's view, these creative acts to which all values owe their being have the characteristic peculiarity that they transcend reality, reality which is the product or sediment of earlier creative acts. And we can never reach the point where no creative act has occurred. It is of the essence of man to create a world, for the world, which we regard as being in itself, and merely the object of human perception and discovery, is primarily the product of human creation or interpretation. Men create such worlds and yet strive beyond them. And this is what Nietzsche has in mind when he speaks of the will to power, the overcoming of what is, the transcending of what is, and not because of any defects which the actual worlds possess, because then history would be a rational progressive process. That he indicates by the term "will to power."

Nietzsche took a further step. Having believed himself to have discovered the will to power, the root of all human history, he universalized that. All beings are characterized by the will to power. In other words, he arrived at a metaphysical doctrine, old-style. But here was the great difficulty: what was the status of that metaphysical doctrine? Is it an interpretation, a subjective act of the thinker Nietzsche? Or is it an historical, objective truth? And this is not clear. Nietzsche felt the necessity of having recourse in the last analysis to an objective truth. One can say that Nietzsche relapsed into metaphysics. Nietzsche's effect on our age is due to the apparent necessity to preserve Nietzsche's understanding of history, without following him in his relapse into metaphysics. The most famous name for that is "existentialism," which preserves Nietzsche's view of the subjectivity of the fundamental truth but frees it from metaphysics. And I can only speak in very general terms of that; otherwise it would lead us too far afield.

The fundamental defect of all metaphysics, according to this view, is the assumption that there are eternal, or sempiternal, truths. And from this point of view, the significance of history allegedly cannot be understood. The natural sciences create no difficulty, because, as Nietzsche has said before, and has now repeated: Every physics depends on a metaphysics, and the question is, exactly: What is it that causes these metaphysics? Here there cannot be historical objectivity: all understanding of historical phenomena is relative to the standpoint of the present thinker or historian. It is impossible to understand the thought of the past exactly as the thinkers of the past understood it; nor is it possible to understand it better than they. One can only understand it differently, in such a way that you cannot say that the understanding reached, say, fifty years from now will be better than the understanding which we now have. All understanding of another's thought means a "melding," as it has been called (I think a rather bad metaphor) of horizons.[33] That of our horizon with the horizon of the Greek thinkers. But since these horizons differ from age to age, there can never be the same understanding; there can never be historical objectivity.

Now here there are very great difficulties, which show to me, at any rate, most manifestly the inadequacy of this historical perspective. But before I go on, I will try to make it somewhat clearer by speaking of an English thinker who has presented an approximation to this view. I would like to see whether I have made myself clear enough. Or rather, I am sure I have not made myself clear enough . . . Let me repeat the main point: that here in this radical historicist position, as sketched first by Nietzsche, the whole realm of science, of rational knowledge, is understood to be itself dependent on nonrational presuppositions, which belong to a certain historical period, shorter or longer, and having no validity in themselves. The utmost we can reach is an understanding of these ultimate presuppositions, which we may also call "absolute" presuppositions, and their sequence, or more precisely, the realization that this is the character of human thought, of the human condition: never to reach anything which can be called eternal or sempiternal.

STUDENT: Could you go over again what is the validity, then, of this historical insight? Where does that validity come from? How is that separated from the other part?

LS: What do you mean by that? How one establishes the fact?

SAME STUDENT: Yes.

LS: Well, let us take this very simple example we found in Nagel. We found that he said the fundamental principle of modern science was the principle of causality. This principle is not self-evident, but is logically arbitrary. And in addition, it emerged at a certain time, in the seventeenth century; this fact implies there was a different understanding of causality before then. And there is no difficulty in assuming that there were a variety of understandings of causality in different times and different cultures, and also, therefore, why not in the future? This fundamental contingency of the principles of thought and action—that is the premise which they assume, of course: that they[34] have been established. But even a man like Nagel, who is very much opposed to historicism, admits, as you see, the great plausibility that this possesses in our age. And then one must think about that and try to understand all our fundamental concepts in redefinitions, in reinterpretations: above all, the concept of truth. I mean, truth can no longer simply mean what it had originally meant, if the highest principles have this contingent character. The question would then be to understand what is the root of the creative act, of this act of creating historical worlds. I can say to you the mere words in which this question has been formulated, but I do not know whether this will help. It is the following: all beings, I mean the totality of things— with these, understanding is in principle concerned. Now the question arises: traditional metaphysics, which is still, according to a well-known view, underlying even our physics, which is allegedly nonmetaphysical, was the quest for the most fundamental being or beings. Whether it is god or atoms does not affect the character of the question. But there is a primary question which is not faced by traditional metaphysics, namely: What is a being? What is a being?

Now let me discuss this a bit more. When Aristotle discusses the question regarding numbers and his difference from Plato in this respect, he says that the issue is not the being of numbers, what numbers are, but the manner of their being.[35] Now what does he mean by that? The primary question for Plato, from Aristotle's point of view, is: What is it? The so-called essences, like cats, dogs, prime numbers, what have you. But there is a more subtle question, namely, the question of the manner of being. For example, a number *is* not in the manner in which a living being is. Do you see that? So therefore the question of the manner of being is a more fundamental question, of course, raised by Plato and by Aristotle. But this is now taken in a much more radical sense. And the final formulation is this: *to be* is not a being, and that *to be* is the most fundamental question never properly raised in metaphysics. As a matter of fact, that is the definition of metaphysics, that it never raises this question. Now this has become difficult to express in English. In German one may use *Sein* and *Seiendes*. It was then also translated into French, *être* and *étant*. In English it is hard to say the difference. But still, that is the formula which I present to you only as an indication of the problem. Now the key point is this: this *to be*, this *Sein*, which is to begin with a wholly mysterious thing, is the ground of history, and only of history, historical work. And therefore, only in the light of this revelation of *to be* can one understand anything, including the objects of natural science. Forget about these terms, which would lead too far; but the creative act, not so much of men but going on somehow through men and within men, these are the ultimate things beyond which we cannot go, and these the fundamental questions. History is, so to say, the only theme of philosophy, but history understood by itself: not the battle of Waterloo or something of this kind, but the fundamental changes in human understanding of the world. Also, if you want to use the traditional term, the categories in which men understand change from historical epoch to historical epoch, and this change of the categories and their ground, this is the theme of philosophy. All the traditional themes are mediate ones, relegated to a very secondary or tertiary state by this fundamental change.[36] This is the only way in which the historicist position could be maintained, and all simpler versions are subject to great difficulties. I may make it a bit clearer if I speak of that English version (which is earlier) of historicism and—we can come back to that later. Yes, Mr. Glenn?

MR. GLENN: Earlier you said that a historian truly couldn't understand the past unless he committed himself. Why is that?[37]

LS: ... philosophy. We can make bibliographies which can be very useful, but you must admit that is not history of philosophy. So that if he is a man who does not have sympathy for political life, for political motivations, can he be a political historian? Again, he can be an excellent bibliographer, no doubt, and typist and what have you, but he cannot possibly be more. Now the key point that is made here by these people is that if you are only a bystander, if you stand outside of the process, you cannot understand the process itself.

STUDENT: To understand the process means that you understand that these commitments are purely subjective and your choice—why do you have to choose them to understand that other people do?

LS: Well, since I am not a historicist, I am perhaps not the best defender of this position. Still, there is doubtless some element of truth in that. There is an old saying, of very early times: Similar things are understood only by similar things. One could make this objection to Nietzsche: these merely objective historians whom he attacks were in all interesting cases not merely objective historians. They were all dedicated to certain ideas, whether that of political progress or of German nationalism, or whatever. The strictly objective historian barely existed, and even today is hard to find. Is there not a necessity for empathy in order to be a good historian? If he is entirely indifferent to his subject matter, can he be a good historian? In other words, if he studies some particular subject and he could as well study any other subject, is there not a certain deficiency there? Must there not be some reason which makes this particular subject important to him? This is not necessarily true on every level, but can there be a great achievement of a historian without that?

I do not believe that this concerns a fundamental issue, except that, in this case, the question is: Is objective knowledge ultimately possible? That is the key point. The traditional view from the Greeks on is that it is possible. It is possible to devote one's life to seeing things as they are. Nietzsche has a very simple but true presentation of the issue. The traditional notion of knowledge—here [LS writes on the blackboard] the pure mind intuits the pure ideas, in spite of many changes, very profound changes, in all respects. The pure mind has been replaced to a certain extent by experience (and of course, who believes in Platonic ideas?) but fundamentally, this notion: something in man is open to the truth, in a fundamentally receptive manner. As the tradition has it, the adequation of the intellect to the thing . . . this is the view of objective truth. And what became doubtful in the nineteenth century and more so in our age is whether this is the true view of knowledge and therewith the true view of the situation. The opposite view would be stated as follows: knowledge is fundamentally spontaneous. Kant says that it is understanding which prescribes nature its laws. It is not the understanding which perceives, grasps, the laws of nature, but by its spontaneity the understanding prescribes, it creates a framework within which we can interpret the sense data rationally, intelligibly. This framework is not within what we perceive; it is a spontaneous act of the understanding. Now, radicalize that in the light of the so-called "experience of history." These interpreting frameworks change from epoch to epoch; and then you have creative acts, which ultimately cannot be explained, because every explanation is in terms of specific categories, of this or that category—which categories are now questioned, and not the unquestioned premise. The ultimate supposition, the ultimate fact at which we arrive, is the unaccountable contingent change of these frames of reference. Yes?

STUDENT: I am confused now as to the relationship, or the difference, between existentialism and historicism.

LS: That is a very long issue. There is a certain arbitrariness of usage. Existentialism, in many interpretations which the word has had, has nothing to do with historicism, I know that. But in the philosophically most important form which existentialism has taken, it is identical with the most radical historicism; therefore I prefer to speak of historicism. One must mention the name of Heidegger, by far the greatest thinker of this school, even of our age—but in Heidegger's thought, existence and historicity are inseparable. In order to keep up the connection with the historical movement of the nineteenth century, and to remind myself in other ways, I prefer to speak of historicism. I quote to you one sentence. Heidegger says somewhere, in one of his first great works: it is self-evident, or obvious, that every science of an age depends on the *Weltanschauung* of that age. That is crucial. By this very fact, the derivative character of all science, including mathematics and natural science, is admitted. Science,[38] according to the older view which Heidegger's teacher Husserl maintained: here is science, here is *Weltanschauung*. And even today that is the commonsense view. Heidegger says from the very beginning: No, that is a dependence of science on *Weltanschauung*. That means the *Weltanschauung* rests on acts of the will and is not merely a theoretical matter. It is clear that knowledge of the most important things is not purely theoretical but at the same time has an element of will in it. I can only remind you of the simple scheme suggested by Nietzsche, which is historically correct. This was the old view: knowledge, I mean the highest knowledge, is of something independent of the human will, and this knowledge is fundamentally receptive. (How much spontaneity might be required for getting into the state of receptiveness—) And the opposite view is rejection of that—that the truth is primarily due to such creative acts. Vulgar historicism is traced to man; in the subtle and theoretical historicism of Heidegger, it is traced to what he calls *Sein*, which is x, the ground of all history, working in and through man. Yes?

STUDENT: You said that the existentialists could not accept Nietzsche's metaphysics, and I'm not clear as to where Nietzsche presents a metaphysics.

LS: Nietzsche has a doctrine of the will to power, and he saw in the will to power (whatever that may mean) the essence of every being. I mean not only of man, but of every being. Now the starting point of existentialism is that there is a radical difference between man and nonman, so that no such formula applies to both. The manner of being of man differs radically from the manner of being of anything else. This alone would be a reason against Nietzsche. But the will to power has the same status in a way as the pure mind in Hegel, or in a different way in Aristotle: something which is eternal. The key point in this radical historicism is that there is nothing eternal, at least that we do not know of anything eternal, and cannot know of it, and what we can reach is ultimately this ground for the creative acts underlying all historical worlds, which Heidegger calls *Sein*.

Now I would like to turn here to an English writer, because this is much more simple when we are speaking in English, who I think is the clearest representative of historicism in the English tongue, and that is R. G. Collingwood, who was formerly professor at Oxford. He wrote a book, *The Idea of History*, which is a detailed discussion of the problem of history, but it suffers from the great defect that it was not edited by Collingwood but by some of his students from his papers, and it is surely not a finished, complete book. But he wrote earlier, and published himself, an autobiography, which is of course much more sketchy than that book on history is, but at the same time it was finished and made ready for publication by Collingwood.[39] I will read to you a few passages.

His work in archaeology—Roman Britain was his subject—which he conducted, however, in a way in which very few archaeologists do, namely, reflecting on what he was doing and reflecting on that in a philosophical manner, led him to a question of logic.

> The *Novum Organum* of Bacon and the *Discours de la Méthode* of Descartes[40] began to have a new significance for me. They were the classical expressions of a principle in logic which I found it necessary to restate: the principle that a body of knowledge consists not of "propositions," "statements," "judgments," or whatever name logicians use in order to designate assertive acts of thought,[41] but of these together with the questions they are meant to answer; and that a logic in which the answers are attended to and the questions neglected is a false logic.[42]

This is the starting point of his own turning. Logic must be a logic of question and answer, and the primacy is given to the question. The answer can be understood only in terms of the question. You will see very soon how important that is.

> For a logic of propositions [the traditional logic, and in a way present-day logic too—LS] I wanted to substitute what I called a logic of question and answer. It seemed to me that truth, if that meant the kind of thing which I was accustomed to pursue in my ordinary work as a philosopher or historian—truth in the sense in which a philosophical theory or an historical fact[43] is called true,[44] the proper sense of the word—was something that belonged not to any single proposition [like "Caesar was killed on the Ides of March"—LS] nor even, as the coherence-theorists maintained, to a complex of propositions taken together; but to a complex consisting of questions and answers. The structure of this complex had, of course, never been studied by propositional logic; but with help from Bacon, Descartes, and others I could hazard a few statements about it. Each question and each answer in a given complex had to be relevant or appropriate, had to "belong" both to the whole and to the place it occupied in the whole. Each question had to "arise"; there must be that about it whose absence we condemn when we refuse to answer a question on the ground that it "doesn't arise." Each answer must be "the right" answer to the question it professes to answer.
>
> By "right" I do not mean "true" [but "relevant," "pertinent"—LS].[45]

Now what has this to do with the question of history? Propositional logic, as he calls it, dealing with true propositions, with that which makes them true, has no obvious relation to history. But if you understand a proposition in terms of the primacy of human questions, things will look different. The question "To what question did so-and-so intend this proposition for an answer?" is an historical question and therefore cannot be settled except by historical methods. I think the time will be sufficient to read you one passage which indicates to you how much this affects us. We can discuss this at greater length next time. The people whom he opposed (and they were not very impressive men) happened to take the traditional view of knowledge. They

> thought that the problems with which philosophy is concerned were unchanging. They thought that Plato, Aristotle, the Epicureans, the Stoics,[46] the Cartesians, etc., had all asked themselves the same set of questions, and had given different answers to them. For example, they thought that

the same problems which are discussed in modern ethical theory were discussed in Plato's *Republic* and Aristotle's *Ethics*; and that it was a man's work to ask himself whether Aristotle or Kant was right on the points over which they differ concerning the nature of duty.[47]

There are still such people around [laughter] and I would not altogether condemn them, but there is a great difficulty nevertheless.

The first point at which I saw a perfectly clear gleam of daylight was in political theory. Take Plato's *Republic* and Hobbes's *Leviathan*, so far as they are concerned with politics. Obviously the political theories they set forth are not the same. But do they represent two different theories of the same thing? Can you say that the *Republic* gives one account of "the nature of the State" and the *Leviathan* another? [The ordinary, vulgar view.—LS] No; because Plato's "State" is the Greek *polis*, and Hobbes's is the absolutist State of the seventeenth century. So the vulgar answer is easy:[48] certainly Plato's State is different from Hobbes's, but they are both States; so the theories are theories of the State. Indeed, what did you mean by calling them both political, if not that they were theories of the same thing?

It was obvious to me that this was only a piece of logical bluff, and that if instead of logic-chopping you got down to brass tacks and called for definitions of the "State" as Plato conceived it and as Hobbes conceived it, you would find that the differences between them were not superficial but went down to essentials. You can call the two things the same if you insist; but if you do, you must admit that the thing has got *diablement changé en route* [has in a devilish way changed on its way—LS] so that the "nature of the State" in Plato's time was genuinely different from the "nature of the State" in Hobbes's. I do not mean the empirical nature of the State [in other words, that they were small in Plato's time and large in Hobbes's time—LS]. I mean the ideal nature of the State [that which they regarded as the best—LS]. What even the best and wisest of those who are engaged in politics are trying to do has altered. Plato's *Republic* is an attempt at a theory of one thing; Hobbes's *Leviathan* an attempt at a theory of something else.[49]

There are no eternal problems. The problems change from epoch to epoch. This does not mean there is no connection, but as he makes clear, and as we will discuss next time, if you have a problem P—$p_1, p_2, p_3,$ and so on—they differ very greatly from each other, and you understand very little and almost nothing of, say, Plato or of Hobbes if you say: Well, they call it P.[50] Now if the problems differ, then of course the answers must differ. But the fundamental point is not the difference of answers but the difference of questions, and the necessity that the starting point, i.e., the questions, would differ from epoch to epoch. Collingwood develops this further, and we will speak of that later. But let us discuss this quickly in the few minutes we still have. Is there something very important here in what Collingwood says? Is not the vulgar view, the very common view, that all philosophers deal with the same problems and look in fundamentally the same directions, is there not something objectionable in that?

STUDENT: It seems to trivialize the history of thought. No sense of any continuity.

LS: Oh, continuity is not identity. And in addition, I could say: Why should not one trivialize the history of thought? Where is it written that the history of thought is so important? You know, Aristotle and Descartes and quite a few others didn't give us the history of thought, yes? I mean, one would have to argue somewhat differently. Mr. Shulsky?

MR. SHULSKY: Well, that particular example was annoying because he didn't make the necessary argument for it. If he had said that Plato and Hobbes were in disagreement because they thought of different ideal states as being the states, so they could never get together, that would be one thing, but instead he seems to say that they don't contradict each other, whereas if the two came together they would have an argument as to how men should live.

LS: That they contradict each other, everybody would see that. But the question is whether they contradict each other by applying, as it were, different predicates to the same thing. And Collingwood says: Is it the same thing? Well, I would say, very simply stated—as a practicing historian, I would say that it is a very grave matter if someone translates *polis* by the word "state." A very grave matter. And sometimes, in order to get a better conscience, they apply the term "city-state." This means there is one universal, called "state," which consists of a variety of particulars: city-states, territorial states, empire states, and what have you. One doesn't understand "state" by this. I will take this up at greater length, but when people speak of "state" as they mean it today in the modern centuries, they mean it in contradistinction to society. *Polis* excludes this distinction. One has to dig deeper. I think that Collingwood has a better understanding of the requirements of history than his opponents; the question is only whether the conclusions which he draws from that are well founded. Yes?

MR. LEVY: Couldn't you get out of that difficulty, as a vulgar person, by saying that the laws laid down by Hobbes that the ruler should give and the laws that Plato lays down that his ruler should give are different, but they are both concerned with laws and rulers? And both mean the same thing by "law," namely, that—well, at least controls that are enforced behind their law. Maybe Hobbes had more persuasion behind his law than Plato had behind his, but force is present in both sets of laws.

LS: Well, there is another way of evading it—I see your point—for example, say, let us not speak of "state" but let us speak of "commonwealth." And this makes perfect sense, to understand the *polis* as commonwealth, and Hobbes speaks specifically of commonwealth, so there is no difficulty. But this does not go to the root of the matter because of the fact that after the First World War, people thought (and, even today, think) in terms of states, with its various connotations. There is nothing of this kind in Plato and Aristotle, and this must be faced. I think it can be faced and can be solved, but if one does not take the additional trouble, one has no right to maintain that the philosophers deal ultimately with the identically same problems. That must be proven. I would say this is a very simple objection to the crude view: How do you know? Only after you have studied them can we say in fact that they deal with the same problems. Good.

Now next time I will speak of Collingwood and then gradually turn to the historical question proper.

7   R. G. Collingwood as an Example

LEO STRAUSS: We are discussing now the position called historicism. We can say there were two forms of it: a primary or naive historicism, and a radical historicism, the latter being started by Nietzsche. The primary or naive historicism asserts that the historian is a spectator of the historical process, who sees that all principles of thought and action come into being and perish. But he exempts *himself*, his principles of thought and action: he stands on the banks of the river, not in the river. The radical historicist asserts that this is impossible; there is no place outside of the stream. The consequence is that the pride of the naive historian in historical objectivity proves to be unfounded. All knowledge is relative to the historical situation, and this applies to the historian's knowledge as well. There is no objectivity, or what we call objectivity is only a derivative mode of a certain kind of subjectivity. Now I have begun to try to explain historicism somewhat better, in greater detail, by beginning to speak of Collingwood. I limited myself to the *Autobiography*, but in the meantime I thought I should say something about his *Idea of History*, his larger work. This is simplified by the fact that many years ago I wrote a long review article on it, and I will quote from that a few passages.[1]

Now what Collingwood tried to do is to develop what he calls the philosophy of history. Philosophy of history as he understands it necessarily entails a complete philosophy conceived from an historical point of view, for the discovery on which philosophy of history is based concerns the character of all human thought, and not merely of historical thought. It leads therefore to an entirely new understanding of philosophy. In other words, it was always admitted that the central theme of philosophy is the question of what man is, and that history is the knowledge of what men have done. But now it has been realized that man is what he *can do*, and the only clue to what man can do is what he has done. Therefore, the so-called science of human nature, or of the human mind, resolves itself into history. Philosophy of history is identical with philosophy as such, which has become radically historical. Philosophy as a separate discipline is liquidated by being converted into history. These are very extreme, but therefore clarifying, formulae.

One can say historicism is characterized by the fact that the traditional, and to common sense so obvious, distinction between philosophy and history, between philosophic and historical questions, is abandoned: a fusion of philosophy and history, a complete fusion, is intended. Now whether that is feasible remains to be seen. Now the question consists of two parts: Why is history necessarily philosophic, and why is philosophy necessarily historical? The first question, why is history necessarily philosophic, Collingwood answers: All history is history of thought, by which he means this. Let us take something so seemingly unphilosophic as the Battle of Trafalgar. But what does it mean to understand the Battle of Trafalgar? Collingwood asks. It means to understand the thought of Nelson, to understand human thought. In every historical investigation, even in archaeology, archaeology of Roman Britain, which was Collingwood's special interest—when he tries to understand the meaning of fortification, what does it mean? What is this fortification for, i.e., what was the thought of the builders? This is a partial explanation of why history is necessarily philosophic, since it is understanding of human thought.

Another conclusion: Since all thinking is critical thinking and not a mere surrender to the object of thought, rethinking of earlier thought is identical with criticism of earlier thought. The point of view from which the scientific historian criticizes the past is that of the present, of his civilization. Scientific history is therefore to see the human past in its entirety as it appears from the standpoint of the present of the historian's civilization. That is to say, history is self-knowledge, and what is more philosophic than the attempt to know oneself? Yet history will not be self-knowledge if the historian sees the past in the light of the present of his civilization without making that present his primary theme. He must know what the present of his civilization is, in order to understand it. The scientific historian starts, therefore, to show how the present of his civilization, or the mind of the present day, or that determinate human nature which is his civilization, has come into existence. Philosophy being fundamentally self-knowledge (because what does it mean to raise the question of what is man?), this is not feasible according to Collingwood except through history. The consequence of this is that all history, and all philosophy, is relative to the present. Now how can this be justified? Now an analysis would show that two premises are involved: in the first place, an assumption of the superiority of the present. The point of view of the present is the highest point of view that ever existed, and therefore we don't lose anything by looking at the past from the point of view of the present. The second reason, however, which differs from the first, is the equality of all ages. I read to you: "Augustine looked at Roman history from the point of view of an early Christian. And Gibbon did so from that of an enlightened eighteenth-century Englishman: 'there is no point in asking, which was the right point of view. Each was the only possible for the man who adopted it.'"[2]

Correspondingly, the present-day historian who looks at the past from the present-day point of view cannot help looking at the past from the present-day point of view, and in this decisive respect, all ages are equal. There is here a difficulty. If the insight into the equality of all ages is the decisive insight, then our age is nevertheless superior to all other ages because only our age has that insight. Is this clear? I have stated it as follows.

> The belief in the equality of all ages is only a more subtle form of the belief in progress. The alleged insight into the equality of all ages which is said to make possible passionate interest in the thought of the different ages, necessarily conceives of itself as a progress beyond all earlier thought: every earlier age erroneously "absolutized" the standpoint from which it looked at things and therefore was incapable of taking very seriously the thought of other ages; hence earlier ages were incapable of scientific history.[3]

Now in his *Idea of History*, Collingwood gives us a specimen of his own historical work, because he writes a history of history, of historical understanding throughout the ages. And what one can say of that history is only that it is extremely poor as a historical work. Collingwood simply does not take seriously, say, Thucydides, or Tacitus, or Herodotus, and one can understand that because he is so certain of the progress made by nineteenth- and twentieth-century scientific history. Hence we draw this conclusion: in order to take the thought of the past seriously, as he *wishes* to do, one must doubt the superiority of present-day thought. Otherwise you do not have an incentive for taking seriously the thought of the past. History, in other words, is required not simply for the sake of self-knowledge but also and above all for the sake of self-criticism— not only to find out that Plato and Aristotle, for example, contributed their share to that beautiful and complete wisdom which we possess, but also that we have forgotten many things which Plato and Aristotle knew. And this is at least as important a function of the historian, to recover that loss.

Only a few more points which I wish to make in this connection. Now if this is so, if it is necessary for understanding ourselves and for understanding our limitations to understand the thought of the past, it follows indeed that a fusion of philosophy and history is inevitable, and to that extent I would agree with Collingwood. There is a simple indirect proof. When you look at present-day literature on political and social matters, one observes the shallowness of those present-day thinkers who lack a historical perspective. It is obviously necessary for us to have this historical perspective, and to that extent it is simply true that a fusion of philosophy and history is inevitable. But we must not deceive ourselves about the crucial implication of this seemingly trivial point. In our age the fusion of philosophy and history is necessary, as everyone will see if he begins to think about any question, whether it is democracy or sovereignty and so on. When he wants to have clarity, he has to engage in historical studies. Mostly, people do not engage in historical studies but look up the next encyclopedia or dictionary and get their facts as it were from there, which are in all cases then of course simply very secondary, not to say tertiary, results, i.e., reflections of what some historians (perhaps good ones) have found out.

The mere fact that such a fusion is today practically inevitable implies a radical break with traditional philosophy, in which such a fusion was inconceivable. Now one could say, and this is a common view, that this is a progress beyond traditional philosophy: traditional philosophy lacked that peculiar reflectiveness which we have and which induces us to engage in historical studies. But this phenomenon can also be viewed from a very different point of view. Let us take the example of Thomas Aquinas. His political thought was based to a considerable extent on Aristotle. So he had studied Aristotle, he had him at his elbow, we may say. But this was not historical study. Aristotle was "the Philosopher," the authority in these matters. The basis of his thought, we can say, was contemporary with Thomas Aquinas. Whether he read Aristotle in Greek or Latin is very unimportant here.

But we in our age are in that situation that the bases of our thought are not contemporary with us, and the reason for that is the fact and the notion of progress. Certain crucial decisions were made, say, in the seventeenth century. This was continued. An enormous structure arose. We are high up in that structure, but we are not directly confronted with the foundations. The way of progress, we can say, is this [LS writes on the blackboard]: ever higher and higher. But this implies blindness about the foundations, if this process is not accompanied by an inverse process, the digging up and the understanding of the hidden foundations. So, while we modern men are by virtue of this "progress" in need of historical studies in order to see again the hidden foundations of our thought, this was not so in all ages. In other words, the fact that we need—*we need*—this fusion of philosophy and history does not mean by itself that our thought is superior to that of the past, in which such a fusion was not necessary and not even possible.

I return now to Collingwood's *Autobiography*. I have read to you a few passages in which Collingwood indicates his starting point, namely, a revision of logic, a substitution of a logic of questions and answers for the propositional logic of the past. And I have indicated how this change in logic, the insight into the primacy of questioning, is connected with his historicism. I will now continue. This *Autobiography* is a very spirited book. He was a fighting man, obviously, and the men whom he fought were a school who called themselves "realists." Let us see what these people say about the word, because the word "realism" has infinitely many meanings.

Cook Wilson[4] (by the way, a man well known in Platonic studies; he is one of these realists) asserted: "Knowing makes no difference to what is known." In other words, this piece of furniture is wholly indifferent to my knowing it. This behind me, the blackboard, is the same blackboard whether I view it or not, and the simple proof is that if I turn around I know I will see it. Knowing makes no difference to what is known, a commonsensical view, which doesn't necessarily mean that it's true. Collingwood regarded this assertion as meaningless.

> I argued that anyone who claimed, as Cook Wilson did, to be sure of this, was in effect claiming to know what he was simultaneously defining as unknown. For if you know that no difference is made to a thing θ by the presence or absence of a certain condition c, you know what θ is like with c, and also what θ is like without c, and on comparing the two find no difference. This involves knowing what θ is like without c; in the present case, knowing what you defined as the unknown.[5]

Is this clear, what the argument means? When you say that knowing makes no difference to what is known, you imply that you know the thing in its status of not-knownness, and this is absurd. For by knowing it, you always know it as known. This is the simple refutation of realism. And this has of course most crucial implications, because the view which Collingwood ascribes to these men in Oxford is the view of the whole premodern tradition: the view expressed in the definition of truth as the adequation of the intellect and the thing. My thoughts are true if what is in my mind, say, about this piece of furniture, agrees with the thing, the piece of furniture itself, and all imperfections of knowledge are those in which my thoughts do not reflect, do not reproduce, the character of the thing. To think truly means to think what is, to look at what is. Knowledge is fundamentally receptive, in spite of all nonreceptive, spontaneous activities which might be required in a subsidiary fashion.

Now what do we say to Collingwood's argument? I would put it this way: I don't believe it settles the issue. Precisely if it is impossible to say whether truth stems from the human mind or not—because that is of course what Collingwood implies: since we cannot possibly know the thing as it is outside of all relations to the human mind, the truth originates ultimately in the human mind. Now precisely if it is impossible to say that, one must leave the question open. Every one of us finds, even in the greatest disturbances which we can imagine, an order: cats are not dogs; trees are not brutes; stones are not trees; and all these things behave in a peculiar manner, to say nothing of man and the various differences among men. The key question is this: Does this order, this *taxis*, originate in the human mind, or does man, in the process of learning and knowing, awaken to a *taxis*, to an order which is independent of man? Differently stated, the latter view is identical with the view that man is a microcosm, that man is a being privileged by nature to understand, or to be open at least to all things, whereas brutes are incapable of that, whereas the other view is that there is no such privilegedness of man by nature, but man, a being among all kinds of beings, is the only one capable of producing an intelligible order.

Now Collingwood contends, and this is by no means so clear, that the view that nothing is affected by being known leads to consequences both regarding human action and regarding political theory in particular. Now he speaks there of certain developments in Oxford at that time, after the First World War, which run parallel to things with which we are now very familiar, which are now known in England as the various philosophies, analyses, of language. It was not yet called that way at that time, but Lord Russell played a great role already at that time, and he is a great living link between that diluvian era and our age. I read to you just a passage for illustration.

> Moral philosophy, from the days of Socrates down to our own lifetime, had been regarded as an attempt to think out more clearly the issues involved in conduct, for the sake of acting better. In 1912 one of these men[6] announced that moral philosophy as so understood was based on a mistake, and advocated a new kind of moral philosophy, purely theoretical, in which the workings of the moral consciousness should be scientifically studied as if they were the movements of the planets, and no attempt made to interfere with them. And Bertrand Russell at Cambridge proposed in the same spirit, and on grounds whose difference was only superficial, the extrusion of ethics from the body of philosophy.[7]

Well, this has of course happened in the meantime, only what is called "ethics" has no longer to do with ethics; it is no longer a normative discipline but is merely an analysis of ethical language.

> The "realist" philosophers who adopted this new program were all, or nearly all, teachers of young men and young women. Their pupils, with habits and characters yet unformed, stood on the threshold of life; many of them on the threshold of public life. Half a century earlier, young people in that position had been told that by thinking about what they were doing, or were about to do, they would become likely on the whole to do it better; and that some understanding of the nature of moral or political action, some attempt to formulate ideals and principles, was an indispensable condition of engaging creditably in these activities themselves.[8] The "realist"[9] said to his pupils, "If it interests you to study this, do so; but don't think it will be of any use to you. Remember the great principle of realism, that nothing is affected by being known. That is as true of human action as of anything else. Moral philosophy is only the theory of moral action: it cannot therefore make any difference to the practice of moral action."[10]

Now whether this follows truly from the principle of realism I have my doubt, because Aristotle was a realist in that sense, and Plato too, and yet they had no doubt that knowledge does make a great difference regarding action, although it does not affect things which cannot possibly be affected by human action, like the course of the planets, to take a simple example.

The same happened, of course, also to political theory, that it lost all its use and reasonableness. We come to a more interesting and more immediate problem, to which I alluded last time. The realists, who were in these matters old-fashioned people, however strange this may sound in the case of Russell, took, for example, for granted the distinction between philosophy and history, and denied that there is a fusion between them, possible or necessary. The realists thought that the problems with which philosophy is concerned were unchanging. This is a point which I read to you last time, which Collingwood questions radically.

> Was it really true, I asked myself, that the problems of philosophy were, even in the loosest sense of that word, eternal? Was it really true that different philosophies were different attempts to answer the same questions? I soon discovered that it was not true; it was merely a vulgar error, consequent on a[11] kind of historical myopia which, deceived by superficial resemblances, failed to detect profound differences.[12]

And now there comes a passage which I read to you about the people who say Plato's *Republic* and Hobbes's *Leviathan* deal with the same subject, the nature of the state. And he wonders: How can you translate *polis*, the subject with which Plato is concerned, by "state"? And there is of course something very important implied.

> There is, of course, a connection between these two things [between the thing about which Plato speaks and the thing about which Hobbes speaks—LS] but it is not the kind of connection that the "realists" thought it was. Anybody would admit that Plato's *Republic* and Hobbes's *Leviathan* are about two things which are in one way the same thing and in another way different. This is not in dispute. What is in dispute is the kind of sameness and the kind of difference. The "realists" thought that the sameness was the sameness of a "universal" [let us say, commonwealth—LS] and the difference the difference between two instances of that universal.

The commonwealth understood as *polis*, the commonwealth understood as a modern state.

But this is not so. The sameness is the sameness of an historical process, and the difference is the difference between one thing which in the course of that process has turned into something else, and the other thing into which it has turned. Plato's *polis* and Hobbes's absolutist State are related by a traceable historical process, whereby one has turned into the other; anyone who ignores that process, denies the difference between them, and argues that where Plato's political theory contradicts Hobbes's one of them must be wrong, is saying the thing that is not [the Swiftian formula for a lie, for an untruth—LS].[13]

Now here of course we reach a point where Collingwood's thesis ceases to be clear, where he is compelled to admit that there is no contradiction between Plato's doctrine and Hobbes's doctrine because they answer entirely different questions, as if it were not possible to raise the question: Whose question is the more profound one? I mean, it may be that given the Hobbesian question, it could not be answered in Plato's manner—I gladly grant that—but the question concerns then the rank, the order of rank of the questions. Here Collingwood stops. He gives here another example.

It was not difficult to see that just as the Greek *polis* could not be legitimately translated by the modern word "State" [which I think is true—LS] except with the[14] warning that the two things are in various essential ways different, and a statement of what these differences are; so, in ethics, a Greek word like *dei* cannot be legitimately translated by using the word "ought," if that word carries with it the notion of what is sometimes called "moral obligation." Was there any Greek word or phrase to express that notion, namely, of moral obligation?[15] The "realists" said there was; but they stultified themselves by adding that the "theories of moral obligation" expounded by Greek writers differed from modern theories such as Kant's about the same thing. How did they know that the Greek and the Kantian theories were about the same thing? Oh, because *dei* (or whatever word it was) is the Greek word for "ought."[16]

In other words, this Greek word, which has the primary meaning, "something is lacking, is needing," of course does not in itself mean "ought," but in certain connections it can approach that meaning.

But the fundamental point which he makes—you have no right to assume that an earlier great thinker *must* have dealt with what *you* regard as the fundamental question—is of course simple common sense. I will read you the conclusion. "Ideals of personal conduct are just as impermanent as ideals of social organization. Not only that, but what is meant by calling them ideals is subject to the same change." Of course. I mean, try to translate the word "ideal" into classical Greek: you wouldn't succeed. There is an equivalent for it, or a half equivalent, but that shows the great difference. "Something for which you would wish or pray," that would be the equivalent, to some extent, of what we mean by an ideal.[17] But surely there is no connection, as I might mention in passing, between "ideal" as the word is developed in the seventeenth century and the Platonic *idea*. There is a connection of sorts: without the Platonic concept of *idea*, people would never have come to speak of ideals. But these are very different things.

> The "realists" knew that different peoples, and the same peoples at different times, held different views, and were quite entitled to hold different views, about how a man ought to behave; but they thought that the phrase "ought to behave" had a meaning which was one, unchanging, and eternal. They were wrong. The literature of European moral philosophy, from the Greeks onwards, was in their hands and on their shelves to tell them so; but they evaded the lesson by systematically mistranslating the passages from which they might have learned it.[18]

And here Collingwood alludes to a very well-known fact, or I think it should be well known: that we are the slaves of the translators. And the translators are in most cases men of an impossible innocence in these matters. They are not aware of what they are doing by translating an important word by the most convenient equivalent in present-day, everyday usage. That's impossible. And that is the reason why it is necessary, if for one reason or another one wants to see the truth about these matters, to learn at least as much of these languages that one can check, with the help of dictionaries, the work of the translators.

We come now to the core of Collingwood's teaching. Traditionally, the central discipline of philosophy was metaphysics. What happened to metaphysics on the basis of the insight into the historicity of all human thought?

> It became clear to me that metaphysics (as its very name might show "after physics," though people still use the word as if it had been "paraphysics"

"by the side of," like "parapsychology")[19] is no futile attempt at knowing what lies beyond the limits of experience, but is primarily at any given time an attempt to discover what the people of that time believe about the world's general nature; such beliefs being the presuppositions of all their "physics," that is to say,[20] their inquiries into its detail. Secondarily, it is the attempt to discover the corresponding presuppositions of other peoples and other times, and to follow the historical process by which one set of presuppositions has turned into another.

In other words, the central and highest philosophic discipline, metaphysics, is nothing but the understanding of our fundamental presupposition, seeing it together with other cultures' or other peoples' fundamental presuppositions, and the movement from one set of presuppositions to another. This is indeed a radical statement. Collingwood calls these presuppositions, to make it quite clear, the "absolute" presuppositions.

> The question of what presuppositions underlie the "physics" or natural science of a certain people at a certain time is as purely historical a question as what kind of clothes they wear. [In other words, it is not in any peculiar sense philosophic.—LS] And this is the question that metaphysicians have to answer. It is not their business to raise the further question whether, among the various beliefs on this subject that various peoples hold and have held, this one or that one is true. [Whether, say, the Babylonian or Greek or Hebrew absolute presupposition is true or untrue.—LS] This question, when raised, would always be found, as it always has been found, unanswerable; and if there is anything in my "logic of question and answer" that is not to be wondered at, for the beliefs whose history the metaphysician has to study are not answers to questions [which therefore can be criticized: are they correct answers to the question or not?—LS] but only presuppositions of questions, and therefore the distinction between what is true and what is false does not apply to them, but only the distinction between what is presupposed and what is not presupposed.[21] The beliefs which a metaphysician tries to study and codify are presuppositions of the questions asked by natural scientists, but are not answers to any questions at all. This might be expressed by calling them "absolute" presuppositions.[22]

Now this is of course a crucial point. All human thought rests ultimately on absolute presuppositions, which differ from historical epoch to historical epoch, and regarding which the question of truth or untruth cannot be raised. This does not lead by itself to relativism and nihilism—that is what Collingwood implies—because we cannot help believing in the absolute presuppositions of our society, and therefore, practically the question doesn't arise. But the great question is whether there are not grave crises in cultures or societies where the absolute presuppositions become questionable. And there, of course, there is no way out thinkable. Collingwood has no doubt that this state of affairs affects the possibility of historical objectivity regarding the absolute presuppositions. In other words, historical thought is also human thought, therefore dependent on absolute presuppositions differing from historical situation to historical situation. Therefore, historical thought is open to the same difficulty that it cannot have objectivity proper. We look at the absolute presuppositions, say, of Plato or Hobbes, from the point of view of our absolute presuppositions. The only objective knowledge of a philosophic character is that of the series of absolute presuppositions which we discern in history. Of course, there cannot be an ethics or political theory proper, for they depend on questionable absolute presuppositions. Now let me pursue that.

From all I have said before, it follows that a rapprochement between philosophy and history is absolutely indispensable in Collingwood's view: a new kind of philosophy. A new kind of philosophy. Now what is that?

> Soon after the beginning of the seventeenth century,[23] a number of intelligent people in Western Europe began to see in a settled and steady manner what a few here and there had seen by fits and starts for the last hundred years and more: namely that the problems which ever since the time of early Greek philosophy had gone by the collective name of "physics" were capable of being restated in a shape in which, with the double weapon of experiment and mathematics, one could now solve them [whereas hitherto they had been insoluble—LS]. What was called Nature, they saw, had henceforth no secrets from man; only riddles which he had learned the trick of answering. Or, more accurately, Nature was no longer a Sphinx asking man riddles; it was man that did the asking, and Nature, now, that he put to the torture until she gave him the answer to his questions.[24]

Now this grave change, this great progress made in the seventeenth century, is the model for that new, great change which Collingwood plans to help to bring about. This statement about modern physics and the revolution of the seventeenth century clearly implies that the absolute presuppositions underlying modern physics are superior to the absolute presuppositions underlying Greek physics. And therefore this contradicts flatly the statement of the equality of the absolute presuppositions or, in other words, that the question of truth cannot arise regarding the absolute presuppositions. Now something analogous to what Bacon and Descartes and Galileo did regarding nature must now be done in regard to history. That is very urgent. Why? "It seemed almost as if man's power to control 'Nature' had been increasing *pari passu* with a decrease in his power to control human affairs."[25] In other words, the well-known fact: the complete chaos, moral chaos, which has arisen in modern times, and Collingwood expects that the new philosophy, i.e., a philosophy which is radically historical, will solve this problem created by man's increasing his power through modern physics and technology.

The usual view is: Well, we only have to develop scientific psychology. They will take care of the problems caused by modern physics and chemistry by enabling us to manipulate men better, so that they behave more reasonably, and so on. Collingwood has very sensible things to say about this point. Psychology cannot do the job. He says it in very general but clear terms: psychology deals with the soul in contradistinction to the mind, and since the questions of true and untrue, good and bad, are questions for the mind, psychology is incompetent to deal with them. That is very abstractly stated, but I think fundamentally sound. But the question is whether history can do the job—an intelligent or philosophic history—which psychology admittedly cannot do.

> Was it possible that men should come to a better understanding of human affairs by studying history? Was history the thing which in future might play a part in civilized life analogous to that of natural science in the past? . . .
>
> The historian is a person whose questions are about the past. He is generally supposed to be a person whose questions are exclusively about the past; about a past, namely, that is dead and gone, and in no sense at all living on into the present.

This view Collingwood denies: "The past which an historian studies is not a dead past, but a past which in some sense is still living in the present." Therefore the historian alone can help us in understanding the present, the present having the past within itself: "So long as the past and the present are outside one another, knowledge of the past is not of much use in the problems of the present."

But the case is radically different from the other point of view. He gives this example:

> "Nothing here but trees and grass," thinks the traveller, and marches on. "Look," says the woodsman [the trained man—LS] "there is a tiger in that grass." The historian's business is to reveal the less obvious features hidden from a careless eye in the present situation. What history can bring to moral and political life is a trained eye for the situation in which one has to act.

And therefore historical understanding is the only way in which we can get clarity about what we have to do. Acting well means acting according to the situation, especially to such situations where we do not have the help of *rules*, i.e., of universals: "If ready-made rules for dealing with situations of specific types are what you want, natural science is the kind of thing which can provide you with them." He gives here an example of where general rules are of no help.

> Everyone has certain rules according to which he acts in dealing with his tailor. These rules are, we will grant, soundly based on genuine experience; and by acting on them a man will deal fairly with his tailor and helps his tailor to deal fairly by him. But so far as he acts according to these rules, he is dealing with his tailor only in his capacity as a tailor, and not as John Robinson, aged sixty, with a weak heart and a consumptive daughter, a passion for gardening and an overdraft at the bank. The rules for dealing with tailors no doubt enable you to cope with the tailor in John Robinson, but they prevent you from getting to grips with whatever else there may be in him. Of course, if you know that he has a weak heart, you will manage your dealings with him by modifying the rules for tailor-situations in the light of the rules for situations involving people with weak hearts. But at this rate the modifications soon become so complicated that the rules are no longer of any practical use to you. We have got beyond the stage at which rules can guide action, and you go back to improvising, as best you can, a method of handling the situation in which you find yourself.[26]

Now this is a key example, and therefore we have to look at it for one moment. Is it true that only knowledge of the situation—replace the tailor by a complicated political situation—that knowledge of the situation as such, without any universals, can guide us? It may be true that all the rules are insufficient. Mr. Levy?

MR. LEVY: The example, I guess, would be Montgomery as a general, or even maybe Churchill as a leader. Did Montgomery have to know anything about Aristotle to win the battle of El Alamein? And yet he had great practical wisdom, as shown by his memoir and his victory in that battle. And did Churchill have to know anything about Aristotle, which he seemed not to know very much about, except for the *Ethics*?

LS: Yes, well, that is an entirely different question, whether "rules" means "rules to be found in this or that book."

MR. LEVY: I was just using that as an example of a rule, of rules, *any* rules, besides that of practical experience as a—

LS: Yes. Well, there was one thing, I believe, which was quite clear in the case of Montgomery, apart from the situation, although it constituted the situation, namely, that he had to win it: victory. Now in the case of politics as distinguished from generalship, the end is somewhat more complicated, complex—you know, because the political good consists of a number of ingredients which cannot be reduced to the simple formula, *victory*, and therefore there are all kinds of considerations. Which of these ingredients is at the moment the most important or the most urgent? This is another point.

But if you look at this case of the tailor John Robinson, it is perfectly clear that it is a matter, first of all, of dealing fairly by him and he should deal fairly by you, that universal fairness is essential for acting properly. And secondly, here, human kindness, which is not the same as fairness, is not the rule, but modifies it. In other words, every situation demands of us that it be developed in one or the other direction. The question of the direction in which it should be developed is ultimately a question of universals, not necessarily universal *rules*, without which we could not act. And this question is simply lost in the historicism of Collingwood as well as in others. For Collingwood, as he makes clear—I'll give you one example: the question of what is the *summum bonum*, the highest good, is for him simply a pseudo-question, just as the question of what is knowledge, or what is art, because all questions must be understood situationally. I must say that in this respect the ordinary positivistic social scientists, with their emphasis on the value questions, are preferable, in my opinion, to Collingwood. I mean, what speaks against them I have tried to state, but in Collingwood the question of the ends in their universality simply disappears in the concern for the situation in which you act. The question of the good life cannot be simply replaced by the question of "What shall I do here?," although the question of the good life becomes sterile if it is not specified by me in this situation, in accordance with that situation. But perhaps Collingwood would say that the question of the good is a pseudo-question because it is already answered by the absolute presuppositions of the society to which we belong, and therefore it cannot arise. But there we come up against a great question: What if the culture or society to which we belong is in a state of crisis, and we lose our morals? This is not in any way faced by Collingwood. He ends the book with a discussion of the political situation at the time of the Spanish Civil War, in which he takes a rather simplistic view of the situation: he takes it for granted that Neville Chamberlain was a crypto-fascist, and other things, which means the situation alone is a poor and insufficient guide for taking one's bearings, both in private and in public matters.

So I will leave it at these points, and . . .[27]

. . . mean the understanding of the human product, thought and so on, of the past. That is the common meaning, and this can be practiced on the basis of various philosophic assumptions. Historicism is something much more specific. Historicism is the assertion that all human thought rests ultimately on presuppositions which differ from epoch to epoch, and which are not susceptible of any criticism.

STUDENT: I see. Then Collingwood was concerned with both of these two things.

LS: Yes, Collingwood became entangled in this difficulty: that while he has to assert the equality of all absolute presuppositions, he cannot help asserting the supremacy of that absolute presupposition which goes together with historicism. In other words, all other cultures or historical periods depended on such absolute presuppositions, but *his* situation, the situation of his thought, goes together with an awareness of this fact. This is a radical change in the situation. That is the difficulty which exists from the very beginning. Mr. Shulsky?

MR. SHULSKY: Is it true, though, that his awareness of the historicity of thought is in fact a big change, especially when it comes to the actual writing of history? Because it would seem that even if a modern historian is aware of historicism, he is just as culture-bound, so to speak, in writing history as anyone else was, so that this progress is so to speak external to the actual writing of history, or understanding history—

LS: That may be so, but still—I mean, let us assume that the historian is not affected by that, although it would be strange if the historicist insight, if it is an insight, did not have an effect on the writing of history. The key point is the philosophic question: Must not historicism be applied to itself? That is to say, historicism too is historical, that is to say, it belongs to a specific historical situation. Is it not necessary? That is of course not in itself fatal if it is properly thought through, provided the thinker in question implies that the situation to which the historicist insight belongs is a privileged moment, let us say the absolute moment, the moment in which man becomes aware for the first time of *the* fundamental basis of all human thought and action. And of course he would have to make this intelligible; the mere assertion would not mean anything. He must show how come this foundation of all foundations, which men never saw as such before, became visible in the twentieth century. What is the peculiarity of the twentieth century that it became visible here and now? That he must answer. Yes, Mr. Devereaux?

MR. DEVEREAUX: As far as I understand, you agreed with Collingwood in saying that it was necessary today for a rapprochement between history and philosophy. Do you mean that in contrast to the premoderns, we simply have more obstacles to overcome? Or did you mean something else, more than that?

LS: Well, I meant it in the first place as a strictly empirical assertion in the old sense of the word, where an empirical assertion means that I know that it is so, and I do not know the reason. What they call a "hard fact." A hard fact is a fact where you do not know the reason, because if you know the reason, it is no longer so hard, ya? [Laughter] That is so that whenever I read something, an analysis of some of the fundamental concepts with which political scientists are concerned—of course the mere historical knowledge which is thoughtless and undigested is of no value, I am speaking only of the other way around—but if someone does not go into the genesis of these concepts, then he is simply a superficial analyst. One can state it formally and therefore very simply as follows. As men of science, we are all concerned with knowledge about the things of which we have primarily only opinions, and if we want to proceed in a perfectly aboveboard and clean manner, we must first make clear to ourselves what our opinions are. We must clarify our opinions. Now if we begin to do that, we see very soon that our opinions are in very large part opinions which we share with our contemporaries and, even more, inherited opinions. But think of such a thing like political freedom. While there are some features, perhaps, which have emerged in the last generation, fundamentally that concept is an inheritance. Now if we want to clarify our opinion, we must therefore also go into this whole history of "political liberty." So the strictly philosophic concern with clarifying our opinions changes necessarily and even insensibly into historical study. This is, I think, an empirical fact which every one of us who is doing some thought, some reflection about it, simply experiences.

Now when we look, say, at Aristotle, and we see that in order to clarify his opinion he does not engage in any kind of historical studies (disregarding all differences of rank between people like ourselves and Aristotle entirely, because even the greatest men now living would have to engage in historical studies, whereas Aristotle did not), then the first impression one gets, and this is supported by powerful prejudice, is that Aristotle, however great he was, lacked the awareness of a certain dimension, of the historical dimension, and which awareness is the preserve of the nineteenth and twentieth centuries, somehow prepared by people like Vico— and you know the usual litany you get. Then that is a question or should be a question, at least: Is this interpretation correct? Is the acquisition of that sixth sense, the historical sense, an enrichment of man's understanding, or a corrective to peculiar defects of modern thought? That is the question. And I think that however we will answer it, we are wiser if we have raised that question and not simply accepted the view now prevailing, because when we accept the view now prevailing, we simply accept the prejudice. Now a prejudice may be true, but if I realize that it is true, it is no longer a prejudice. Accepting prejudice as such is a questionable thing, for academic people, at least. Yes?

MR. DEVEREAUX: You say that in order to investigate our opinions, we must go into the origins and so on. Does one ever get to the end of this, or are you constantly in this historical investigation?

LS: Well, that is a very difficult question. We must never lose a certain common sense. In other words, for a given purpose it may be perfectly sufficient to stop at a certain point, and it may be relatively easy, but other questions are very . . . I could tell you some stories from my private experience where I was sure I had clarified something, a concept which I thought was relatively important, and then I found that further studies are still indicated. But it all depends what the immediate purpose of the study is, if one is . . . That is exactly the point with which we are confronted when we advise students regarding doctor's theses. Let us assume that the subject is of interest, and then the question arises: Is it manageable? Now what is true of students is true in a modified manner also of professors and even of old professors, who are supposed to be able to manage problems which a doctoral candidate cannot manage, but even they, and precisely they, will also come across questions which cannot be managed, and therefore they have to find some defensible and not arbitrary division of the subject matter so that they can do that. Whether a full clarification is in fact possible, that is a very long question. And to the extent to which historicism means only this, that a full clarification is not possible, to that extent it has a point. But the question is whether one has to be a historicist in order to admit the infinity and the elusiveness of the truth. Do you see how this is implied? Yes?

STUDENT: If I understood what you said about Collingwood correctly, he would say that you can't say whether Plato or Hobbes, for example, which one of these was right, because each one asked an essentially different question. Then you said, in contradistinction, that you can still ask which question is higher or more worthy. But wouldn't Collingwood say this doesn't make any sense, because the worth of a particular question is only relative to the particular age in which it was asked?

LS: Yes, but then Collingwood goes on to say that there is something more fundamental than all questions, what he calls the absolute presuppositions, on the basis of which questions arise. And he says, regarding these absolute presuppositions, you cannot say whether the absolute presupposition of Plato or that of Hobbes is true or not. It seems simple enough. But then he discusses the question of modern physics, seventeenth century and so on, which is based on specific absolute presuppositions. But here we see the very strange fact: that modern science represents a progress beyond earlier science insofar as it can solve all kinds of questions which were insoluble in the past. Or nearer home: the most fundamental insight possible on the basis of Collingwood is the insight into the historical character of all thought, the insight that all human thought is based on absolute presuppositions. I would say this is the absolute presupposition of absolute presuppositions. The absolute presuppositions of the first order cannot be said to be true or false, according to Collingwood: the absolute presupposition of absolute presuppositions is *true*. I mean, what do you care about the absolute presuppositions of the first order, if you have a much more fundamental insight of which you can be sure that it is true? Do you see that point? I think the position as Collingwood stated it is not tenable. It was developed much more subtly and profoundly on the basis of Nietzsche by Heidegger (the talk of which I spoke last time), and here the difficulties also appear in a peculiar way.

Well, I would like to mention only one point. Fundamentally, what Collingwood says about absolute presuppositions would be accepted by Heidegger. Heidegger only states it differently, and Heidegger is much more concerned with the connection between thought and language. Language is of course always the language of this or that people, with this and that peculiar tradition. Therefore when we think traditionally of truth, we mean the universality of truth, say, today in mathematics: this is a universal language. But philosophy as philosophy can of course never take on this mathematical character. It is always linked to a specific language, whether it is German or Greek or English, and so on and so on: necessarily particular. Now today, men, all inhabitants of this globe, are for the first time brought into contact with one another, and the question of the universalism of thought, with which the philosophers and the scientists were always concerned, has now become a grave practical problem. I would like to state it as simply as possible, since it is a very complex thing. In brief, Heidegger links up the historicist insight with an insight into the essential defect of all previous philosophy, of all philosophy of Greek origin. There was fundamentally something narrow about the traditional view which implied that history is philosophically irrelevant. Now this enlargement is somehow connected in Heidegger's view with the need today to start an intellectual meeting with the Far East. I mean not Mao, but with the Chinese tradition.[28] And of course not with those people who run around in America and say that what Confucius said is what Thomas Jefferson said. Not these, but the people who really understand that tradition and know that this is nonsense.

Now that a dialogue between Westerners of great depth and thoughtfulness with Easterners of the same character could contribute to enlarge, to free the West from its peculiar defects—on a very low level, that is suggested by Northrop, of whom many of you—but there is no comparison between the two, I must emphasize that.[29] And now here is the interesting point. You could say that then you reach here at the end a truly universal understanding, where Westerners and Easterners see the same thing in the same manner. But here is the point: the difference in the dialogue between the Westerner and the Easterner—there is an understanding, they understand each other, but in a way they remain of course the same. Each is enlarged: the Westerner is enlarged by the

Easterner, the Easterner is enlarged by the Westerner, but the starting point, that the one is a Westerner, the other is an Easterner, remains. In other words, the universal regarding which they agree still looks different from the two different points of view. Do you see that? That is, I think, the most extreme attempt of which I am aware of trying to reconcile historicism with this universalism, without which human thought is not possible.

STUDENT: It is true that Hobbes's state and Plato's state would not be the same thing, yet it seems as though they had contradictory notions not only of what the state was, but what people were, what human nature is? And those surely—human nature was not fundamentally different necessarily, but their understanding was.

LS: Yes, but that's the point.

SAME STUDENT: How would Collingwood get around that, or explain that problem? I mean, is man fundamentally—does he seek his own self-preservation?

LS: No, no, no. That is much too superficial from Collingwood's point of view. Man is a being which is essentially historical. Man has always, as he puts it, a determinate nature. You don't find man nude, so to speak, man without having interpreted himself and the world. Proof: language. On every stage which we find, man has a language, and this language means a complete interpretation, on whichever level, of human life and the whole. Behind that you cannot go. You cannot speak of human nature, the naked human nature, so to speak; you can never find it. That is radically inaccessible, and therefore all general science of man, like biology or psychology, would remain below the level of this whole problem, because the argument would be that biology and psychology always rest themselves on premises which they cannot substantiate and which are somehow dependent on what Collingwood calls the absolute presuppositions regarding which the question of truth and untruth cannot be raised. Yes, Mr. . . . ?

STUDENT: As I understand Heidegger's attempt, that would seem to me to be only of practical, in other words, not philosophical relevance, unless you conceive of that reconciliation, enlargement, between East and West as the absolute moment that becomes the whole, what has been missing in the tradition.

LS: No, it is of course of theoretical importance, because the Westerners learn something which they do not know from their own tradition, just as the Easterners learn something in their dialogue which they do not know from their tradition. And the sentences, so to say, which Heidegger has devoted to this subject go easily on a single page. He only alludes to that, but I believe that is very important for the horizon in which he thinks. The key point is this: under no conditions a return to past ways of thinking; that's reactionary. That is so in Heidegger, as well as in people much lower than he is. In former times, sometimes people had the view (it was very common in the West) that there is a Greek way of thinking, which is deficient and must be supplemented by the biblical way of thinking, which is also in a way "East," Palestine being situated in Asia. But this is out, for Heidegger. In this respect he simply follows Nietzsche: Christianity is not acceptable to him in any way. And he seeks, for this supplement to the West, not even in India, but in the Far East. No reasonings, only allusions to these things are given, but I think what interested me only was this peculiar universalism. I mean, on the level of positivism, universalism is no problem. Proof: Chinese who are biologists, mathematicians, and so on, as any Westerner. Truth, science, is essentially universal. But this becomes a problem when one reflects about the fact that modern science, while being accessible to every human being of certain gifts, is of Western origin and somehow dependent on absolute presuppositions of Western origin. I mean the thing which people bring out about Parisian nominalism, and other things as the basis of modern science, and there are lots of things, rightly or wrongly,[30] and therefore this will not do. Or this understanding of engineers all over the globe, this doesn't go to the fundamental human questions. Nor is it possible, according to this kind of people, that there is a universal morality, because if you look at the moralities, in a crude way they might agree—you have to behave decently and in more or less gentlemanly manner, and so they agree on the whole—but when you come to more subtle questions or more detailed questions, you get a great variety of answers. And this leads first to the doubt of any possible universal morality, and yet ultimately the need, not only the practical but in the first place the theoretical need, of universalism asserts itself. Very simply, the historicist thesis is a universal thesis. No one can run away from that. Colloquially, one says we cannot run away from reason, and the simple proof of this is that in the end we cannot run away from making universal assertions. And even if we supply them with some question marks and so on, that doesn't affect the fundamental situation. Good.

Now I will leave it at that, and would like to say how I intend to go on. After having considered positivism and historicism, the two prevailing ways of thinking in the West today, and furthermore the fact that both are incompatible with political philosophy, with the idea of political philosophy, I have to raise the question whether there is not some common ground between political philosophy and the views now prevailing. And the answer is: There is one. It is the history of political philosophy. This is not denied by any serious man, that the history of political philosophy is possible and necessary, however impossible political philosophy itself may be. And we will start on this basis, on an irenic basis, and forget about . . .

II

Why Studying the
History of Political
Philosophy Is
Necessary Today

8 On the Difference between the Ancients and the Moderns

LEO STRAUSS: At the beginning of this course I said I would try to make visible to you the air which we all breathe whether we know it or not, and I believe I did that by presenting to you the issue of positivism on the one hand, and historicism on the other. This was necessary because political philosophy as the quest for *the* just or *the* good society has become incredible in our age owing to positivism and historicism. I cannot repeat, naturally, what I said in these seven long sessions. Positivism leads to the contempt or neglect of the political philosophies of the past. Historicism, on the other hand, must cultivate the history of political philosophy, although it can no longer recognize the possibility of political philosophy proper.

Yet closer inspection shows that even positivism cannot leave it at that contempt if it wants to fulfill its self-imposed duty. For the study of human societies, political societies, cannot limit itself to the study of institutions, etc. It must also take into consideration the ideologies, and within this context it is compelled to discuss the political philosophies of the past. To take a simple example, which I believe I have used before: in order to understand the United States Constitution as it is now, one must of course understand it as it was understood by its framers, the original framers. And if one tries to do that, one is driven back in the first place to Montesquieu, the theoretical authority for Hamilton and Madison, and Montesquieu himself does not reveal his full message if we do not contrast his teaching with that of certain ancient thinkers, among them the historian Polybius. More generally stated, every attempt at rational knowledge, philosophic or scientific, consists in replacing opinions by knowledge. This cannot be conscientiously done if one does not first know the opinions from which one starts. But these opinions are only partly our opinions. Their most important part, or their largest part at least, is inherited. What we regard as our opinions consists to a considerable extent of the sediments of past discussions, discussions which were conscious, which were the focus of attention in earlier centuries, and now we live on their results; hence the nonhistorical concern with the clarification of our opinions insensibly shifts into historical studies. And to that extent, historicism is right in the assertion that philosophic or scientific questions cannot be separated from the historical questions, or that a fusion of philosophy and history is indispensable.

Historicism is superior to positivism, owing to this awareness. In fairness to the founder of positivism, Comte, one must say that Comte was perfectly clear on this point. According to Comte, one cannot make clear what the scientific spirit is, except by means of a history of the human mind. One must see the earlier alternatives, the theological and the metaphysical mind, if one wants to see the scientific mind in its peculiarity and the superiority of the scientific spirit to the spirit of theology and metaphysics. There is an external sign of the fact that this need for historical studies is felt more and more within science. I have not made any statistical studies, but from some facts which have come to my attention it seems that the interest in the history of science, i.e., of modern science, is now much greater than it was, say, fifty years ago. That a physicist of the rank of Einstein took the trouble of writing a history of physics is, I think, one of these straws in the wind.

Now regarding historicism, we have seen that, according to it, the fundamental fact is a change in the absolute presuppositions. To use the term coined by Collingwood, we can say it's a change in the categories. Change cannot be explained; that is the reason why it is a fundamental fact. For any explanation means the use of categories, of specific categories, and the validity of these categories is exactly the problem on the basis of historicism. You remember what I quoted to you from Nagel about the logically arbitrary and historically contingent character of the principle of causality as understood by modern science. Marxism, for instance, believes it is able to explain the change of categories, of the principles of understanding and action, by tracing them to the relations of production, ultimately. But the question is whether the assumption of the primacy, of the fundamental character, of the relations of production is not itself historically relative, i.e., plausible under the conditions of the nineteenth and twentieth centuries but not simply true. The difficulty regarding historicism is this: that despite the fact that the change of absolute presuppositions is not a rational process, a progress from lesser to greater rationality, yet *our* absolute presuppositions, which include and which consist in the historical awareness, are of course said to be superior to all earlier thought. Now that superiority is identical with the discovery of the historical character of all human thought or, as people say, with the experience of history as history, or of historicity. This experience, whatever that may mean, is based somehow on historical evidence, and here we see again the fusion of philosophy and history. Historicism cannot clarify itself except through clarifying the position which it replaces: the nonhistoricist philosophy.

At any rate, there exists agreement today as to the necessity of the history of political philosophy, on the basis of the belief in the impossibility of political philosophy proper. In order to be reasonable, moderate, not extremist, or however you would like to call it, it is safest to begin therefore with the history of political philosophy, a subject the legitimacy of which is not denied by anyone today except by people who are very obviously lacking in simple coherence of thought. But still there will be one difference between the way we—"we" is not *pluralis maiestatis*, but I mean "I and some people who think like me"—we, in contradistinction to the positivists and historicists, approach the history of philosophy while we are open to the possibility that political philosophy as such is not impossible. And so I believe that this approach is less prejudiced, more open-minded than the positivist and the historicist approaches.

Now let us proceed in an orderly manner. We turn to the history of political philosophy, to the *whole* history of political philosophy, in principle at least. The first thing you have to do in such an enterprise is to divide it into periods; otherwise, how can we find our bearings in this infinite mass of material? The initial division into periods must not be arbitrary. How can we make it nonarbitrary? I would suggest: if we do not rely on our own poor judgment but follow the views, the consciousness, of the actors—in this case, of the great political philosophers. Now if we turn to them, we learn, as good children do, that we have first to be docile and to listen to our betters, and later on we of course may also criticize them.

Now we learn from Cicero that the founder of political philosophy was Socrates. Socrates was the one, according to Cicero, who brought philosophy down from heaven, brought it down to earth and introduced it into the cities and houses of men, and compelled it to think about good and bad and so on.[1] So the whole story of political philosophy seems to begin with Socrates. But here we are in an embarrassing situation, because Socrates did not write. The only things which he did write, as far as our knowledge goes, were two letters. When he held a discussion about justice and injustice, he drew up a list for the discussion, and wrote out,

in Greek letters of course [LS writes on the blackboard], justice and injustice. Then he asked the interlocutor to enumerate the points. But at
any rate, Socrates did not write books, so the oldest books available are
those by Plato, Socrates's direct pupil, and by Aristotle, Plato's pupil. After Aristotle's time, almost within his lifetime, a new school emerged, because Plato founded a school, the Academy, whereas Aristotle founded a
school called the Lyceum. And the third, later school is the so-called Stoic
school. Here we know nothing: we have only fragments, and we have to
rely chiefly on Cicero, who gives us coherent presentations, if very summary presentations, of the Stoic moral-political doctrine.

Now all these developments from Socrates to the Stoics, this I propose
to call classical political philosophy. By this I do not wish to minimize the
differences between Plato, Aristotle, and the Stoics, but they have something fundamentally in common: they all build on a foundation laid by
Socrates. This classical political philosophy is the only political philosophy prior to the modern age. As for medieval political philosophy, we
must distinguish within it between political theology, a political teaching
based on revelation (which as such does not fall within the province of
political philosophy), and political philosophy proper. Now the political
philosophy proper of the Middle Ages is fundamentally based on classical political philosophy, especially Aristotle. One of the boldest medieval
thinkers—Dante, in his *Monarchy*—speaks of the absolute novelty of his
enterprise in that work. Yet one has only to begin to read it to see that it
is based on Aristotle. Aristotle is *the* philosopher for Dante. And however
original the proposal made in the *Monarchy* may be, the foundations are
Aristotelian.

At a certain moment a break occurred. Again, we do not trust our
own impression but look around and listen to these voices of the men of
the past, who claimed to have done away completely with this political
philosophy founded by Socrates, root and branch. And the loudest and
clearest voice—there cannot be the slightest doubt about that—is that
of Thomas Hobbes, and so until further notice we will assume that *the*
break with classical political philosophy occurred in the work of Hobbes.
And as I will already say now, closer study would show that the break
had occurred prior to Hobbes, in the work of Machiavelli, but in Machiavelli the claim to a radical break is by far not as audible and powerful as in Hobbes. So we have then this very simple division from which
we start: classical political philosophy or premodern political philosophy,
and modern political philosophy. And the question which concerns us,

since we are not merely historians, we cannot afford to be merely historians, this question is for us a quarrel: Which of the two is right? And this is a quarrel of the ancients and the moderns: *la querelle des anciens et des modernes*, as it was called in the seventeenth century. At that time the famous quarrel was the quarrel about whether, say, Dryden or Corneille were as good dramatists as Sophocles and Euripides, or Molière as good a comedian as Aristophanes. In other words, it appears to be primarily a literary question, but it is much more than that. The fundamental quarrel was that between modern philosophy, which includes modern natural science, and classical philosophy and classical science. The most famous document in the English language of that quarrel is Swift's *Battle of the Books*, and for those who read more carefully, Swift's *Gulliver's Travels*. But this I cannot go into now.

Now Hobbes questions all preceding political philosophy. They all were wrong, and worse than wrong: sophists. In the present-day textbook version, which is of course not entirely unreasonable (it is very hard to say something which is entirely unreasonable) but nevertheless it is misleading: there was another tradition stemming from the sophists, via the Epicureans and so on. This thing didn't exist for Hobbes: that was not political philosophy; that was a teaching which destroyed civil society and not one which tried to show a way toward the good or just civil society, let alone was political philosophy in Hobbes's sense. Now Hobbes gives a long list in various places of these men, and Socrates, Plato, Aristotle, and Cicero are of course the greatest names. He doesn't say anything about the Scholastics, because he wrote in a Protestant country, and you can say the Reformation had taken away this problem from Hobbes, although that's not quite true because Richard Hooker was also an Anglican, and he made a great use of Thomas Aquinas. And he[2] has a discussion of Cardinal Bellarmine, but in a very special context, the context of ecclesiastical power, where he has to take issue with the claim of the Catholic Church as stated by Bellarmine, that all ecclesiastical power is concentrated in the hands of the pope.

Now what is wrong with these people: Socrates, Plato, Aristotle, and so on? Hobbes says they are teachers of anarchy, anarchists—a very strange assertion, it seems, Aristotle as anarchist. What does Hobbes mean by that? They laid the foundation for criticizing their governments. From the point of view of Socrates, Plato and Aristotle, and Cicero, and so on, it is legitimate to criticize the governments if they misbehave, which does not necessarily mean that they justify rebellion, but they made it possible, theoretically, to criticize their governments. Think only of the concept of tyrant, and you have it very clear. In other words, they laid the foundation for a possible appeal from the law laid down by government, the positive law, to *natural law*. That is historically correct. But Hobbes says, opposing them, that the command of natural law is to obey the positive law; therefore there is no possibility of appealing from the positive law to the natural law. And in the particular form which Hobbes gave this thought, it means (and this is in a way implied in what I said): government must be absolute, in order to be government. And an absolute government is as such uncriticizable. Now this criticism of Hobbes's is crude criticism, but not groundless criticism, hence an important implication: that Hobbes to a considerable extent agrees with the tradition which he attacks, namely, like the tradition, he recognizes natural law. For how could he otherwise say *the* command of natural law is to obey the positive law? So the difference between Hobbes and the tradition comes first to sight as a difference within the context of natural law. Now what is that difference? In the epistle dedicatory of his *Elements of Law Natural and Politic*, Hobbes says: "From the two principal parts of our nature, reason and passion, have proceeded two kinds of learning, mathematical and dogmatical." It is obvious that mathematics comes from reason and dogmatical from passion.

> The former is free from controversies and dispute, because it consists in comparing figures and motion only, in which things truth and the interests of men, oppose not each other. But in the later, in dogmatical learning,[3] there is nothing not disputable, because it compares men and meddles with their right and profit: in which, as oft as reason is against the man,[4] so oft will a man be against reason. And from hence it cometh that they that have written of justice and policy in general, i.e., the political philosophers,[5] do all invade each other and themselves with contradiction. [In other words, there doesn't exist any political philosophy worthy of the name.—LS] To reduce this doctrine to the rules and infallibility of reason, there is no way but first to put such principles down for a foundation as passion, not mistrusting, may not seek to displace; and afterward, to build thereon the truth of cases in the law of nature, which hitherto have been built in the air, by degrees, till the whole be inexpugnable.[6]

So what is the difference? Traditional doctrine, political philosophy, was under the spell of passion and therefore not rational. As they say today, it was ideological. But there was nevertheless a reason which is slightly different: the foundations were wrongly laid because the principles laid down by Socrates and his successors were distrusted by passion. And Hobbes wants to reform, to revolutionize, natural law doctrine, and thus make it a scientific doctrine for the first time by laying down foundations which are agreeable to passion, in harmony with passion. Natural law must be in harmony with the passions, not against them. That is the first, of course very insufficient, statement. Hobbes will be compelled to make a distinction between passions with which one must be in harmony and passions which must be fought; that is the second step. But the first point is that the foundation must be a passion. That is the first point I would like just to read to you.

Now let me read to you another statement in the same work, *Elements of Law*, part 2, chapter 9, the heading of section 8, where he speaks of the duties of government. "The institution of youth in true morality and politics necessary for keeping the subjects in peace."

The subjects must be taught true morality. This is very traditional. But these *Elements of Law*, from which I quoted, are Hobbes's earliest work, which on the whole is the most traditional version. Let us see how he speaks in a later work, *Of the Citizen*, how he calls it there. In *Of the Citizen*, chapter 13, section 9, the heading: "The correct institution of the citizens[7] in political doctrine is necessary for the preservation of peace." Here he does not speak anymore of true morality. Shortly after him a very great political thinker, of whom you will all have heard, John Locke, said: "However strange it may seem, the lawmaker hath nothing to do with moral virtues and vices," but only with security of life and limb and property.[8] Now this is clearly implied already in Hobbes, and even stated to some extent: the government is concerned with nothing but the preservation of peace. Accordingly, moral virtue in Hobbes's sense is nothing but the human habits conducive to peace: peaceableness and all its implications. Virtues which have no direct relation to peace, such as courage, intelligence, wisdom, even temperance, are not strictly speaking moral virtues from Hobbes's point of view. Now if we take these two points I mentioned together, building on the passions and narrowing down the sphere of moral virtue so that moral virtue is nothing but the habits conducive to peace, we can say that what Hobbes achieved and wished to achieve was a lowering of the standards set up by Socrates and his successors. Of course, he believed that the older standards were foolish, but still, that is exactly part of the quarrel: Were they foolish? At first glance, we see that the standards are much lower, much more pedestrian. Winston Churchill somewhere speaks of "low but solid grounds." This is a clear formulation of what was in the minds of men such as Hobbes and Locke, though Churchill didn't mean these men. "Low but solid," versus high but unsolid—building in the air, as Hobbes said.

This is a crucial part of the fundamental layer of modern political philosophy. Now why is it necessary to lower the standards, as I called it? Let us consider a few remarks of Hobbes. In *The Citizen*, chapter 1, section 2: "Of those which have written something about states, the majority presuppose or assume or postulate, that man is an animal born apt to society. The Greeks say, *zōon politikon*, the political animal, and build on that foundation the civic doctrine . . ." and so on.[9] And Hobbes tries to show that this is absurd, that man is by nature not apt for peace and peaceable living together, but rather the opposite. And he concludes this paragraph with the remark: "the origin of great and lasting societies cannot be sought in men's dutiful benevolence or friendliness," as Cicero for example said, "but only in mutual fear."[10] Man is by nature antisocial, which Hobbes identifies with asocial. As he puts it, nature dissociates man. And the fundamental error of the tradition was that it believed that nature made men by nature social. Nature is not a kind mother but a stepmother, even an enemy. This is quite obvious when you think of Hobbes's famous doctrine of the state of nature. Everyone has heard these beautiful four adjectives: the state of nature is characterized by the fact that man's life is solitary, nasty, brutish, and short. This is the condition in which nature has placed us. All blessings of life we owe to action against nature, human action against nature.

Now another point connected with that is the following one, which Hobbes states most clearly in *The Citizen*, chapter 2, paragraph 1. There he speaks about how the authors define the law of nature, and he says most people assume that the law of nature is identical with the common opinion of mankind, or at least of the wisest and most civilized nations. In other words, there is a natural understanding, a natural awareness of the principles of right and wrong, and this shows itself even in savage nations to some degree. Hobbes simply rejects this: no trust whatever in common opinion, in the common sayings of the human race. And here we must remind ourselves that Hobbes was a contemporary of and in a way a competitor with Descartes. Now Descartes began, laid the foundation for, the enterprise of modern philosophy with his famous universal doubt, his doubt of everything. Hobbes absolutely agrees with this point of Descartes, that one must begin with universal doubt: he even says, in a somewhat unfriendly, nonmagnanimous manner, that this is elementary, everyone knows that. But what is the meaning of that? There have been doubters all the time. They were called skeptics. The difference between Descartes and the skeptics is this. The skeptics drew the inference that human knowledge is not possible, and we have to live with these probabilities, with these guesses, as Mr. Popper seems to say now. But Descartes was the opposite of a skeptic. He believed that if we want to have a solid foundation for science or philosophy, we must build on a foundation which is not exposed to any possible doubt, so that the extreme skepticism is the foundation for an absolutely watertight dogmatism. In this point Hobbes is in fundamental agreement with Descartes.

Now among the arguments which Descartes uses in order to justify the universal doubt, the following is most revealing. He says there might be a very powerful evil genius who wishes to deceive us. Now this might be the situation of our intellect, the situation of man, and therefore we must think as if this were the case in order to be free even from the power of such a very powerful evil demon. And when someone says, "There is no such evil demon, that is nonsense," Descartes says that doesn't make any difference, because if you speak of natural causes (natural causes in the sense in which we now speak of it) of our perceptions and conceptions, they are as little concerned with our realizing the truth as this evil demon would be. No trust in our natural faculties: we have to find a new foundation. In some respect, Hobbes is even clearer here than Descartes. But the point which I wanted to make is that the lowering of the standards has to do with a profoundly changed posture toward nature: no trust in nature. Now if we want to understand Hobbes somewhat better, we have to consider an earlier thinker, to whom I have already referred, who stated the crucial point before Hobbes. As far as I remember, Hobbes never mentions him, and this is in itself quite interesting. You know, today it is customary that you quote or mention names, but in the past this was, in some writers at least, a very great art: whom to mention, whom to honor by mentioning, and whom not to mention. The man I mean is Machiavelli. And here *the* fundamental text regarding modern political philosophy occurs in his *Prince*, chapter 15.

It now remains to be seen what are the ways and rules for a prince as regards his subjects and friends, as distinguished from his enemies [he had discussed this before—LS]. And as I know that many have written of this,

I fear that my writing about it may be deemed presumptuous [you see, he is much more modest than Hobbes is—LS], differing as I do especially in this matter from the opinion of others. [He doesn't say "of all others."—LS] But my intention being to write something of use to those who understand, it appears to be more proper to go to the real truth of the matter than to the imagination thereof. And many [he doesn't say "all"—LS] have imagined republics and principalities which have never been seen or known to exist in reality. For how we live is so far removed from how we ought to live, that he who abandons what is done [the ordinary practice—LS] for what ought to be done, will rather learn to bring about his own ruin than his preservation. A man who wishes to make a profession of goodness in everything must necessarily come to grief among so many who are not good. Therefore it is necessary for a prince who wishes to preserve himself to learn how not to be good, and to use this knowledge and not to use it, according to the necessity of the case.[11]

In other words, the prince must use virtue *and vice*, according to the circumstances. Good action is no longer virtuous action but shrewd action. Here we have a decisive opposition of the two considerations: a political teaching which takes its bearings by how men *ought* to live, and a teaching which takes its bearings by how men *do* live. This is not the same as our present fact-value distinction, because Machiavelli's teaching is as normative as that of Plato, only the norms are very different because according to him the Platonic or other norms are based on the assumption that men are good, and he starts from the opposite assumption, that at least most men are bad—which is a very inadequate analysis, of course, but I leave it at this for the time being.

Now in the *Discourses*, book 1, chapter 46, he quotes from a Roman historian, Sallustius. And in quoting Sallustius he changes somewhat the text. And the prevalent view today is that he wrote it from memory and it has no importance. I have come to doubt of this assumption. At any rate, the passage as misquoted or amended by Machiavelli is: "All evil stems from good beginnings." All evil stems from good beginnings. Now surely the biblical view says that the beginnings were good. The relation to classical philosophy is somewhat more complicated. All evil stems from good beginnings, i.e., we must start from bad beginnings, if we want to build up a stable society. Well, this has become elementary in modern thought: the beginnings are bad, savage, preliterate, underdeveloped, and what have you. At the beginning (we can state Machiavelli's thought), there was not love, but terror. And by opposing that fundamental terror, the terror of the state of nature in Hobbes's language, men build up civil society, and they will do it better the better they know that they have to count only on themselves. Since he speaks of evil examples, I would like to remind you of what Machiavelli says about good examples. Good examples, Machiavelli says, arise from good education, and good education is a consequence of good laws, and good laws ultimately go back to good founders of societies, or legislators. But who are these model founders? Well, men like Cesare Borgia, if this name means anything to you, or the Roman emperor Septimius Severus, whom Machiavelli himself calls a criminal and a mixture of a fox and a lion.[12] So in other words, the roots of goodness, of that kind of goodness of which man is capable, are laid by people who are the very opposite of good.

Now incidentally, the passage which I read to you from the *Prince*, chapter 15, is used in Spinoza's *Political Treatise*, chapter 1. And here that is very interesting, because Machiavelli is not, according to the official cataloging, a philosopher, but Spinoza is. But Spinoza takes over this whole statement about the errors of the past and in what they consist: we have to take men as they are and take our bearings by that. Now, colloquially or vulgarly, we may say what is characteristic of men like Machiavelli and Hobbes is that they claim to oppose a realistic teaching to the idealistic teaching of the past, and I think as a provisional formulation that this is even indispensable. But we must not forget for one moment that what they tried to do was to erect on this so-called realistic basis an ideal order, so much so that Hobbes at the end of chapter 31 of the *Leviathan* compares his *Leviathan* in a certain respect to Plato's *Republic*. It has this in common with Plato's *Republic*: that it is a blueprint of a perfect society. The perfection is much lower than that aspired to by Plato, but perfection it is. According to a very common view, this modern development was an idealistic development. Carl Becker wrote a book, *The Heavenly City in the Eighteenth Century*,[13] but what is forgotten here is the difference between the heavenly city of the eighteenth century and the heavenly city of Plato and Aristotle—that the foundations of the heavenly city of the eighteenth century were lower, the foundations of the heavenly city of Plato and Aristotle were higher. Plato and Aristotle, we may say (and of course that is true of the whole tradition of these great men), wanted to delineate the character of the just society by taking their bearings by men's perfection, by the highest in them. And these modern thinkers, trying to think in low but solid terms, tried to take their bearings by the lowest, but for this very reason the most powerful, in man. The perfection of man, the highest perfection of man, is very rare, as everyone has admitted at all times; therefore you cannot count on it. But can you not find something which is very common, which you can find very powerful in every man, or almost every man? And if you build on that a civil society, then you have built upon a solid foundation.

Now this solid foundation is according to Hobbes man's urge, necessity, to preserve himself, meaning the individual's urge to preserve himself, in other words, his fear of death and more specifically, since we are speaking of social matters, his fear of violent death, of death at the hands of other men. Hobbes is not particularly interested in death due to disease or illness. (There are some very amusing documents of that.) The only violent death which interests him is that coming from the hands of other men. And Hobbes waxes poetic when he begins to speak of the fear of death and its majesty as *the* solid foundation of civil life. But speaking now wholly unpoetically, the fear of violent death is only the worst side of the desire for self-preservation. In the traditional scheme, most clearly presented in this point by Thomas Aquinas, the desire for self-preservation is of course recognized as a fundamental inclination of man. But there is another one, the inclination towards society, which occupies a higher rank; and the third and highest is the desire for knowledge of God, or desire for knowledge generally speaking. These higher stories are out: they do not play any role in Hobbes's construction of civil society. This only confirms what I said before, the lowering of the standards. The higher ones must somehow shift for themselves.

There is another implication which I can only mention here, but I think I must mention it. In the traditional doctrine, especially as presented by Thomas Aquinas, these natural inclinations of man give rise primarily to duties. I mean, it goes without saying that self-preservation is a duty, as is shown by the fact that suicide is a sin. The rights are somehow derivative from the duties. This is radically changed in Hobbes. The fundamental phenomenon is not any duty but the right to preserve myself, and any duties which come in are derivative from the fundamental right. And this we find nowhere with such clarity as in Hobbes. Here you can also see the "realistic" character of this modern doctrine. That people should do their duties, one can only hope. But that they should be concerned with their rights, and fight for them: this is a much safer, more realistic, assumption. In Edmund Burke we find very beautiful remarks about this philosophy of the rights of man, as I quote from memory:

"The catechism of the rights of man is easily learned; the conclusions are in the passions."[14] You don't have to think about it. But it would be more precise to say: the premises are in the passions, and the passion of fear of violent death.

I must say something, as a matter of fact quite a few things, about the developments after Hobbes; otherwise we will not understand the whole issue of the quarrel between the ancients and the moderns and what is its subject, its fundamental subject. I must of course limit myself to the most telling and striking facts; therefore I will not speak now of Locke but I will turn immediately to Rousseau, because Locke, however important he is—in many respects the fundamental scheme of Locke is not so different from that of Hobbes, as one would assume. The practical consequences which Locke drew from it are totally different, we can say, from the practical conclusions which Hobbes drew. But the theoretical differences are not so great. I would like now to make a pause and see whether there is any point you would like to take up at this point. It might help me to clarify it, and it might help also you to clarify your thought. Yes, Mr. Levy?

MR. LEVY: Could you just repeat once more the reasons why scientists want to know the history of science, as shown by Einstein writing that book?

LS: I said the mere fact, the brute fact, that there is today a much greater interest in the history of science. In Wisconsin there is an Institute for the History of Science. I do not know when that started. It was rather recently founded.

MR. LEVY: I just wondered what the reason for that is.

LS: I believe it has something to do with the so-called crisis of modern thought, that certain things which were indubitable and a matter of course are no longer so. Whether that is a conscious motivation in every historian of science is a different story. Yes?

STUDENT: How is it that . . .[15]

LS: . . . which would compel us to qualify his statement. There was a tendency that still exists, I believe: you know when people today who have no knowledge of earlier thought—say, they know nineteenth- and twentieth-century thought to some extent, and they read Hobbes for the first time. And that is of course all very outlandish, very medieval, and now they look at a medieval text and say: Oh, yes, that is much more medieval than one would think. In the case of Spinoza, who was also a very revolutionary thinker, a very competent and very learned man has presented him as the last of the medievals.[16] So why did these people make these mistakes? Because they didn't listen to what Hobbes and Spinoza themselves said about what they were doing.

STUDENT: I see. That's why, then, you use this standard provisionally.

LS: Yes, sure. But I must say, I believed Hobbes for quite some years until I began to understand Machiavelli, and then I saw that the fundamental step was taken by Machiavelli, with this not unimportant difference: that Machiavelli simply was uninterested in the whole issue of natural law and natural right, whereas Hobbes was interested. And therefore Hobbes as it were tried to apply Machiavelli's insight, stated in this chapter 15 of the *Prince*: let us take our bearings by how men live and not by how they ought to live. Hobbes tried to apply this Machiavellian insight to natural law. That is the peculiarity of Hobbes. But the first decisive step was taken by Machiavelli, but that took some time. I could explain, but that would be better discussed in a seminar on Machiavelli than here. Good.

Now then I will turn to Rousseau, because in Rousseau this kind of political philosophy, which Hobbes had started, reached its first crisis. Rousseau's argument is in a way very simple. Hobbes had said: man is by nature asocial, presocial. And yet Hobbes took it for granted that these presocial men, who led this life that was solitary, nasty, brutish, and short, were able to enter civil society by making the social contract with one another. Rousseau as it were says to Hobbes: Look, if man is by nature presocial, then he is by nature prerational. He cannot have reason if he doesn't use language, and these people in the state of nature, each in his foxhole and with no communication with the others, of course would not have a common language. They might have common sounds, but not a common language. Therefore, Rousseau takes this great step of questioning, what Hobbes did not do, the traditional definition of man as a rational animal. Rationality is an acquisition of man, it does not belong to his nature, and he suggests provisionally but nevertheless importantly that the true definition of man is that man is a being endowed with *freedom*, as distinguished from rationality. We will see later on that this was a very important and powerful change. Now, but if the state of nature is a state in which men are presocial and prerational—that means in which man is a stupid animal, as Rousseau himself says—how can one gain a standard for human conduct by looking at man in the state of nature? That seems to be absurd.

Furthermore, according to Hobbes, man has no natural end. That was understood in the whole tradition, in spite of certain differences of opinion: that man has a natural end, or rather a variety of ends, which, however, lead up to one highest end or highest good. Now I will read to you what Hobbes has to say about this matter. *Leviathan*, chapter 11, "Of the Difference of Manners": "By manners, I mean not here decency of behavior, as how one man should salute another, or how a man should wash his mouth, or [laughter] pick his teeth before company, and such other points of the small morals; but those qualities of mankind that concern their living together in peace and unity."

In other words, I think Hobbes underestimates the importance of decent behavior for men living together in peace and unity. I don't want to— you easily know the examples of what men could do in company which would make their company unbearable. [Laughter]

> To which end we are to consider that the felicity of this life consists not in the repose of the mind satisfied. For there is no such *finis ultimus* (utmost aim), nor *summum bonum* (greatest good), as is spoken of in the books of the old moral philosophers. [This keystone of the whole tradition: out.—LS] Nor can a man any more live whose desires are at an end, than he whose senses and imagination are at a stand. Felicity is a continual progress of the desire from one object to another, the attaining of the former being still but the way to the latter . . . So that, in the first place, I put for a general inclination of all mankind, a perpetual and restless desire of power after power, that ceases only in death.[17]

I think we can leave it at that. There is no highest good, there is nothing in which men's desire could find repose, could come to an end. But this desire for power after power is of course infinite, and only externally cut off by death. But we must have some fixed point to take our bearings. Since this cannot be found in the end of man, Hobbes finds it in the beginning, by which I do not mean a baby now born, but men at the beginning, man in the state of nature. This beginning is in a way the end, because by being so abysmally bad, it points away from itself to civil society. In a negative way, surely it is an end.

Now Rousseau goes much beyond this than Hobbes in this direction, for, as I said, in Hobbes the state of nature points toward civil society, but not in Rousseau. According to Rousseau, the state of nature is good, and hence why should any sane individual wish to leave it? On the contrary, since the state of nature is good and we do no longer live in the state of nature, the formula would rather be "Let us return to the state of nature," which formula is used by Rousseau, and it needs a long commentary, but it is not entirely wrong. Incidentally, when Rousseau treats childhood with unusual respect in his pedagogical work the *Emile*, that has also to do with the questioning of teleology. From the traditional point of view, childhood is the preparation for adulthood: childhood is teleologically ordered toward adulthood. But if there is no teleology, childhood is as perfect as adulthood, and therefore childhood has a value for itself and not merely as a preparation.

Now the state of nature in Rousseau undergoes a variety of modifications of a fundamentally accidental character, and with the consequence that the state of nature becomes eventually like Hobbes's state of nature and therefore must be abandoned. To that extent he rejoins Hobbes in this point. Yet in spite of that, the state of nature remains the standard in Rousseau, since just civil society comes as close to the state of nature as civil society possibly can. For what is the peculiarity of the state of nature? That man is not subject to any authority, that he is free in this sense. Now Rousseau's formula is that by entering civil society, man must remain as free as he was theretofore, i.e., in the state of nature.

Now let us consider this somewhat more closely to understand it better. The construction of Hobbes was this. Man has by nature the right to self-preservation; therefore he must have the right to the means of self-preservation, say, a stick, or a gun or whatever, or, for that matter, also food—which was less important for Hobbes than it was for Locke; it's one of the great differences between the two men. Where Locke also is the more realistic one, as you will see—what is the use of all the sticks in the world or guns in the world if you don't have food and water? This is, then, the key question in this argument: means may be apt or inapt, and a reasonable man would say that man, if he has a right to the means of self-preservation, has of course only a right to apt means of self-preservation. But here judgment comes in: some people are good judges and others are bad. Who is going to judge of the means of self-preservation? The Hobbesian answer: everyone must be the judge, and not merely the wise man. And the reasoning can be stated very simply as follows: the wise man has better judgment, but he has much less interest in the self-preservation of the fool than the fool himself; therefore let the fool be the judge. Everyone is the judge.

Now Rousseau, starting from this, makes this crucial step beyond Hobbes and Locke: this right of the judgment of self-preservation must be preserved *within* civil society, whereas Hobbes and Locke had said or implied that this right to judge ceases in the moment men enter civil society. Now what are these judgments on the means of self-preservation in civil society? What is their popular name? Laws. Therefore, according to Rousseau, justice demands that in civil society everyone subject to the law must have had a say in the making of the law. That is a strictly necessary consequence. This may be very just; but still, if the majority are fools, as Rousseau would admit (and would even emphasize), what kind of laws will we get, if everyone has the same say as everyone else? Mind you, there is no representative or parliamentarian democracy here, but direct democracy. Direct democracy. Rousseau must therefore say that if this provision is accepted, the justice or reasonableness of the positive laws is guaranteed. If no one is subject to the law who did not have a say in the making of the law, then the justice or reasonableness of the laws is guaranteed. In his terms, the general will, the will of the legislator, cannot err. Or, the sovereign is always what he ought to be. A sovereign in the strict sense can only be a community consisting of free and equal members; otherwise it wouldn't be a sovereign but a tyrant, according to Rousseau. Now if this is so, if the general will cannot err, it follows that there is no possibility nor need for ever appealing from the positive law to the natural, obviously. I mean, if you have a mechanism which produces invariably just and wise laws, you don't have to appeal from these laws ever to a higher law.

A society constructed according to natural law never has to appeal to natural law; that is what Rousseau wants to say. And this of course gives a high degree of legal clarity: the positive law is unquestionable from any consideration of justice. Here we see again, in a different way, what I called the "realism," in quotation marks: the coincidence of the Is and the Ought. The sovereign is always what he ought to be, which when you hear it first sounds sheer insanity. According to the traditional view, men's desire must be subject to a vertical limitation. [LS writes on the blackboard.] Here is man's desire, and then there comes a limitation from above, either from the divine will or from man's perfection—it does not make any difference. What Rousseau, and by implication Hobbes and Locke, had in mind is that this is out. How did Machiavelli put it? This leads to the notion of imaginary principalities and imaginary commonwealths. For Machiavelli, the kingdom of God would of course also be an imaginary kingdom. The only limitation which we can trust is the horizontal one: the will of others. The will of others. They will react and prevent us from [general laughter]—I am reduced to the status of certain animals. [LS apparently refers to his gesticulation; further laughter.] In other words, the vertical limitation is only an Ought and as powerless as Oughts are. The vertical[18] limitation, consisting in man's desire limited by the desires of his fellows, this is in principle sensible. But of course this can also lead in itself to chaos: my desires are thwarted by those of others, and I thwart those of others, etc. How can this be done rationally? That is Rousseau's question. Or, and this is the same question, only another formulation: Why is the general will beyond error? The answer of Rousseau is this: by generalization. But I have to explain it. I have desires, all kinds of silly, foolish, irrational desires, and the same is true of my fellows. But then we introduce a mechanism. We say: The ultimate judgment of which desires are legitimate and which are illegitimate depends on the law, the making of which will depend on your vote as much as on that of anybody else. Simple example: I enter the assembly, the town meeting, with the irrational desire not to pay any taxes. I can't stand up and say: I don't want to pay no taxes. [Laughter] I have to say: There ought to be a law that no one should pay any taxes. In other words, in the moment I conceive of my desire in terms of a law, in the moment I express my desire in the terms of a law, I become already more reasonable, to say the least, than I was before. So the generalization of my particular foolish, vicious will is almost the fully sufficient remedy for my unreasonability.

You see here again, in this concrete example, I do not hold my desire against a natural law, an unwritten eternal law. What is sufficient to bring about justice, rationality, is the mere form—generality—which is of course rationality. Reason always speaks in general or universal terms. In other words, the rational order, the order of the just society, is not the order according to nature in any sense. The natural order as Rousseau understands it is radically conventional, counterrational. Counterrational. By nature, men are unequal according to Rousseau, but the social contract replaces the natural inequality by conventional equality, and that is justice. You remember what I said before about certain changes regarding the concept of nature. Keep this in mind; I will later bring it together.

Now if this is so, if my will, my desire becomes rational by taking on the form of a law, then I may say that by obeying the law, everyone obeys himself. He obeys the law which he has imposed upon himself. He is free because he does not obey any other man. Freedom, obeying the law which one has imposed on oneself, is self-determination. There is no reference to something outside of man in any manner or form. But there is a serious difficulty here which I would like to present to you in Rousseau's own words. *The Social Contract*, book 1, chapter 8.

The transition from the state of nature to the state of civil society produces in man a most remarkable change. It substitutes in his conduct justice for instinct, and gives to his actions the morality which they previously lacked. [In the state of nature, there was no morality.—LS] Only at that moment does the voice of duty replace the physical impulse, and right replace appetite. And hence man, who hitherto had been only self-regarding, sees himself compelled to act on other principles, and to consult his reason before listening to his inclinations.

So the state of civil society is a state of reason, as Hobbes has said before.

Although he deprives himself in this state of many advantages which he had from nature [against Hobbes—LS] he regains therein so great ones. His faculties exercise themselves and develop themselves. His ideas extend, his sentiments become ennobled, his whole soul rises to such a point that if the misuses of that noble condition did not degrade man often beyond that state which he left, he would bless unceasingly the moment which liberated him from it forever, and which from a stupid and narrow animal, made him an intelligent being and a man. [A human being: in other words, presocial man, prepolitical man, is not truly a man.—LS]

Let us reduce this whole balance to terms easy to compare. What man loses by the social contract is his natural freedom, and an unlimited right to everything which tempts him and on which he can lay his hands. What he gains is civil freedom, and the property, the true ownership, of everything he possesses. In order not to deceive oneself in these points, one must well distinguish the natural liberty which has no limits except the forces of the individual from the civil liberty which is limited by the general will [i.e., by law—LS].

One could add to the acquisitions of the civil state a second point: moral liberty, which alone makes man truly master of himself. [Moral liberty is not civil liberty; it is more than civil liberty.—LS] For the impulse of appetite alone is slavery; and the obedience to the law which one has prescribed to oneself is liberty. But I have already said enough on this point, and the philosophic sense of the word liberty is here not my subject.[19]

Well, the difficulty here is this. Moral liberty is something very radically different from civil liberty. Civil liberty can be understood fundamentally in Hobbesian terms as derivative from self-preservation. Can this be done regarding moral liberty? In an important part of his *Emile*, the profession of faith of the Savoyard vicar, Rousseau has presented this issue of moral liberty in terms of a traditional spiritualistic, or dualistic, metaphysics, in other words, God and the soul as a substance different or radically distinguished from body or matter. The question concerns the status of this metaphysics. According to Rousseau himself, that metaphysics is exposed to insoluble objections. What is the tenable basis of moral freedom if it cannot be found in traditional dualistic metaphysics? This is the question. Rousseau has not developed this theme sufficiently, and one reason, and perhaps the decisive reason, is this: because Rousseau saw a moral alternative, if we may say so, to moral liberty, to the life of duty or of virtue. And this he called goodness. Goodness, as he understands it, is strictly natural, i.e., not acquired by human effort, and something fundamentally different from virtue and duty. To elaborate that would take an infinite time.

By virtue of his doctrine of goodness, which one can call a very sentimental doctrine—this kind of goodness which is perfectly compatible with doing rather terrible things, as Rousseau himself did; I mean, that he sent his children away to an orphanage was surely not a virtuous action, as he admitted, but it was perfectly compatible with his goodness, which gives you an idea of how far this goodness can lead. But however this may be, Rousseau's concern with this difference between goodness and virtue is the explanation, I believe, why he did not elaborate, or try to find a new basis for, moral liberty as distinguished from civil liberty, and a basis different from traditional metaphysics. The man who did this, on the basis of Rousseau, was Kant. And we cannot understand the whole issue if we do not consider, briefly at least, Kant's solution to that problem.

I see it is now time. I would like to mention only one point regarding Rousseau, which may explain the situation somewhat better. Hobbes had started from self-preservation, preservation of the existence of each, as *the* fundamental thing. Again, Rousseau thinks here more deeply than Hobbes does on the Hobbesian basis. He raises this question: Must you not presuppose that life or existence is good if you attach to self-preservation, to preservation of life, the importance which you do attach to it? How do you know that life, sheer life, mere life, mere existence, is good? Rousseau says, "I know it," and he refers to something which he calls the sentiment of existence, in which man becomes aware, senses directly, the goodness of life as life. It is possible that this is the first reference to the whole question of existence which is now in the center of discussion. At any rate, to remain with the key to the issue of greatest concern to us, we shall follow up next time the problem of Rousseau by seeing in a very provisional manner how Kant solved Rousseau's problem, and put therewith moral and political philosophy on an entirely new basis, and the net result—I think that I should not keep you in wholly unnecessary tension—the key point which I am trying to make is this. The result of Kant's work is that from Kant on, the moral law is no longer a natural law, what it still was up to Kant. Nature has nothing whatever to do with morality—an exaggerated formula, but a sufficient one. To live according to nature, which was the formula of the ancients, becomes a meaningless phrase. The depreciation of nature, which is already clearly visible in Hobbes, as seen in the very notion of the state of nature as used by him, becomes decisive for modern thinking, and this is the substantive reason why political philosophy as originally understood by the classics has become incredible. So in other words, after I have presented some important stages of modern thought, we are somewhat better prepared for understanding the beginning of classical political philosophy.

III

The Origins of
Political Philosophy

9 *Physis* and *Nomos*

LEO STRAUSS: Now I led up to the point that the possibility of political philosophy is today controversial, but on the other hand the possibility and necessity of the history of political philosophy is generally admitted. I showed then that the primary theme of the history of political philosophy is the quarrel between the ancients and moderns. This issue, the quarrel, is necessarily seen to begin with from the modern point of view, for the ancients could not possibly know of the quarrel which the moderns would raise. In the first stage, indicated by the names of Hobbes and Machiavelli in particular, we find what we provisionally and colloquially call realism opposing itself to the imagined, imaginary principalities and republics of the classics. We might say that men like Hobbes and Machiavelli, and many in alliance with them, oppose the utopianism of the classics. The term utopia was coined in 1516 by Sir Thomas More in his *Utopia*, and More is on the side of the classics. That was an act of irony, to speak of the utopia, but not an act of rebellion against the classical tradition. The meaning of that attack was that the classics aimed too high, ultimately because they had an unfounded trust in human nature and in nature in general. It suffices to remind you again of Hobbes's expression, "the state of nature," the state in which nature put man—a most undesirable state. In his *Discourse on the Origin and the Foundation of Inequality among Men*, Rousseau uses as a motto a statement from Aristotle's *Politics*: "What is natural must be viewed not in depraved things, but in those which are according to nature." Now he quotes it in Latin translation. One could as well have said in Latin: not in depraved things, but in those which are in their natural state, in *status naturalis*, the state of nature. This is the old meaning of the state of nature according to which the state of nature is the state of health, of perfection. Even in Hobbes, "state of nature" has sometimes this meaning, but this is of course the old meaning, not the meaning peculiar to Hobbes and also to Rousseau. Let us keep this in mind. Ultimately, at the root of the whole dissent we find a radical change regarding nature.

I spoke last time especially of Rousseau's critique of Hobbes. In this critique, the project of Hobbes and Locke and other men of that generation experienced its first crisis. Rousseau argues that precisely if the state of nature is presocial or asocial, as Hobbes had asserted, it must be prerational. Hence man in the state of nature, strictly understood, must have been not yet a true human being, but a stupid animal. Here the question arises immediately: How can the state of nature any longer be used as a standard, if the state of nature is subhuman? The state of nature was a kind of standard for Hobbes (for Locke too), but negatively: since it was so terrible—nasty, brutish, and short—let's get out of it as fast as we can. It pointed away from itself to the state of civil society. Furthermore, according to Rousseau, the just or healthy society no longer needs or permits an appeal from the positive law to the natural law. That's another sign of the depreciation of nature: the appeal to the natural law is no longer possible or necessary. But still we want to have just positive laws, not unjust ones. Now the justice of the positive laws is guaranteed according to Rousseau by the mere form of law: the law is made by the citizen-body; everyone subject to the law must have had his say in the making of the law, and the law pronounces only on general subjects. This guarantees the justice of the positive laws. So the form of law, the mere fact that it is general, is sufficient: you do not have to have recourse to human nature and to a natural law.

But there remains a great obscurity in Rousseau regarding the relation between political liberty and moral liberty, or between law and morality in general. Morality proper, according to Rousseau's presentation, is based on a dualistic metaphysics, a metaphysics which distinguishes between corporeal and incorporeal substances, the latter being God and the souls. But that dualistic metaphysics, according to Rousseau, is exposed to insoluble objections. Now these difficulties, which Rousseau encountered but did not solve, were solved by Kant. Kant is the greatest pupil of Rousseau. There is an autobiographic diary utterance of Kant to the effect that it was Rousseau who brought him into the right shape—a statement which he has not made about any other man. There is a very famous statement of Kant about what he owed to Hume: Hume awakened him from the dogmatic slumber, Kant said, but this is not comparable in breadth to what Kant says about what he owed to Rousseau.[1] Now we have therefore to turn to Kant and mention the bare minimum without which we cannot understand anything.

Now according to Kant, morality cannot be based on this dualistic metaphysics, which according to Rousseau is exposed to insoluble objections. God and the soul are unknowable. This does not mean that the opposite view, say, materialism, the view that everything that is is corporeal, is true. Materialism, or the view underlying modern physics, has as its premise the principle of causality. And this principle of causality, on which the whole edifice rests, had been subjected to a radical critique by David Hume. One can reduce the gist of Hume's critique to this formula. Science, rationality in the highest sense, rests on an irrational foundation: custom, mere custom, not rationality, is underlying our thinking in terms of causality. Kant, opposing Hume and trying to save the dignity of science, asserts that science is rational but it is limited to the phenomenal world, which Kant distinguished from what he called, with a strange expression, the "thing in itself," meaning beings as we cannot know them but which must be supposed to underlie the things which we know, the phenomenal things. Reason supplies only the form of knowledge; for its content, it depends on sense experience. Hence there cannot be knowledge of nonsensible things because we do not have any sense data regarding God and the soul. More precisely, that which makes possible knowledge of the phenomenal world is the understanding in contradistinction to reason. It is the understanding which prescribes nature its laws. By "nature" Kant understands here the totality of phenomena, of things of which we can have, directly or indirectly, sense experience. Reason proper, that in man which is not and cannot be dependent on or cooperative with sense experience proper, supplies only so-called regulative principles, not the constitutive principles, not the principles underlying the understanding of phenomena in common sense or in science.

Now, while pure reason—the title of Kant's book was *The Critique of Pure Reason*—is so weak in the sphere of theory, it is sufficient for man's guidance as practical reason in the practical sphere. Reason as practical reason depends in no way on experience, whereas all theoretical knowledge depends directly or indirectly on experience. Practical reason prescribes, without any borrowings whatever from experience, universally valid laws of action. The only access to the absolute—one could say, to the infinite—we have according to Kant is through the moral law, not through science. Now this implies that the laws prescribed by practical reason—think of such laws as "Thou shalt not lie"—the moral laws are not based in any way on knowledge of nature, and in particular of human nature. Hence the moral law can no longer be called, as it had been called before, the natural law: the natural laws from now on are laws like the Newtonian laws, whereas in the older usage, the moral law was called the natural law. Now why is this?

The moral law must be valid not only for men but for *all* intelligent beings, that is to say, for God too. And hence, how can it be based on the understanding of human nature? And the reason which Kant would give is this: if God's actions are not to be understood in terms of the moral law, then God might conceivably do things which are unjust. Think of the great difficulties regarding the sacrifice of Isaac, or any other problems of this kind. This tendency of the whole eighteenth century to subject God to the moral law reaches its climax in Kant's teaching. Furthermore, the moral law must be universally valid, without any ifs and buts. For example, thou shalt not murder: no ifs and buts. Thou shalt not lie: no ifs and buts. But knowledge of human nature is based on experience, and experience cannot supply universally valid or apodictic laws. Experience can tell us only that this was so always hitherto. But that doesn't tell us anything about the future, and if you think of the importance of the future, especially of the social future, for moral orientation, that is of course an enormous liberation for all kinds of things which seem to be denied by any previous experience of men. The moral law cannot be based on anything else or cannot be deduced from anything else. It cannot be derived from nature or from God: not from nature because we have only empirical knowledge of nature; nor from God because we do not have any theoretical knowledge of God. The moral law therefore liberates man from the tutelage of nature, which includes here also previous custom. If the moral law were a natural law, Kant asserts, nature would impose a law on man. Therefore, there would be what Kant calls heteronomy of the will: the will dependent on something outside of the will. The will would not give a law to itself; nature would give it to you. And therefore there would not be self-legislation strictly understood, or autonomy. If freedom is autonomy, the will must give a law to itself and must not borrow it or take it over from any other source.

Now how is such a moral law possible? The moral law is the law of reason, pure reason, in no way dependent on experience in any shape or form. Where does it get its content? Kant's answer is this: the *form* of reason supplies the content. The form of law—and law means generality, universality, rationality—is sufficient to supply the moral law. And this is formulated by Kant in what he calls the categorical imperative, which claims to be an authentic interpretation of what we all experience when we have a bad conscience, for example. It is that in us which reminds us of our duty. Now the categorical imperative says: Act in such a way that the maxims of your action can be made and be understood as universally valid laws binding all intelligent beings. That reminds of Rousseau's more narrow consideration regarding the positive law. I remind you of that example. I enter the assembly with the desire not to pay any taxes, and then I have to express this desire in the form of a law: From now on, no one has to pay any taxes. [LS taps on the table for emphasis.] I am replaced by "anyone," that's the generalization. And then I can see perhaps that my desire is foolish, because if no one pays any taxes there will be no roads, and no hospitals, and what have you.

Now Kant radicalizes this profoundly. He speaks not of my desire but of my maxim, implying that in all our actions, we make use of general principles whether we are aware of it or not. Maxims of the syllogism. For example, some people act on the maxim: I want to get along in the world by hook and by crook. They may not even know that they are acting on that, but they could know. And now, Kant says, we make an experiment. Let us conceive of this or any maxim as a universally binding law: Every man is morally obliged to get ahead in the world by hook and by crook. Not only permitted but obliged, that is the meaning of law. And then we can see, Kant asserts, that this is impossible as a universal law. Men could not live if they were all obliged to act in this manner.

If this is the character of the moral law, which has infinite political implications, it is impossible to criticize political proposals, such as universal peace, United Nations, or in whichever form these things may appear, on the grounds that they disagree with human nature or with experience because experience means previous experience. And what can we possibly know of what man is capable of in the future? Morality as Kant understands it liberates man from the tutelage of nature. That man is able to do what he is morally obliged to do goes, for Kant, without saying. "Thou canst what thou oughtst." Man is capable, therefore, for example of establishing perpetual peace. The only criterion which remains here, since no recourse to human nature is possible, is that of sheer self-contradiction. So in other words, sheer self-contradiction, i.e., formal irrationality, this is a clear sign that the law in question cannot be a moral law. The fundamental concern is with the moral law. That means also it is not with the good, or in particular with the highest good, or the end. I read to you a passage last time from Hobbes where he rejects the notion of the *sum-mum bonum*, in *Leviathan*, chapter 11. In a different way, in a very different way but still not entirely unconnected, Kant rejects the starting of moral reflection from the good. No concept of the good, including the highest good, as an object must determine the moral law, but the moral law in its turn determines the concept of the good.

The traditional view from classical antiquity was: To live well means to live according to nature. In order to understand Kant's reasoning, we raise this simple question: Why is this so? Why is living well living ac-cording to nature? Why is the natural order, granted we know it, in a way, good? Which is after all presupposed. Are not the basest and most destructive passions as natural as the noblest thoughts? In other words, we would have to raise the question: Which natural inclinations are to be respected, and which are to be rejected? This question is answered by Kant's categorical imperative. The natural order is to be respected. It is good to the extent to which by transgressing it I will something which I cannot will to be a universal law. For example, if I desire food, food which I need for the sustenance of my life, I can easily see that a moral law com-manding everyone to seek food for the sustenance of his body is compat-ible, is thinkable, as a law obliging all men. But if I desire to be superior to others and transform this into a universal law, "Everyone should strive to outdo everybody else," then I see chaos. The only thing which we know to be irreducible to anything else, or to be of absolute worth, is the moral law, or a will agreeing with the moral law, a good will. Kant believes this is to act in agreement with our ordinary, everyday, prephilosophic moral understanding. We take it for granted that we should be decent, and if someone raises the question "But why should I be decent?," he has already ceased to be decent. That makes sense. And if this is properly elaborated, we arrive at the view that the law that we ought to be decent does not have a Why. It cannot be reduced to anything else. Man owes his dignity to the moral law alone.

From this one can draw the conclusion, which Kant himself did not yet draw but Fichte, a famous successor of Kant, did: Man's duty consists in subjugating everything else, in him and without him, to the moral law, because everything else has no intrinsic worth.[2] Let us assume that the moral law demands from everyone virtuous activity in the sense of full and uniform development of all his faculties and the exercise of the fac-ulties jointly with others, which would be compatible, which would be susceptible of the universalization spoken of. But is such a development possible? As long as everyone is crippled as a consequence of the division of labor or of social inequality, then how can he develop all his faculties jointly with others in such a condition? A difficulty raised by Fichte. From here there is only one step to what one can call Marx's moral principle. Marx speaks very emphatically of the pushing back of the nature-limit. Nature is only an obstacle to be overcome or a thing to be used for man's moral purpose: nature does not supply a guidance in any way. The foundation for that was laid by Kant more than by anybody else.

I would like to mention only a few points regarding the later development. In the eighteenth century, prior to Kant, a new discipline of philosophy emerged: aesthetics. This thing did not exist in the past. There are discussions of the beautiful, and that was a very important theme in the Platonic and Aristotelian traditions. But now a new science emerges, not metaphysics, which deals with the beautiful, and that is aesthetics. The name comes from the Greek word *aisthēsis*, sense perception, and it is indicated that the beautiful is the sensuously beautiful. In the Platonic tradition it was understood that you cannot understand the sensuously beautiful except in the light of the intellectually or, let us say, ideally beautiful. This connection is divorced: the sensuously beautiful—sounds, colors, and so on—are to be understood on their own terms. This is the theme of aesthetics.

Now in the post-Kantian development of aesthetics (and the greatest of them is probably Hegel's aesthetics), it is still admitted that there are things by nature beautiful, say, human bodies, horses, certain breeds of dogs, and so on, but all things by nature beautiful are infinitely less important from the point of view of beauty than works of art. It is for this reason that today "aesthetics" means for all practical purposes the philosophy of fine art and has no longer anything whatever to do with things by nature beautiful.

I will read to you a few more passages from a much later thinker, but belonging to the same tradition. Nietzsche's *Beyond Good and Evil*, number 9.

"According to nature" you wish to live? O, noble Stoics, how your words deceive! Think of a being like nature, immoderately wasteful, immoderately indifferent, devoid of intentions and considerateness, devoid of compassion and a sense of justice, fruitful and desolate and uncertain at the same time. Think of indifference enthroned: how could you live in accordance with this indifference?[3]

In other words, the thought of living according to nature is based on a total misunderstanding of how nature truly is. There is another paragraph
in the same work of Nietzsche, number 188:

> Every morality, in contrast to *laisser aller*, is a work of tyranny against
> "nature," and also against "reason"; but this is not an objection to it, not
> unless one wished to decree, proceeding from some kind of morality, that
> all types of tyranny and irrationality are to be forbidden. What is essential
> and of inestimable value in each morality is that it is a long-lasting re-
> straint. To understand Stoicism or Port-Royal or Puritanism, it is well to
> remember the restraints under which any language hitherto has reached
> its peak of power and subtlety—the restraint of metrics, the tyranny of
> rhyme and rhythm.
>
> How much trouble have the poets and orators of each nation always
> taken—not excepting several of today's prose writers with an inexorable
> conscience in their ear—"for the sake of a folly," say the utilitarian fools,
> who think they are clever. "In deference to arbitrary laws," say the anar-
> chists, who imagine they are free, in fact free-thinkers. The strange fact,
> however, is that everything of freedom, subtlety, boldness, dance, and
> craftsmanlike certainty that one can find on earth, whether it applies to
> thinking or ruling or speaking or persuading, in the arts as well as in codes
> of conduct, would never have developed, save through the tyranny of such
> arbitrary laws. Indeed, the probability is strong that this is "nature" and
> "natural"—and not *laisser aller*.

Since not everyone knows French, what's the ordinary English translation
of *laisser aller*? "Let things go." And so he develops it at relatively great
length in this paragraph.

> Look at any morality, you will see that it is its nature to teach hatred of
> *laisser aller*, of too much freedom, and to implant the need for limited ho-
> rizons, for the nearest task. It teaches the narrowing of perspectives—in
> other words, stupidity in a certain sense, as a necessary condition for life
> and growth.
>
> "Thou shalt obey—someone or other and for a long time: if not, you
> perish and you lose your last self-respect"[4]—this seems to be the moral
> imperative of nature. It is neither "categorical" to be sure, as old Kant de-
> manded (observe the "if not") [the categorical imperative doesn't say "if
> not"—LS] nor is it directed to any individual (but what does nature care

about an individual?). But it is directed to peoples, races, times, classes—
and above all to the whole animal known as man, to mankind.[5]

Now this paragraph is remarkable for other reasons too, not directly connected with what I am discussing now. But the remarkable thing here is
this: throughout the paragraph, Nietzsche uses the word "nature" in quotation marks, except in the last statement, where he mentions nature. And
Nietzsche was an extremely careful writer, and this is not an accident. In
this strange use or nonuse of quotation marks, a profound difficulty reveals itself. Nietzsche cannot strictly speak anymore of nature; therefore
the quotation marks. And yet he needs nature.[6] He cannot speak anymore
of nature strictly speaking. Nature has become for him radically problematic. That which for Kant was the justification of nature, namely, that
nature is the only rational interpretation of sense data, of the phenomenal
world (and only the phenomenal world)—this has become doubtful for
Nietzsche. We can say that the understanding of things in terms of modern science or, for that matter, in terms of Greek or Babylonian science
(whatever you take) is a historically contingent way of interpreting things,
to use the most general term we can use here—in other words, the phenomenon which we have discussed under the heading *historicism.* Now
if we draw a conclusion from these remarks, from these examples which
could be considerably enlarged, we may make this tentative suggestion
and I believe surely a worthwhile suggestion: that what is characteristic
of modernity from its beginning until the present day is the questioning of nature as it was understood in classical and premodern times in
general.

Now this seems to be an absurd, not to say idiotic, statement. Who
does not know of the immense importance of natural science, the science
of nature, in the modern world? But the question is: On what is the emphasis, when we speak of natural science in modern times and in premodern times? "Natural science" is used by the Greeks as well as by the
moderns. But in premodern times, the emphasis is of course that it is
the science of *nature.* The emphasis is altogether on nature. In modern
times, the emphasis is altogether on *science,* so much so that we don't even
bother to add *natural* science. When a man is a scientist, he is of course
a natural scientist; when he is a scientist of another kind, then we say
he is a social scientist. This is a qualified scientist, not a scientist simply.
In other words, reminding you of some things I have alluded to before,
the great questions of nature: whether nature, as the concern of modern

natural science, is not a human construct and by this very fact not nature proper. I am aware of the fact that there is, or at least was, a school in this country in this century which called itself Naturalism. Now this seems to show that nature is very important and crucial, also for moral orientation, in our time. But this can easily be shown to be incorrect because the characteristic thesis of Naturalism is: nature is not a term of distinction. In plain English: everything that is is natural. But if everything that is is natural, that makes nature questionable the other way around, which we shall see very soon when we consider the rudiments of the original conception of nature. This was indeed a most important ingredient of the whole modern development. I quote to you a sentence from Spinoza, *Theologico-Political Treatise*, chapter 4: "All things are determined by the laws of universal nature, both regarding existence and operation, in a certain and determined manner."[7] In other words, every event—every event, whether it is a human action, or lightning, or whatever you have—is determined and must be understood ultimately in terms of the universal laws of nature. In the formulation of Naturalism: nature is not a term of distinction. And we will see later on, as I indicated, when we turn to the Greek notion of nature, the premodern notion, we shall see immediately that even for so-called materialists, "nature" is a term of distinction: not all things are natural. We are of course familiar with that fact without any learning, from ordinary understanding: "this is not a natural thing proper, it is an artifact." But I will have to take this up in a broader context.

Now after this general remark, necessary for the reason indicated about the modern development, I would now like to turn to the beginning, to Greek or classical political philosophy. But before I do that, I would like to find out whether there is any point you would like to raise now. Mr. Glenn?

MR. GLENN: From what little I know of John Dewey, I don't think he fits into the modern Naturalism—

LS: I think he does—well, I don't claim to be an expert in that matter, but this sentence which I quoted, I found in a book, *Naturalism*, edited by people who were affiliated with Dewey.[8]

MR. GLENN: I think he still looks to nature for a guide to moral activity.

LS: Yes, well, that is quite true, and I see now what you mean. That is quite true, that there is, at least in Dewey's *Human Nature and Conduct*, which is I suppose his most important ethical work—this has a formal character which reminds of Aristotelian ethics.[9] It's undeniable. To that extent he indeed uses nature as a guide. The content, the substance, is wholly un-Aristotelian, what he says—you know this book, I take it— what he says about the cooperation of impulse and custom or, rather, custom and impulse, how they must cooperate and how they must be balanced to one another: this is somehow based on the nature of man or on the nature of human society. But he can reconcile this with his general historicism or relativism by leaving it entirely open what kind of custom and what kind of impulse it is in principle. In other words, you know, in every stage of human development, except perhaps in very stationary societies, there is custom. And there is also impulse, individual impulses partly generated by the very custom which rebels against it. And now what is necessary is to strike a reasonable balance between the two which would make possible the highest growth of the individual as well as of the society. But we would have—Mr. Glenn, *all* my statements are in need of long footnotes. I mean, I am familiar with the fact that the Aristotelian tradition, in a way the same as the Thomistic tradition, lasted very long into modern times. I am not speaking now of Catholic universities, but even in the Protestant universities of Germany the prevalent view in the eighteenth century prior to Kant was a modified Thomistic view. I am not speaking now of the theological teaching proper but the philosophic teaching. The orientation by the natural perfection of man was still there. But these men—the most famous name was Christian Wolff—are practically forgotten.[10] The men who molded modernity were those who opposed the classical tradition, and only in very rare cases are these reactionaries remembered. I think the most famous case is that of Swift, at least in the English-speaking countries.[11] Good. Is there any other point you would like to raise?

STUDENT: Maybe you're going to come to this, but how would Aristotle respond to the modern view of nature? He surely must have recognized these—

LS: Not quite, no. Let me state it as simply as I can. Such a thing as the view that there are only bodies or bodily things was of course known to Aristotle. Let us call this view materialism as it is ordinarily called. That he knew. Furthermore, he knew of philosophies which try to understand the whole somehow in mathematical terms. The Pythagoreans are the most well-known example. But the combination of corporealism with mathematics and, in addition, something which did not exist in classical antiquity, the modern experiment, namely, the experiment which is artificially planned. The word "experiment" means originally simply an experience. I go around and see a strange animal and describe it: that is an *experimentum*, but this is of course not the modern experiment. The modern experiment is what Bacon called something which comes out when you torture nature, put her to the question. That is to say, you try to bring about conditions which never or very rarely are to be found in nature—say, a completely airless motion, a fall without any air—and use these extreme cases, which strictly speaking occur never, as the key to everything. This would have been the Aristotelian reaction: How can you make an impossibility the key to what is actual? And roughly, the resistance of the Aristotelians to the moderns, the primary resistance, had to do with that.

SAME STUDENT: On a lower level, though, Aristotle surely must have known that nature was not simply teleological, that there was a lot of, as Nietzsche says, waste—

LS: No, he would not have granted that. I am sure that he would have tried to show that what we call waste is based on a very superficial understanding. To take one example which is quite well known: the enormous waste of human sperma for the generation of a single child, and it may not even lead to that intended result. I think Aristotle would say: How could it be otherwise, given the situation in the uterus and so on and so on, that you have to waste very, very much in order to give a single sperma the chance to fertilize an egg? He would not have admitted that. And so on, but you have to ask someone who knows much more of modern science and understands Aristotle's *Physics* and biological writings, to answer that question properly.

I will now begin with my discussion of the classical thought, and I begin from the beginning. Since we seem to have observed that the key question concerns nature, we begin with the very first mention of the word "nature" in available Greek literature, and this is in Homer, in *The Odyssey*, book 10, the only mention of nature in Homer. The story is told not by Homer himself but by Odysseus. And Odysseus says that his comrades had been captured by this goddess-witch Circe, and Odysseus tried to liberate them. But then a divine helper, the god Hermes, comes and warns him of the terrific powers of that witch and wishes to protect him. Hermes says to Odysseus (but we know it of course only through Odysseus):

> "I can keep you clear of harm, and give you safety. Here, take this potent
> herb and go to Circe's house. This shall protect your life against the evil

day. And I will tell you all the magic arts of Circe. She will prepare for you
a potion and cast drugs into your food. But even so she cannot charm you,
because the potent herb which I shall give will not permit it. And let me
tell you more. When Circe turns against you her long wand, then draw the
sharp sword from your thigh and spring upon Circe as if you meant to slay
her. She then will cower and bid you to her bed. And do not you refuse
the goddess's bed. But that so she may release your men and care for you.
[Odysseus was a married man, and this is not unimportant here.—LS]
But bid her swear the blessed ones' great oath, that she is not meaning now
to plot you a new woe, nor when she has stripped, to leave you feeble and
unmanned."

As he thus spoke, Hermes gave the herb, drawing it from the ground,
and pointed out its *nature*. Black at the root it is, like milk its blossom; and
the gods, who have a different language, call it Moly. Hard it is for a mortal
man to dig; but the gods can do everything.[12]

Now this is a remarkable story. "The gods can do everything." The gods
are omnipotent. But this is obviously not meant, because the gods are omnipotent as a consequence of their knowledge of the natures of things, and
over these natures they do not have any control. This is the first statement,
and it is rich in implications, some of which we will gradually make clear.

Things have their natures, which means here they have certain looks,
and they have certain powers. This one has the power to protect one
against Circe's charm. Looks and powers—in Greek, *eidos* and *dynamis*—
are already here implied.

I give you another wholly unscientific or unphilosophic statement
about nature, which is much later, but still relatively early. Thucydides
speaks somewhere in his *History* of the nature of a locality or a place,[13] by
which he means that they landed in enemy territory and it is important
for them how the nature of the place is, obviously—whether it is a jungle
or it is a place where you can see, etc. Now then he changes the expression,
and instead of speaking of the nature of the place, he says: the place itself.
The nature of the place is the place itself as distinguished from something
which is not the place itself but something added to it. What could be
added to it? Now in that case it is clear: fortifications, which they built in
order to strengthen the place the more. More generally stated, the nature
of the thing, the thing in itself, is understood in contradistinction to human art, to *technē*, from which such words as "technical" and "technology"
are derived.[14]

... he is a just man. In addition, he is a human being, and he has this and this color of the hair, and God knows what—this and this property. Justice itself, nothing added to it, and nothing lacking, because this just man may not be of perfect justice. That is the same as nature; therefore for Plato the ideas are the natures, however unintelligible that may sound at first hearing. But let us only keep this simpler Thucydidean passage in mind, where it is clear that the thing itself, the nature of the thing, is understood in contradistinction to what men make of it, to human art.

Now we may say that thus far the notion of nature as discussed is commonsensical, prephilosophic, or prescientific. But here we must remind ourselves for a moment of our historicist friends who say: This was *Greek* common sense, not common sense without qualification, because not all languages, even those of very highly civilized peoples, have a word for nature. My favorite example is the Old Testament, where there is no such word. The point is that nevertheless the distinction is immediately intelligible to us today, I take it, and it was also without great difficulty intelligible to other nations who did not know Greek. The thought was easily translatable with the help of artificially coined words, for example into Hebrew and Arabic. Up to this point, there is nothing particularly striking.

I remind you again of the fact that we owe this interesting story to Odysseus. Now Odysseus is one of the many Homeric heroes, but he is a peculiar man. He is very wily, as we know, but I am now concerned with another characteristic of his: he is the greatest traveler among the Homeric heroes. You know what happened to him on his way back, and he stayed longer away from home than anybody else. And there were other Greek travelers on all kinds of levels, but the most famous of them after Odysseus probably is the historian Herodotus. Now let us see how nature appears in the light of travelers' experiences. I am speaking of very simple ones. The traveler, let us say, goes to Persia, and there he makes the observation that fire burns in Persia just as it burns in Greece. The example is taken literally from Aristotle.[15] But why is this so strange? Because many things in Persia are so different from the way they are in Greece, for example, say, the laws regarding inheritance. I know nothing about them, but I suppose they were different in Persia from those in Greece. Surely the forms of government were manifestly different, and last but not least, the gods worshiped by the Persians differed from the gods worshiped by the Greeks. All these things, if we generalize, differ from country to country, whereas the characteristics of water, fire, and so on do not differ.

(I hope you will not hold against me that there might be hot springs in a given country and no hot springs in another one, but this is only a slightly complicated case. It doesn't affect the fundamental things.)

Now this leads to another distinction which is much more fertile in consequence: the distinction not between nature and art, which is elementary—the skin or the hide of the shoemaker, and then the shoe— but the distinction between nature and [LS writes on the blackboard] *nomos*. One can translate it to begin with by "law," "custom," "convention." The meaning is this. There are things which are by nature, say, dogs, light- ning, and what have you. Then there are things which are by virtue of hu- man making: shoes, chairs, etc. But there is a third kind of thing: things which are only by virtue of being held in reverence or, more generally stated and perhaps more precisely stated, by virtue of being *held*—using "holding" here in the sense in which it is used of judges, the holding of a judge, but not quite the same. Of being held, of being believed in. In the accusation of Socrates, it is stated that Socrates commits an unjust act by not believing in, by not holding in reverence, by not holding the gods held by the city. At this point we go beyond that which is the merely prephilo- sophic and prescientific understanding of nature, and this is decisive for the emergence of political philosophy. I will give you an example of that distinction which is at first glance perhaps not recognizable.

At the beginning of the seventh book of Plato's *Republic* you find the simile of the Cave, a simile which is meant to show man what his situa- tion is in regard to true education, i.e., philosophy. Men are primarily cave dwellers, not in the sense of what modern prehistory tells us, but *we*, here, in the civilized country or wherever we are—we are cave dwell- ers. We don't see the light of the sun, the natural light. We see nothing but the shadows of artifacts, and this we do only because there is an ar- tificial light somewhere. Nothing but the shadows of artifacts. Artifacts remind us of course of the distinction between nature and *technē*, but the shadows of artifacts remind us of something which is in a way even less substantial, less fundamental, than *technē*. What Plato means to suggest is that men see primarily everything in the light of authoritative opinions— *authoritative* opinions, not just fabricated things. These opinions are in a sense man-made; therefore Plato speaks of artifacts. But they are not known to be man-made.

Now this distinction between *physis* and *nomos* is absolutely crucial. According to a well-known textbook version, this is an invention of the sophists, of certain more or less unscrupulous moneymakers and prestige hunters of the fifth century—of whom we have no writings left, by the way, or hardly any, and we know chiefly through Platonic dialogues. But this is historically simply not true. This distinction between *physis* and *nomos*, between nature and convention, is essential to classical political philosophy itself and even to the whole tradition, and there is a very simple proof. As long as the classical tradition lasted, a distinction was made between the natural law and the positive law: the natural law, which is by itself, and the positive law, which has its ground in human decisions, human opinions. This distinction was crucial. I will indicate this briefly, postponing a development of that until next time.[16]

Once this distinction had sunk in, the question arose: What about morality (as we call it)? The Greeks said: What about the just and the noble? Is this merely by convention, or is it at least partly natural? And this became, to begin with, the key issue. And one can say that classical political philosophy, the political philosophy founded by Socrates, constituted itself by establishing the view that the just and the noble are fundamentally natural and not merely conventional. And the modern view, as we have already indicated, modified that very profoundly, of course not in the sense in which the sophists had understood that.

Before I go on I would like to read to you a remark of Hegel, which is very helpful for clarifying the difference between the ancients and the moderns. Now this sentence reads as follows, and you must listen carefully because Hegel's sentences are quite complicated, and even the English translation, which I haven't made, has given the Hegelian sentences the simplicity of sentences of Addison.

> The manner of study in ancient times is distinct from that of modern times, in that the former, the study in ancient times,[17] consisted in the veritable training and perfecting of the natural consciousness. ["Natural consciousness" means here the primary consciousness, not yet specialized.—LS] Trying its powers at each part of its life severally, and philosophizing about everything it came across [in other words, proceeding in a very unsystematic manner—LS], the natural consciousness transformed itself into a universality of abstract understanding which was active in every matter and in every respect. [Although it was unsystematic, it was universal: there was no question which it didn't address.—LS] In modern times, however, the individual finds the abstract form ready made.[18]

This, rightly understood, is very true. What happened in classical philosophy, especially political philosophy, is the primary acquisition of concepts, that is to say, of philosophic or scientific concepts, as distinguished from the use of concepts already acquired—not to say the transformation of concepts already acquired. This is, I think, the peculiar charm which everyone experiences when reading a Platonic dialogue, but I think also when reading very important parts, at any rate, of the Aristotelian writings: this way which is not systematic, methodical in our sense, and yet very open-minded, and starting from scratch. Regarding classical political philosophy in particular, we must say that it is therefore, for the reason indicated by Hegel, closer to political life than modern political philosophy. This may sound strange, given the utopianism of the classics and the realism of the moderns, but you have only to make one simple experiment. The most realistic and tough studies of political bosses, and any other kind of unsavory things, are written of course in a certain language. I am not speaking now of what someone in a political campaign does—these are not scientific studies—but you have read such studies, and this language is surely not the language of the political arena. Whereas the Platonic-Aristotelian analyses, however far away they might lead from what everyone in the political arena knows and admits, are written in a language which is fundamentally that of everyday life. One can say that there is not a single technical term in the properly political writings and parts of writings of Plato and Aristotle, whereas surely in modern times—to some extent already in the premodern tradition, but surely in modern times—a scientific or philosophic language takes over. If you take, for example, such distinctions as Hobbes's state of nature, state of civil society, as meant by Hobbes, no one would have ever thought of these things in political debate proper, whereas all the terms used by Plato and Aristotle for designating political phenomena are everyday terms. What they do, especially Aristotle, is to define them more precisely, and this more precise definition became then the great heritage of the West. But the starting point is ordinary understanding which we can with not too great difficulty reactivate for ourselves. Partly it is necessary for the purpose to learn something of Greek, so that one is not completely at the mercy of the translators. And one must take some other efforts—I have indicated the question when I spoke about Collingwood's partly justified criticism of modern philosophers.

After the foundation was laid, fundamentally after Aristotle, the relation of the political philosophers to political life was always mediated by an already existing tradition of political philosophy. No such tradition interfered at the beginning, in the founding epoch. Now this has a broader basis. Classical philosophy in general is not based on that peculiar skepticism on which modern philosophy is fundamentally based, as is most clearly shown in the case of Descartes. It is not based on a distrust of our primary awareness of things and people; therefore you can take over these terms. You have to make them clearer, avoid the ambiguities and so on, but fundamentally it is the same way of understanding. I will give you a simple example of the peculiar artificial character which modern thinking about this matter has as contrasted with the classical. Descartes began to speak of "the ego," and in some European languages, they use even not the Latin word *ego*, but *le moi*, or in German, *das Ich*, in English, "the I"—only in English you can't use it well because people might think of this part of the body; therefore you have to say "the ego." But look at the formation from a linguistic point of view. Who speaks in ordinary life, if he is not corrupted, of "the ego"? And even here today, especially in half-psychoanalytical language—"inflated ego" and so on— this has something very strange and surely very artificial about it. People know of the ego not from ordinary experience but via science. Their understanding of their fellow humans is mediated by certain sciences, true or pseudoscience.

Now people became aware gradually, especially in the nineteenth and twentieth centuries, that there is something wrong in that Cartesian egocentrism. And people became aware of the fact that I could not know myself as an ego, as an I, except if I recognized another man, at least, whom they called a "thou." And then they may of course also speak of the "we." Now no one would use these terms in everyday language, and we don't need them. But the phenomenon meant by these people who speak of the ego, thou, and we—the true phenomenon of people living together in trust and intimacy—was of course known to men like Plato and Aristotle because this is a necessity of human life. But how did they speak about it? They called it friendship, "friendship" having here the broad meaning where of course the relation between husband and wife would also be a form of friendship. You see here, when you speak of friendship, you are much closer to the phenomenon than if you speak of the I, thou, and we, because when you speak of friendship you only continue what you do in everyday life. You say, "he is my friend," "they are friends." You would never say, except in a very stilted way: He is my alter ego. This can be said, but this is not the ordinary way of talking. When you speak to him, you say "thou"—well, of course, not in present-day English, but in older English and in other languages which make a distinction between the second-person plural and second-person singular.

In other words, in his philosophic discussions, Aristotle (or Plato, too) continues the way of talking about, which is the *ordinary* way of talking about. He does not even try to preserve, in philosophic or scientific discussion, the speaking *to* a friend. That would be absurd, but one could do that—if Aristotle had written his treatises in the form of a letter to Nicomachus or whoever it might be, which also would be somewhat peculiar. By this I mean the direct relation to political and ordinary life, which is preserved in classical political philosophy and which is not existing in modern political philosophy. This is only superficially in conflict with the fact that modern political philosophy is in a way realistic and classical political philosophy is "idealistic." Perhaps the very utopianism of the classics is more in agreement with what is going on in the marketplace than a certain toughness, tough-headedness, aspired to by present-day and earlier academicians. That we must perhaps consider later.

Generally speaking, I would say the point of view which the classical political philosophers take is that of ordinary political life, of the citizen or statesman, and they look in the same direction as he looks—the same perspective. They only try to look further afield, much further afield: it is not a *different* perspective. They do not have the posture of an outside spectator who sees the political arena as one in which the big fishes swallow the small ones, for example, and looking at it from the outside and then trying to learn something about human beings as one can learn about stones and rats, and then apply it. They have their stand in the political sphere and look at it as political men. This leads eventually to some complications, but this is surely the starting point, and we must keep this in mind, if we want to understand. This is so to say the matrix of classical political philosophy.

Well, I will say a few more words about this and then pursue the theme of nature and convention more fully. And then I hope we can have a discussion about *the* classical work of classical political philosophy, Aristotle's *Politics*, and see what kind of a thing that is.

Notes

EDITOR'S INTRODUCTION

1. For a list of the courses Strauss offered at the University of Chicago see George Anastaplo, "Leo Strauss at the University of Chicago," in Kenneth L. Deutsch and John A. Murley, *Leo Strauss, the Straussians, and the American Regime* (Lanham, MD: Rowman & Littlefield, 1999), 14–18. The descriptions of the courses can be a bit misleading. For example, and most relevant to this transcript, the first course listed for spring quarter 1960 as "Introduction to Political Philosophy: Study of Aristotle's *Politics*" was, in fact, a seminar, as the transcript of that course shows. I remembered the winter 1965 course by the same title as being "primarily on Aristotle's *Politics*," as Anastaplo comments. In fact, however, Strauss devoted only seven of the sixteen lectures to Aristotle.

2. Strauss did not associate introductory courses per se with lectures or a survey. He seems to have thought more in terms of the subject matter and the correct approach to take in studying it. At the beginning of the seminar he gave on Aristotle's *Politics* in the spring quarter of 1960, he explained that he called this course an "Introduction to Political Science," because he wanted to make clear that he did "not regard Aristotle's teaching as a historical subject." After presenting a very brief account of the history of political philosophy in his first lecture, Strauss concluded not merely that "the mature approach of present day social science presupposes the experience of the failure of the earlier approaches," but that "we cannot know that [Aristotle's] teaching was wrong if we do not know first what his teaching was." And that "means that we have to understand him in his own terms." Strauss then divided the *Politics* into fifteen segments for the sake of assigning students papers, two per book except for one on book 8. In that seminar he spent much less time than in the 1965 course bringing out the problematic character of the contemporary denial that political philosophy is possible any longer and correspondingly more time on a detailed commentary on the *Politics* itself. As in this 1965 course, so in the lecture course he gave called "Basic Principles of Classical Political Philosophy" in autumn 1961, Strauss began with eight lectures on "the crisis of our times" that duplicate many of the arguments he gives in the 1965 course concerning the problems posed by positivism and historicism, but the treatment he gives of Aristotle's *Politics* in "Basic Principles" does not follow the text as closely as these lectures do.

3. A fuller statement of Strauss's views on education can be found in "What Is Liberal

Education?" and "Liberal Education and Responsibility" in *Liberalism Ancient and Modern* (New York: Basic Books, 1968), 3–25.

4. *Natural Right and History* (Chicago: University of Chicago Press, 1953), 35–80, hereafter *NRH*; "An Epilogue," *Essays on the Scientific Study of Politics*, ed. Herbert J. Storing (New York: Holt, Rinehart, 1962), 307–27; and *What Is Political Philosophy? and Other Studies* (Glencoe, IL: Free Press, 1959), 9–55.

5. Strauss observes in passing that Comte's claim about the questions raised has been refuted by modern biology, but that his thesis about science addressing the question of how rather than why has nonetheless survived.

6. In this respect, Strauss comments, contemporary positivists are truer descendants of Descartes, who introduced the notion that everything must be doubted and all knowledge rationally reconstructed.

7. In his 1960 seminar on Aristotle's *Politics* Strauss suggests that he learned that Simmel was the first man to argue for a value-free social science from Arnold Brecht's *Political Theory*. Strauss responds to Brecht's criticism of his own arguments in *Natural Right and History* later in these 1965 lectures.

8. Strauss makes a similar argument in "An Epilogue." See n. 4 above.

9. Strauss incorporates many of the arguments and some of the same examples he gave in his critique of Weber in *NRH* into these lectures.

10. Arnold Brecht, *Political Theory: The Foundations of Twentieth-Century Political Thought* (Princeton: Princeton University Press, 1959), 262.

11. Ernest Nagel, *The Structure of Science: Problems in the Logic of Scientific Explanation* (New York: Harcourt, Brace & World, 1961), 491–92.

12. Strauss gives a more detailed analysis of Nietzsche's argument and the difficulty in which it culminates in "Note on the Plan of *Beyond Good and Evil*" in *Studies in Platonic Political Philosophy* (Chicago: University of Chicago Press, 1983), 174–91.

13. In chapter 6 Strauss comments: "Vulgar historicism is traced to man; in the subtle and theoretical historicism of Heidegger, it is traced to what he calls *Sein*, which is *x*, the ground of all history, working in and through man" (page xx).

14. *NRH*, 25–33.

15. Speaking as a historian, Strauss agrees with Collingwood that the ancient *polis* and the modern state are not the same. He uses the opportunity, in fact, to urge students to learn as much of the original languages as possible so that they will not remain victims of well-intentioned but often inaccurate translators.

16. Strauss explicitly incorporates sections of his review of Collingwood's *Idea of History*, "On Collingwood's Philosophy of History," *Review of Metaphysics* 5 (1952): 559–86.

17. A historicist can avoid this contradiction, Strauss observes, if he argues that his age constitutes an "absolute moment" at which the truth about the historicity of all thought becomes (and can only become) clear, and gives reasons for that conclusion. In "Philosophy as Rigorous Science," *Studies in Platonic Political Philosophy*, 32–33, Strauss attributes such an argument to Hegel, Marx, Nietzsche, and Heidegger. In these lectures he states that Heidegger developed the historicist argument much more subtly than Collingwood. He refers particularly to Heidegger's call for the initiation of a dialogue between East and

West. Such a dialogue would expand the horizons of both the Easterner and the Westerner, Strauss suggests, but Heidegger does not think that either would ever have the same view as the other. Strauss also comments on the significance of Heidegger's calling for a dialogue between the Far East and the West in "Existentialism," the first of "Two Lectures by Leo Strauss," ed. David Bolotin, Christopher Bruell, and Thomas L. Pangle, *Interpretation* 22 (1995): 317.

18. Strauss presents a fuller version of this argument in *NRH*, chapters 4–6, and "The Three Waves of Modernity," in *An Introduction to Political Philosophy: Ten Essays by Leo Strauss*, ed. Hilail Gildin (Detroit, MI: Wayne State University Press, 1989), 81–98.

19. I do not know of any other place that Strauss emphasizes Kant as the turning point away from a notion of nature as a source of standards of right except the transcript of the seminar "Kant's Political Philosophy" the year after these lectures.

20. *Nicomachean Ethics* 1134b25–27.

21. Strauss here gives an extremely abbreviated form of the argument he presents more fully in chapter 3 of *NRH*, "The Origin of the Idea of Natural Right," 81–164.

22. In his *Nicomachean Ethics*, which constitutes the first part of Aristotle's study of politics, Aristotle insists (1.1094b13–29) that the study of any subject must be suited to the character of the subject. Later in these lectures Strauss observes that the *Politics* contains the only two oaths to be found in Aristotle's entire corpus, and he suggests that the use of oaths reflects the controversial and passionate, because partisan, character of political arguments.

23. Strauss admits that Aristotle's critique of Hippodamus's proposal seems to contradict what he says later (*Politics* 3.1287a30) about law as reason (*nous*). But, Strauss notes, in the *Nicomachean Ethics* (10.1180a22) Aristotle says that law is speech derivative from *some* practical wisdom. There is moreover another reason for the difference between the Thomist and the Aristotelian teaching concerning the relation between reason and law. According to Aristotle, laws differ according to regime, and most regimes are defective. Hence their laws cannot be simply reasonable.

24. This emphasis on the essentially controversial, because divisive, character of political life and debate most distinguishes Strauss's attempt to revive an Aristotelian understanding of politics from the attempts of contemporary scholars such as Alasdair MacIntyre, *After Virtue* (Notre Dame: University of Notre Dame Press, 1981), and Martha Nussbaum, *The Fragility of Goodness* (Cambridge: Cambridge University Press, 1986), to revive Aristotelian "virtue ethics."

25. Athenian democracy was not, in fact, as purely democratic as Aristotle's description, Strauss observes, but Aristotle's "democracy" is not an "ideal type." It was not Aristotle's discovery; he simply took the claims democrats actually made and extended and clarified them. Modern readers tend to take their understanding of Athenian democracy from Pericles's funeral oration, but according to Thucydides (2.65) Athens under Pericles was the rule of one man and a democracy only in name.

26. In the seminars Strauss devoted entirely to Aristotle's *Politics* in spring 1960 and fall 1967 he follows the order of the text indicated by the Bekker numbers and takes up books 4–6 before 7–8. The emphasis Strauss puts on Aristotle's discussion of the best

regime in these lectures distinguishes his presentation of Aristotle's *Politics* here from the chapter "On Aristotle's *Politics*" in *The City and Man* (the only essay Strauss published that was devoted exclusively to Aristotle). In concluding that chapter Strauss observes that "the guiding question of Aristotle's *Politics* is the question of the best regime," but that question is "better discussed on another occasion." *The City and Man* (Chicago: University of Chicago Press, 1964), 48–49.

27. Strauss explains that the "middle class" that holds the balance in such a regime is not "bourgeois." Rousseau coined the term "bourgeois" to distinguish merchants from the "citizens" willing to fight for their country. In ancient cities, Aristotle observes, those who bear heavy arms become citizens (chapter 15, xxx).

28. Cf. *NRH*, 36: "The difference between the classics and us with regard to democracy consists exclusively in a different estimate of the virtues of technology."

CHAPTER ONE

1. Henri de Saint-Simon (1760–1825), social theorist and reformer, founder of French socialism.

2. Jean-Baptiste Lamarck (1744–1829), French naturalist and early proponent of a theory of evolution.

3. The word *mathēmata* (derived from *manthanō*, to learn) initially denoted the various branches of knowledge but came in postclassical ages to mean the mathematical disciplines specifically.

4. Auguste Comte, *Cours de philosophie positive*, vol. 3 (Paris: Bachelier, 1838), 295. The translation here and in subsequent quotations from this work appears to be Strauss's.

5. It is likely that there was a change of tape here.

6. Strauss here passes over in silence a part of this selection from Comte.

7. Strauss says "to establish."

8. Comte, *Cours de philosophie positive*, vol. 4 (Paris: Bachelier, 1839), 690–91.

9. Strauss here omits a part of the quoted material.

10. Here again some of the quoted material is omitted.

11. Comte, *Cours*, vol. 4, 173–74.

12. Some lines are omitted from the quotation.

13. Strauss omits lines from this passage.

14. Comte, *Cours*, vol. 4, 63–64.

15. Franz Josef Gall (1758–1828), German neuroanatomist and physiologist, pioneer in cranioscopy or phrenology.

16. Antoine Destutt de Tracy (1754–1836), French materialist philosopher credited with having coined the term "ideology."

17. The Museum of Science and Industry, near the University of Chicago campus.

18. *NRH*, 8n.

CHAPTER TWO

1. A slightly different translation of the text is quoted on p. 20.

2. Comte, *Cours*, vol. 4, 566.

3. Strauss says they nevertheless constantly "conform to."

4. Comte, *Cours*, vol. 4, 568–69.

5. Ibid., 570.

6. Ibid., 571.

7. *Republic* 369e ff.

8. There was a change of tape at this point.

9. Comte, *Cours*, vol. 4, 189.

10. Comte has "intellectual or material."

11. Comte, *Cours*, vol. 4, 582.

12. There is a break in the tape at this point; the recording resumes in mid-sentence.

13. Comte, *Cours de philosophie positive*, vol. 1 (Paris: Bachelier, 1830), 50–51.

14. There is a break in the tape at this point.

15. The Vietnam War, 1954–75.

16. *Brown v. Board of Education of Topeka*, 347 U.S. 482 (1954).

17. Comte, *Cours*, vol. 4, 655.

CHAPTER THREE

1. William James, *The Varieties of Religious Experience* (New York: Longmans, Green, 1902).

2. Ernst Mach (1838–1916), founder of the modern philosophy of science and forerunner of logical positivism.

3. V. I. Lenin, *Materialism and Empirico-Criticism*, in *Collected Works*, vol. 14 (Moscow: Progress Publishers, 1964).

4. From the essay "On Freedom" (1940), in Albert Einstein, *Ideas and Opinions*, trans. Sonja Bargmann (New York: Crown, 1954).

5. "Meanest Capacities": see *Leviathan*, ch. 15.

6. Georg Simmel, *Einleitung in die Moralwissenschaft*, 2 vols. (Berlin: W. Hertz, 1892–93).

7. Ibid., vol. 1, iii, v. Apparently Strauss's translation.

8. Ibid., 321.

9. Ibid., 322.

10. Strauss leaves out a few of Simmel's words here.

11. Simmel, *Einleitung*, vol. 1, 232.

12. Friedrich Nietzsche, *Daybreak* § 2. Presumably Strauss's translation.

13. Strauss says "low."

14. Strauss says "regarding validity questions."

15. Max Weber, *The Protestant Ethic and the Spirit of Capitalism*, trans. Talcott Parsons (London: Allen & Unwin, 1930). There are many later editions of this work.

16. *Faust*, part 2, act 2, l. 7488.

17. There is a break in the tape at this point; the recording resumes in mid-sentence.

18. American Medical Association.

19. Milton Friedman (1912–2006), who for many years held a position at the University of Chicago, was a tireless and eloquent proponent of free-market capitalism.

20. Alfred C. Kinsey et al., *Sexual Behavior in the Human Male* (1948) and *Sexual Behavior in the Human Female* (1953).

21. Orlando Wilson was superintendent of the Chicago Police Department at the

time. Earlier he had taught at Harvard and Berkeley. Wilson became professor of police administration at the University of California, Berkeley, in 1939 and served as the dean of the university's School of Criminology from 1950 to 1960.

22. Harold Lasswell (1902–78) was a leading member of the behavioralist school of social science in the United States.

CHAPTER FOUR

1. See Strauss's remarks at the end of the preceding chapter.

2. The candidates in the presidential election of 1964 were the incumbent President Lyndon B. Johnson (Democrat) and Senator Barry Goldwater of Arizona (Republican).

3. Decolonization in the British Empire began with the independence of India in 1947. Algeria gained its independence from France in 1962.

4. Strauss says, "will ever come."

5. Friedrich Nietzsche, *Thus Spoke Zarathustra*, Prologue, § 5. Strauss read the entire passage from Walter Kaufmann's translation, available in *The Portable Nietzsche*, ed. and trans. Kaufmann (New York: Viking Press, 1954), 128–30; this is abridged in the text.

6. Nathan Glazer (b. 1924), influential sociologist, editor, and policy advisor, co-author of *The Lonely Crowd* (1950). This paragraph reproduces almost verbatim Strauss's remarks in "Perspectives on the Good Society," *Liberalism Ancient and Modern* (Chicago: University of Chicago Press, 1968), 271–72.

7. In *Liberalism Ancient and Modern* (p. 272) Glazer is quoted so: "'there will be developing . . . good small societies' composed 'of reactionaries and anarchists and radical intellectuals.'"

8. Bobby Baker was a Senate staffer and associate of President Johnson, whose alleged corruption the Goldwater team attempted to exploit in campaign ads throughout 1964.

9. E.g., *Politics* 3.1275b25.

10. *Republic* 619b–e.

11. The Hoover war collection of materials, which Henry Hoover began to collect while he was organizing humanitarian relief for Belgium, was established in 1919 as a library and archives at Stanford University.

12. Max Weber, *The Theory of Social and Economic Organization*, ed. and trans. A. M. Henderson and Talcott Parsons (New York: Oxford University Press, 1947), 358–59.

13. Rudolph Sohm (1841–1917), German theologian, jurist, and historian of law.

14. Strauss apparently has in mind the simile of the line at *Republic* 509d–511e and its recapitulation at 533b–534a. The Greek word in question is likely *pistis* (511e1, 534a1).

15. Spinoza, *Ethics*, part 2, axiom 2.

16. There is a break in the tape at this point.

17. The class sessions on Aristotle are not included in this volume. For audiofiles and a transcript of those sessions, see the Leo Strauss Center website.

18. Bernard Montgomery (1887–1976), general in the British Army during World War II.

19. The main point is that these commonsense judgments mean more, are more, than those limited, conditional judgments such as "if general, he's good." Strauss's point turns

on a distinction between those statements that involve a concept (e.g., *general*), that have criteria built into them, that may be analyzed in a value-neutral sort of way, and those in which some moral attribute or virtue is predicated of a subject as human being or what have you, those that cannot be so analyzed.

20. See *NRH*, 59 ff.

21. R. H. Tawney, *Religion and the Rise of Capitalism* (New Brunswick, NJ: Harcourt, Brace, 1926). Tawney specifically criticizes Weber; see 315n32.

CHAPTER FIVE

1. See the discussion of Simmel in chapter 3.

2. Arnold Brecht, *Political Theory: The Foundations of Twentieth-Century Political Thought* (Princeton: Princeton University Press, 1959), 262.

3. Ibid., 263.

4. Ibid., 263–64.

5. The word in Brecht is "writes."

6. Brecht completes his point: "(which by the way might be much more graphic than speaking of cruelty, A.B.)."

7. Brecht writes "or epigones."

8. Noted in the margin of the transcript source: "Strauss is reading this with suppressed glee."

9. Brecht has "implications" and "possibilities."

10. Brecht, *Political Theory*, 264–65.

11. Brecht has "Leo Strauss resumes his objections in his paper 'Social Science and Humanism' (in L. White, ed., *The State of the Social Sciences*, Chicago 1956, pp. 415 ff.)." This essay is reprinted as chapter 1 of Leo Strauss, *The Rebirth of Classical Political Rationalism*, ed. Thomas L. Pangle (Chicago: University of Chicago Press, 1989).

12. Brecht's references to page numbers of Strauss's paper as printed in White have been omitted.

13. Strauss omits a reference to a book chapter by Paul Edwards here.

14. The words "in the proposition 'Noncannibalism is superior to cannibalism'" are a restatement, not in Brecht.

15. Brecht, *Political Theory*, 549n50.

16. Ibid., 550 n.

17. Nagel quotes from Strauss's "The Social Science of Max Weber," *Measure* 2 (1951): 211–14, which is identical to *NRH*, 50–53.

18. The words "of fact and value" are a restatement, not in Nagel.

19. Ernest Nagel, *The Structure of Science: Problems in the Logic of Scientific Explanation* (New York: Harcourt, Brace & World, 1961), 491–92.

20. Ibid., 494. "Objects," not "subjects," is the word used by Nagel.

21. Ibid., 320. The author quoted is Ludwik Silberstein.

22. Nagel writes not "the discussion" but "this discussion."

23. Nagel, *Structure of Science*, 323.

24. Nagel says "at will."

25. Strauss adds the words "of causality" as a clarification.

26. Nagel has "It is at least plausible to claim, therefore, that the acceptance of the principle of causality as a maxim of inquiry (whether the acceptance is explicit or only illustrated in the overt actions of scientists, and whether the principle is formulated with some precision or only vaguely) is an *analytical consequence* of what is commonly meant by 'theoretical science.'"

27. Nagel writes "a special form."

28. Nagel has "thereby."

29. Nagel, *Structure of Science*, 324.

30. Hans Reichenbach (1891–1953), German-born philosopher of science of the logical-positivist variety.

31. Sc. Nagel.

32. Suggested reformulation: In sum, positivism, for reasons I have not sufficiently explained, involves the abandonment of the original understanding of science, namely, that science is the perfection of human nature; this was so to say the rock on which science was built. And this occurred in connection with the abandonment of the view that there are such things as perfections of nature. This eventually led to the question being raised: What is the basis of science?

33. *Poetics* 1451b5–11.

34. *Summa Theologica* 1a, q1 a2.

35. Giambattista Vico (1688–1744), philosopher of history.

36. *Second Treatise*, sec. 15.

37. *Critique of Pure Reason* A852/B880–A856/B884.

38. Oswald Spengler (1880–1936), historian, author of *The Decline of the West* (1918).

CHAPTER SIX

1. Churchill died on January 24, 1965, the day before this class session took place.

2. Fulton, Missouri: A reference to Churchill's "Iron Curtain" speech, delivered at Westminster College in Fulton in March 1946. Greece: Apparently a reference to British support for anticommunist forces in Greece toward the end of World War II, a policy continued by the United States and subsequently expanded into the Truman Doctrine.

3. Winston Churchill, *Marlborough: His Life and Times*, 2 vols. (Chicago: University of Chicago Press, 2002).

4. The exact wording in Nagel: "Human behavior is undoubtedly modified by the complex of social institutions in which it develops, despite the fact that all human actions involve physical and physiological processes whose laws of operation are invariant in all societies. Even the way members of a social group satisfy basic biological needs—e.g., how they obtain their living or build their shelters—is not uniquely determined either by their biological inheritance or by the physical character of their geographic environment, for the influence of these factors on human action is mediated by existing technology and traditions."

5. Nagel, *Structure of Science*, 460.

6. Ibid., 464.

7. Ibid., 464–65.

8. Nagel writes "must also be recognized."

9. Nagel has "the analysis of actual social phenomena." *Structure of Science*, 465–66.

10. Nagel has "contingent."

11. The plural, "values," is used in Nagel.

12. In original: "adequacy."

13. Nagel inserts here an ellipsis indicating omission of some of the material quoted from Mannheim.

14. Nagel inserts an ellipsis here.

15. Nagel, *Structure of Science*, 498–99.

16. Ibid., 500.

17. The words "of these sociologists of knowledge" are a restatement, not in Nagel.

18. In Nagel: "succeeded in meeting" (not "superseded")

19. Nagel has "a social perspective enters essentially."

20. Nagel has "Is the thesis."

21. In original: "its acceptance as valid is strictly limited to those who can do so, and social scientists who subscribe to a different set of social values ought therefore dismiss it as empty talk."

22. Nagel has "presumably" here.

23. In original: "conclusion."

24. Nagel, *Structure of Science*, 500.

25. A reference to Soviet repression under Stalin and to Nikita Khrushchev's policy of de-Stalinization initiated in the mid-1950s.

26. Post-Hegelian historicists, presumably. Strauss's point seems to be that while both Hegel and his successors understood that people see things differently at different times, this historicist insight became problematic when the successors rejected the Hegelian view of historical progress leading to the "absolute moment" at which it became clear that every truth belongs to its specific circumstances.

27. The transcript has a blank space here.

28. Leopold von Ranke (1795–1886), typically regarded as the founder of modern scientific history as a discipline distinct from Hegelian philosophy.

29. Ruth Benedict (1887–1948), American anthropologist.

30. Strauss begins reading at the start of "On the Thousand and One Goals"; here the passage is abridged.

31. In Nietzsche: "who gave *me* my name—*the name which is both dear and difficult to me.*"

32. Friedrich Nietzsche, *Thus Spoke Zarathustra*, First Part, § 15, in *The Portable Nietzsche*, trans. Kaufmann, 170–72.

33. Strauss seems to be referring here to the argument concerning the "fusion of horizons" put forward by Hans-Georg Gadamer in *Wahrheit und Methode* (Tübingen: J. C. B. Mohr, 1960 [*Truth and Method*, trans. Joel Weinsheimer and Donald G. Marshall, rev. ed. (New York: Crossroad, 1990)]. An exchange of letters between Strauss and Gadamer concerning the interpretation of texts was published as Leo Strauss–Hans-Georg Gadamer,

"Correspondence concerning *Wahrheit und Methode*," *Independent Journal of Philosophy* 2 (1978): 5–12.

34. "They," i.e., the contingency of the principles.

35. See Aristotle, *Metaphysics* 13 and 14.

36. Strauss refers here to the argument made by Martin Heidegger in *Being and Time*, trans. John Macquarrie and Edward Robinson (New York: Harper & Row, 1962).

37. There was a change of tape at this point; the recording resumes in mid-sentence.

38. Sc. is independent of *Weltanschauung*.

39. R. G. Collingwood, *The Idea of History*, ed. T. M. Knox (Oxford: Clarendon Press, 1946); Collingwood, *An Autobiography* (Oxford: Oxford University Press, 1939).

40. Collingwood mentions only the titles of these works; the authors' names are understood.

41. Here Collingwood inserts parenthetically "(or what in those acts is asserted: for 'knowledge' means both the activity of knowing and what is known)."

42. Collingwood, *Autobiography*, 30.

43. In the place of "fact" Collingwood has "narrative."

44. Collingwood inserts here "which seemed to me."

45. Collingwood, *Autobiography*, 36–37.

46. Here Collingwood inserts "the Schoolmen."

47. Collingwood, *Autobiography*, 59.

48. Collingwood has "The 'realist' answer is easy."

49. Collingwood, *Autobiography*, 61–62.

50. See ibid., 69.

CHAPTER SEVEN

1. Leo Strauss, "On Collingwood's Philosophy of History," *Review of Metaphysics* 5 (1952): 559–86.

2. Ibid., 562. Quoted material in the passage is from Collingwood, *Idea of History*, xii.

3. "On Collingwood's Philosophy of History," 574.

4. John Cook Wilson was Wykeham Professor of Logic at New College, Oxford. *On the Interpretation of Plato's* Timaeus: *Critical Studies* (London: Nutt, 1889) was one of the few works published during Wilson's lifetime. Much of his unpublished work appeared in *Statement and Inference*, ed. A. S. L. Farquharson, 2 vols. (Oxford: Clarendon Press, 1926).

5. Collingwood, *Autobiography*, 44.

6. In the place of "one of these men" Collingwood has "Prichard."

7. Collingwood, *Autobiography*, 47.

8. These words are inserted here in Collingwood: "And their teachers, when introducing them to the study of moral and political theory, would say to them, whether in words or not—the most important things that one says are often not said in words—'Take this subject seriously, because whether you understand it or not will make a difference to your whole lives.'"

9. Strauss omits "on the contrary."

10. Collingwood completes the thought: "'People can act just as morally without it as

with it. I stand here as a moral philosopher; I will try to tell you what acting morally is, but don't expect me to tell you how to do it.'" *Autobiography*, 47–48.

11. In Collingwood, "the."

12. Collingwood, *Autobiography*, 60–61.

13. Ibid., 62.

14. In Collingwood, "a."

15. The words "namely, of moral obligation" are a restatement, not in Collingwood.

16. Collingwood, *Autobiography*, 63.

17. Strauss no doubt has in mind the Greek expression *kat' euchēn*, for which see Aristotle, *Politics* 2.1260a29, 4.1295a29, 7.1325b36, etc.

18. Collingwood, *Autobiography*, 65.

19. The words "after physics" and "by the side of, like parapsychology" are not in Collingwood.

20. "to say" is not in the original.

21. Strauss omits the sentence "A presupposition of one question may be the answer to another question."

22. Collingwood, *Autobiography*, 65–67.

23. In Collingwood: "that century."

24. Collingwood, *Autobiography*, 77–78.

25. Ibid., 91.

26. Ibid., 95, 96, 97, 100, 101, 104–5.

27. There was a break in the tape at this point. The recording resumes in mid-sentence.

28. Heidegger begins such a dialogue in "A Dialogue on Language between a Japanese and an Inquirer," in *On the Way to Language*, trans. Peter D. Hertz (New York: Harper & Row, 1971), 1–54. Published in German as *Unterwegs zur Sprache* (Pfullingen: Neske, 1959).

29. F. S. C. Northrop (1893–1992), American philosopher, author of *The Meeting of East and West* (New York: Macmillan, 1946).

30. Michael Allen Gillespie, in *The Theological Origins of Modernity* (Chicago: University of Chicago Press, 2008), has recently made a version of this argument.

CHAPTER EIGHT

1. Cicero, *Tusculanae disputationes*, book 4.

2. Hobbes, *Leviathan*, chapter 42.

3. "In dogmatical learning" is a restatement, not in Hobbes.

4. In original, "a man."

5. "I.e., the political philosophers" is a clarification, not in Hobbes.

6. *The Elements of Law Natural and Politic*, ed. Ferdinand Tönnies (London: Frank Cass, 1889).

7. "A right instruction of the citizens" is the expression used in *De Cive or The Citizen*, ed. Sterling P. Lamprecht (New York: Appleton-Century-Crofts, 1949), xii, an edition based on Hobbes's own translation with spelling modernized. Strauss is probably translating from the Latin edition of *De Cive* (Amsterdam: Elzevir Press, 1647) from which

he quotes in *Spinoza's Critique of Religion* (Chicago: University of Chicago Press, 1965), 285–86.

8. Locke, *An Essay concerning Toleration* (1667), in *John Locke: Political Writings*, ed. D. Wootton (New York: Mentor, 1993), 194–95.

9. *De cive*, chapter 1, section 2.

10. Ibid.

11. Apparently Strauss's translation.

12. For Machiavelli's opinion of these two men, see *The Prince*, chapters 7 and 19.

13. Carl L. Becker, *The Heavenly City of the Eighteenth-Century Philosophers* (New Haven: Yale University Press, 1932).

14. From *Thoughts on French Affairs* (1791). The actual quotation is: "The little catechism of the Rights of Men is soon learned; and the inferences are in the passions."

15. There is a break in the tape at this point.

16. H. A. Wolfson, in *The Philosophy of Spinoza* (Cambridge, MA: Harvard University Press, 1934).

17. *Leviathan*, ed. Michael Oakeshott (New York: E. P. Dutton, 1914 [Oxford: Basil Blackwell, n.d.]), chapter 11.

18. Strauss apparently means "horizontal" here.

19. Jean-Jacques Rousseau, *Social Contract*, book 1, chapter 8. Presumably Strauss's translation.

CHAPTER NINE

1. Strauss is apparently thinking of Kant's comment that "Rousseau set [him] straight" in his "Remarks on the *Observations on the Feeling of the Beautiful and Sublime*" (Ak 20: 44). The comment about Hume is made in the preface to the *Prolegomena to Any Future Metaphysics* (Ak 4: 260).

2. Johann Gottlieb Fichte (1762–1814), German philosopher of the post-Kantian idealist school.

3. Friedrich Nietzsche, *Beyond Good and Evil*, § 9. Apparently Strauss's translation.

4. Nietzsche has "the last self-respect."

5. Nietzsche, *Beyond Good and Evil*, §188.

6. For a more complete version of Strauss's argument, see Leo Strauss, "Note on the Plan of Nietzsche's *Beyond Good and Evil*," *Studies in Platonic Political Philosophy*, 174–91.

7. Benedict Spinoza, *Opera*, ed. Carl Gebhardt (Heidelberg: C. Winter, 1925).

8. *Naturalism and the Human Spirit*, ed. Y. Krikorian (New York: Columbia University Press, 1944).

9. John Dewey, *Human Nature and Conduct: An Introduction to Social Psychology* (New York: Henry Holt, 1922).

10. Christian Wolff (1679–1754), prominent German rationalist philosopher in the period between Leibniz and Kant.

11. Jonathan Swift: see chapter 8.

12. *Odyssey* 10.286–306. Strauss reads from *The Odyssey*, trans. George Herbert Palmer (Cambridge: Riverside Press, 1921), with slight changes.

13. Strauss apparently has in mind Thucydides's *History*, book 4, secs. 3–4.

14. There is a break in the tape at this point; the recording resumes in mid-sentence.

15. *Nicomachean Ethics* 5.1134b26.

16. For a transcript the next session of the course, session 10, see the Leo Strauss Center website.

17. The repetition of "the study in ancient times" is not in Hegel.

18. G. W. F. Hegel, *The Phenomenology of Mind*, trans. J. B. Baillie, 2nd ed. (London: Allen & Unwin, 1931), 94. Translation modified slightly by Strauss "in order to bring out somewhat more clearly the intention of Hegel's remark" (*What Is Political Philosophy?*, 75 n).

Index